Mrs.
COBLIN

CENTENNIAL ALBUM OF THE CIVIL WAR

CENTENNIAL ALBUM OF THE CIVIL WAR

by

Marvin H. Pakula

in collaboration with

William J. Ryan *and* David K. Rothstein

CASTLE BOOKS ★ **NEW YORK**

This Edition Published by Arrangement with A. S. Barnes & Co., Inc.

Printed in the United States of America
Library of Congress Catalog Card Number: 60-11319

To my mother, whose inspired guidance
contributed infinitely to this
commemorative volume

CONTENTS

FOREWORD

At the start of hostilities between the North and South, it was apparent that both forces approached the unforeseen with extreme optimism. The elaborate, Zouave-inspired uniforms of volunteer companies and regiments reflected such optimism and, if I may be excused for noting, just a bit of immaturity.

Undeniably, however, the resulting mixture of style and color gave the contemporary onlooker a unique visual experience. It is the dedicated purpose of this book, and in particular of the color section, to attempt a re-creation of the impact of such style and color on the eyes and mind of the civilian viewer. The rigors of war soon stripped away this touch of glamour and caused General Sherman to remark accurately and concisely, "War is Hell!"

ACKNOWLEDGMENTS

My deepest thanks to the Reverend Cornelius Greenway, who encouraged me to attempt this detailed work and provided me with much portrait material from his large collection of signed "carte de visites." My special thanks also to Mr. George Breitman, who arranged my first meeting with Dr. Greenway as well as the initial one with my collaborators, Dr. Ryan and Mr. Rothstein.

The following institutions, organizations, and departments provided the bulk of reference material invaluable to this volume:

The National Archives, Washington, D.C.; Smithsonian Institution, Washington, D.C.; U.S. Government Printing Office, Washington, D.C.; Office of the Quartermaster General and Military History Branch, Department of the Army, Washington, D.C.; The Confederate Museum, Richmond, Virginia; Valentine Museum, Richmond, Virginia; Battle Abbey, Richmond, Virginia; New York Historical Society; New York Public Library; United States Marine Corps Headquarters, Washington, D.C.; and the Library of Congress, Washington, D.C.

Special thanks also to:

Mr. William M. E. Rachal, Editor, Virginia Historical Society; Mr. Milton Kaplan, Curator, Print and Photograph Division, Library of Congress; Mr. Robert Abels, Military Collector; Miss Josephine Cobb, Archivist-in-Charge, Still Picture Branch, National Archives; Mr. Leon Weidman, Military History Section, New York Public Library; Miss Eleanor S. Brockenbrough, Assistant House Regent, Confederate Museum, Richmond, Virginia; Miss Elizabeth Dance, Assistant Curator, Valentine Museum, Richmond, Virginia; Mr. Milby Burton, Director, Charleston Museum, South Carolina; Major Charles West, U.S.A.R. Vice-President and Secretary, and Mr. W. Ogden McCagg, Administrator, Company of Military Collectors and Historians; Colonel W. M. Miller, U.S. Marine Corps, Head, Historical Branch, G-3 Division, Washington, D.C.; Mr. Arthur Breton, Manuscript Department, and Mr. Joseph Rapport, New York Historical Society; Mr. Martin Traube, 187th Field Artillery Armory, Brooklyn, New York; Miss Charlotte Capers, Director, Department of Archives and History, State of Mississippi; Mrs. Alice Handy Cox, Falls Church, Virginia; Miss Motylewski, Still Picture Branch, National Archives; Colonel D. G. Gilbert, Chief, Historical Services Division, Office of Chief of Military History, Department of the Army, Washington, D.C.; Lt. Colonel James S. Cook, Jr., Chief, Heraldic Branch, R. & E. Division Office of the Quartermaster General, Department of the Army, Washington, D.C.; State Senator MacNeil Mitchell, Albany, New York; Brigadier General George Stevenson, Adjutant General, New York Army N.G., Albany, New York; Colonel Frederick P. Todd, New York Army N.G., Director, West Point Museum; Lt. Colonel John H. Magruder III, U.S.M.C., Director of Marine Corps Museum, Quantico, Virginia; Colonel Allen P. Julian, U.S.A. Retired, Director, Atlantic Historical Society; Dr. James Heslin, Associate Director, New York Historical Society; Commander F. M. Lloyd, Public Information Officer, U.S. Naval Academy, Annapolis, Maryland; Mr. Louis Levy, Free Lance Photographer, Expert on Signatures; Miss Rosanna Blake, Silver Spring, Maryland; Mr. Clarkson A. Collins III, Librarian, Rhode Island Historical Society; Miss Lilla M. Howes, Director, Georgia Historical Society, Savannah, Georgia; Miss Mary G. Bryan, Director, Department of Archives and History, Atlanta, Georgia; Miss Mary B. Prior, South Carolina Historical Society.

MARVIN H. PAKULA

INTRODUCTION

In a few months we will observe the One Hundredth Anniversary of the beginning of the War Between the States. A young nation born in the dark days of the American Revolution, a few millions scattered along the Atlantic seaboard, were to grow, by 1861, into a youthful and strong nation of some thirty millions. But within three-quarters of a century, brothers in blood were to divide into the Blue and Gray. And in a desperate war of some four years' duration the whole government and military structure of the Confederate Gray was to go down in ruins amidst the blood and rubble of the Civil War. Instead of obeying the wise counsel "United we stand, divided we fall," two equally determined and unyielding branches of the same American nation were to fall upon each other and to wage a fierce conflict from Florida to Pennsylvania, from the Mississippi in the West to the outskirts of Washington.

It is no wonder that one is lost in reverence as he stands on the hill called "Little Round Top" and, as the shades of evening creep over the silent and peaceful battlefield of Gettysburg, enshrouded in gloom by the statues of Lee, Sedgwick, Hancock, Warren, and other heroic leaders who fought there, suddenly realizes that he is in another world—a Valhalla of the dead.

Again and again, youth and old age find themselves returning to the fascinating but bloody panorama called the Civil War. "Bulldog" Grant, "rugged" Sherman, and the "dashing" Sheridan, all in blue, match talent and courage with equally able gray-clad warriors like the beloved "uncle" Robert E. Lee, the veteran Jim Longstreet, the fascinating "Stonewall" Jackson, and the dashing "Jeb" Stuart, the "Chevalier Bayard" of the South.

Little did the leaders on either side of the struggle realize the terrible price that was to be paid in the years following the Southern attack on Fort Sumter nearly 100 years ago.

All the great leaders have long since departed the scenes of their triumphs and defeats, and the last soldier of the Civil War has closed his eyes. Let us hope that both Blue and Gray are holding a reunion in eternal peace and that they are tenting on the old camp grounds in happy understanding and mutual friendship.

As one pursues even a cursory reading, or perhaps a re-reading, about the great battles and bouts of the Civil War, there come to mind several practical questions.

Who were these men? What was their general background? Where did they fight? Why did these military leaders, nearly all West Point graduates, and many old friends and classmates—most of them, fellows in arms in the war against Mexico and and officers in the United States Army—why did they choose to take opposite sides in the war?

It took real courage and conscience for Robert E. Lee and several other Southern generals to resign their high commands in the regular army and to offer their services to the Confederacy. Let it be remembered that Lee was Winfield Scott's choice as commander in chief of the Union Army in the early days of the strife. However, Lee, like other Southerners, honorably refused to draw his sword against his own state of Virginia and refused to shed the blood of his relatives. Grant and Lee and the wise and generous Lincoln were aware of this. When Lee fought on hopelessly, his final adversary, Grant, offered generous terms of surrender to a gallant and honorable soldier at Appomattox.

The general works and special biographies written about the Civil War and its leaders are legion, and many volumes continue to pour from the press.

Many of these works are technical in scope and treatment. Others are full of battle maps and statistical data, while still others either give a surplus of detail on certain generals or give a colorful and personal account, almost becoming historical novels.

Many of these works are too expensive for the average pocketbook. In fact, quite a modest outlay is incurred if one wishes to gain a wide acquaintance with the Civil War and its leaders.

Aware of the tremendous interest at present on the subject of the Civil War and of the greater interest that will be stimulated by the observance in 1961 of the One Hundredth Anniversary of the opening of this struggle, the authors of this book offer to the reading public a careful selection of the most prominent military leaders of both North and South. This book presents a gallery of charcoal-drawn portraits, accurately made from the available photographs, together with a profile on each leader, revealing his background and the battles in which he fought. There is also included a fine selection of Army Corps insignia, uniforms, and various kinds of arms used—all in brilliant colors. A ready and practical working bibliography completes the book.

The authors are deeply grateful for the use of sources made available to us by the libraries of New York City and Washington, D.C. They hope that readers will understand the extremely difficult problem involved in selecting and condensing material from the vast amount of literature available in this field.

WILLIAM J. RYAN
DAVID K. ROTHSTEIN

COLOR PLATE CREDITS

KEY

Numbers refer to Color Plate Sources, below.

Plate 1. 1, 2, 3, 4, 9, 21, 22, 23, 27
Plate 2. 1, 2, 3, 4, 10, 11, 14, 21, 24
Plate 3. 1, 2, 4, 7, 11, 12
Plate 4. 1, 4, 7, 10, 12, 21, 26
Plate 5. 3, 4, 8, 14, 21, 23, 24
Plate 6. 1, 2, 4, 8, 9, 11, 21, 22
Plate 7. 1, 2, 3, 4, 7, 8, 14, 23
Plate 8. 13
Plate 9. 13
Plate 10. 13

Plate 11. 1, 3, 5, 20
Plate 12. 3, 5, 6, 7, 16, 20, 25, 27
Plate 13. 1, 3, 5, 7, 10, 16, 20
Plate 14. 1, 2, 4, 10, 16, 21, 26, 28
Plate 15. 1, 2, 4, 5, 6, 21
Plate 16. 1, 4, 5
Plate 17. 6, 16
Plate 18. 11, 17, 18
Plate 19. 11, 19, 23
Plate 20. 2, 3, 4, 15

COLOR PLATE SOURCES

1. *Photographic History of the Civil War*, Francis Trevelyan Miller (New York: Thomas Yoseloff, 1957).
2. New York Historical Society.
3. Smithsonian Institute, Washington, D.C.
4. Company of Military Collectors & Historians, Washington, D.C.
5. Confederate Museum, Richmond, Virginia.
6. The Battle Abbey, Richmond, Virginia.
7. Bannerman's Sons.
8. National Archives, Washington, D.C.
9. *New York in the War of the Rebellion, 1861–1865*, by Frederick Phisterer, 1909.
10. *Uniform Buttons of the Armed Forces of the United States: 1784–1948*, by David Johnson.
11. *Army Lineage Book: Vol. II Infantry Department of the Army*, 1953.
12. Robert Abels.
13. *Flags of the Army of the U. S. During the War of the Rebellion*, Quartermaster General, U. S. Army, 1888.
14. Official U. S. Government Plates, New York Public Library.
15. Charleston Museum, South Carolina.
16. *Confederate Arms*, William Albough III and Edward N. Simmons (Harrisburg, Pa.: The Stackpole Company, 1957).
17. *Women of the Confederacy*, Simkins.
18. *History of South Carolina*, Vol. II, Snowden (Lewis Publishing Co., 1920).
19. *Pictorial History of the Civil War in the United States*, Benson Lossing (George W. Childs Publisher, 1866).
20. Department of Archives and History, State of Mississippi.
21. *A Compendium of the War of the Rebellion*, Frederick H. Dyer (New York: Thomas Yoseloff, 1959).
22. One Hundred and Eighty-seventh Field Artillery Armory (Fourteenth New York Infantry Regiment).
23. New York Public Library.
24. *Philadelphia in the Civil War*, Frank H. Taylor (Philadelphia, 1913).
25. Valentine Museum.
26. Personal Collection.
27. *Generals in Gray*, Ezra J. Warner (Louisiana State University Press, 1959).
28. *Pictorial Battles of the Civil War*, by Benjamin La Bree.

PORTRAIT CREDITS

UNION ROSTER

Anderson, R.   Cornelius Greenway Collection.
Banks, N. P.   L. C. Handy Studios.
Barry, W. F.   Library of Congress.
Birney, D. B.   Cornelius Greenway Collection.
Buell, D. C.   L. C. Handy Studios.
Buford, J.   National Archives.
Burnside, A. E.   Library of Congress.
Butler, B.   Library of Congress.
Canby, E.   Cornelius Greenway Collection.
Crook, G.   National Archives.
Cushing, W. B.   National Archives.
Custer, G. A.   National Archives.
Dahlgren, J. A.   *Mr. Lincoln's Contemporaries* by Roy Meredith (New York: Scribner's, 1951).
Farragut, D. E.   National Archives.
Foote, A. H.   National Archives.
Franklin, W. B.   National Archives.
Frémont, J. C.   National Archives.
Geary, J. W.   National Archives.
Gillmore, Q. A.   National Archives.
Granger, G.   Library of Congress.
Grant, U. S.   National Archives.
Gregg, D.   National Archives, Cornelius Greenway Collection.
Griffin, C.   National Archives.
Halleck, H. W.   Cornelius Greenway Collection.
Hancock, W. S.   Library of Congress.
Heintzelman, S. P.   Library of Congress, *Mr. Lincoln's Cameraman.*
Hooker, J.   *Mr. Lincoln's Contemporaries, supra.*
Howard, O. O.   Library of Congress.
Hunter, D.   National Archives.
Keyes, E. D.   Library of Congress.
Kilpatrick, H. J.   Library of Congress.
Logan, J. A.   Cornelius Greenway Collection

McClellan, G. B.   National Archives.
McClernand, J. A.   Library of Congress.
McCook, A. McD.   National Archives.
McDowell, I.   Library of Congress.
McPherson, J. B.   Library of Congress.
Meade, G. G.   Library of Congress.
Merritt, W.   National Archives.
Osterhaus, P.   National Archives.
Pleasonton, A.   National Archives.
Pope, J.   Cornelius Greenway Collection.
Porter, D. D.   Library of Congress.
Porter, F. J.   Library of Congress.
Rawlins, J.   Cornelius Greenway Collection.
Rosecrans, W. S.   National Archives.
Schofield, J.   National Archives.
Scott, W.   Library of Congress.
Sedgwick, J.   National Archives.
Sheridan, P.   National Archives.
Sherman, W. T.   National Archives.
Sickles, D.   National Archives.
Sigel, F.   National Archives.
Slocum, H. W.   National Archives.
Stoneman, G.   Library of Congress.
Sumner, E. V.   Library of Congress.
Thomas, G.   Library of Congress.
Torbert, A. T. A.   Cornelius Greenway Collection.
Upton, E.   National Archives.
Wallace, L.   National Archives.
Warren, G. K.   Cornelius Greenway Collection.
Webb, A.   Cornelius Greenway Collection.
Williams, A. S.   Miss Georgia Fleming, Bambridge, Georgia.
Wilson, J. H.   Cornelius Greenway Collection.
Wright, H. G.   Cornelius Greenway Collection.

CONFEDERATE ROSTER

Alexander, E. P.   *Photographic History of the Civil War.*
Beauregard, P. G. L.   L. C. Handy Studios.
Bragg, B.   Library of Congress.
Breckenridge, S. C.   National Archives.
Buckner, S. B.   *Photographic History of the Civil War.*
Cheatham, B.   National Archives.
Cleburne, P. R.   *Photographic History of the Civil War.*
Early, J. S.   Library of Congress.
Ewell, R. S.   Library of Congress.
Forrest, N. B.   Library of Congress.
Gordon, J. B.   National Archives.
Hampton, W.   George S. Cook and Eustis Cook, Richmond, Virginia.
Hardee, W. J.   *Mathew Brady—Historian with a Camera* by James Horan (New York: Crown, 1955).
Hill, A. P.   L. C. Handy Studios.
Hill, D. H.   National Archives.
Hood, J. B.   National Archives.
Huger, B.   Library of Congress.
Jackson, T. J.   National Archives.
Johnston, A. S.   *Photographic History of the Civil War.*
Johnston, J. E.   National Archives.
Kemper, J. E.   Library of Congress.
Law, E. M.   L. C. Handy Studios.

Lee, F.   George S. Cook and Eustis Cook, Richmond, Virginia.
Lee, R. E.   *Photographic History of the Civil War.*
Lee, S. D.   Library of Congress.
Longstreet, J.   National Archives. *Photographic History.*
Lovell, M.   Library of Congress.
Magruder, J. B.   *Photographic History of the Civil War,* Battle Abbey Richmond and Ezra J. Warner Collection.
Mahone, W.   Library of Congress.
Marmaduke, J. S.   *Photographic History of the Civil War.*
Morgan, J. H.   Ezra J. Warner Collection.
Mosby, J. S.   L. C. Handy Studios.
Pemberton, J. C.   National Archives.
Pickett, G. E.   L. C. Handy Studios.
Pike, A.   *Photographic History of the Civil War,* Ezra J. Warner Collection.
Polk, L.   Valentine Museum.
Price, S.   Ezra J. Warner Collection.
Robertson, B. H.   Library of Congress.
Rosser, T.   *Generals in Gray.*
Semmes, R.   Valentine Museum.
Smith, E. K.   Library of Congress.
Stuart, J. E. B.   Valentine Museum.
Van Dorn, E.   National Archives.
Wheeler, J.   Library of Congress.

CALL TO THE COLORS!

Plate 1

THE GENERAL OFFICER

The broad category of the general officer opens an avenue of varied data that is especially interesting. The four years of the Civil War produced no less than 2,311 generals between the two armies. Of these, the North listed 1,882 officers ranking as brigadier or major generals; and the South contributed 429 generals in four grades (general, lieutenant general, major general, and brigadier general).

Rapidly expanding armies were forced to promote their young officers quickly and frequently. This resulted in startling age differences among men holding general's commissions. Lt. General Winfield Scott, the senior general of the U.S. Army, was seventy-five before he retired from duty, while a Ninety-seventh Pennsylvania Infantry Colonel, Galusha Pennypacker, became a brigadier general at twenty. While Pennypacker was certainly the youngest wartime brigadier, Major Generals George A. Custer, Emory Upton, and Wesley Merritt succeeded him in rank while in their mid-twenties.

A study of the Confederate generals shows a parallel situation. John Bell Hood was a full general at twenty-nine, Stephen D. Lee was a lieutenant general at twenty-seven, and William Fitzhugh Lee (Robert E. Lee's second son) a major general at twenty-three. In contrast, General Samuel Cooper, the Confederate adjutant general, was sixty-three and Major General David E. Twiggs was seventy-one when they attained their ranks. Aside from the top rank of full general, which contained just eight men, with an average age of forty-eight, and seventeen lieutenant generals whose average age was forty-one, the remaining 404 officers were in the thirty-six to thirty-seven-year age bracket.

There was an unusually high number of combat deaths in the general's rank. The South lost seventy-two officers in action, the North fifty-two.

The first color plate supplements the black and white portraits of specific general officers in both armies.

Figure A presents a Union major general in full regalia. The rich gold appointments on uniform and saddle blanket are well set off by the navy blue background. General Joseph Hooker was the inspiration for this mounted figure.

Various accouterments and insignia of the general officer are shown in Figures B to G. For contrast, the insignia of the lower ranking officers appear in Figures H to M.

Figure B shows a regulation officer's belt buckle, drawn full size.

Figure C shows the hat emblem of the Union officer. Generals wore silver stars within the wreath, according to rank.

Figures D to F are the shoulder bars of the three ranks:
D—Lieutenant General
E—Major General
F—Brigadier General

General Grant, who had the distinction of holding the only Union rank of lieutenant general, commanded all the Northern armies. Individual armies, military districts, corps, and divisions were normally the province of a major general. As suggested by the rank-title itself, brigades were commanded by a brigadier general.

The sword and buff sash are distinctly those of the general officer. Regimental officers wore dark red sashes. The staff officer's sword, shown in Plate 5, is approximately that of the regimental officer. The staff officer carried a sword with a slightly more ornamental counter-guard than the regimental sword.

The color inserts in the shoulder bars of the regimental officers denote the branch of service, as do the collar facings of the Confederate officers shown in Plate 11.

Plate 2

VOLUNTEER REGIMENTS

The Fourth Michigan Volunteer Infantry Regiment (Figure A) was organized at Adrian, Michigan, and mustered into service June 20, 1861. The regiment was assigned to Wilcox's Brigade in Heintzelman's Division of the Army of the Potomac under General Irwin McDowell. It remained with the Army of the Potomac throughout the war, assigned successively to the First Division of the Third and then of the Fifth Corps.

This Michigan unit saw service in every major engagement associated with the Army of the Potomac. When relieved from duty—in the trenches before Petersburg on June 19, 1864—the Fourth Regiment had lost 12 officers and 177 enlisted men in combat, and 1 officer and 107 men through disease. The unit's engagements included: Bull Run, Hanover Court House, Gaines Mill, Malverne Hill, Second Bull Run, Antietam, Fredericksburg, Chancellorsville, Gettysburg, Mine Run, Wilderness, Spotsylvania, Cold Harbor, and Petersburg.

The Sixth Pennsylvania Cavalry (Seventieth Volunteers) was also called Rush's Lancers after its colonel, Richard H. Rush. Supported in its recruiting by prominent Philadelphians, the regiment was able to secure the best of personnel. Their uniform (Figure B), while essentially a standard cavalry outfit, had a slight variation in the collar trim. The center braid consisted of one worsted loop instead of the regulation two. Enlisted men wore the metal crossed sabers on top of their cap crown while officers wore them in front.

The Norwegian fir lances, which gave the Sixth Pennsylvania its nickname, were nine feet long, with an eleven-inch, three-edge metal tip. A scarlet guidon was fastened to the lance just below the tip. These weapons were abandoned in 1863 because of their awkward handling and the fact that the cavalry performed mostly in dismounted service which, of course, limited the value of the lance.

The regiment lost seven officers and seventy-one enlisted men in combat and three officers and eighty-six men through disease. Their record of major engagements includes: Hanover Court House, Gaines Mill, Seven Days' Battle, Antietam, Fredericksburg, Chancellorsville, Gettysburg, Brandy Station, Second Bull Run, Mine Run, Yellow Tavern, Cold Harbor, Five Forks, and Appomattox.

The chevrons worn by the various grades of noncommissioned officers are presented in Figures C to H. Starting with sergeant major (Figure C) the chevrons are colored in pairs to represent the infantry, artillery, and cavalry branches of service in that order. Figures G and H are both cavalry chevrons with Figure G the earlier issue. Army regulations later specified that yellow rather than orange be the official cavalry color.

Starting left to right, the rank and service of the chevrons run:

C—Sergeant Major, Infantry
D—Quartermaster Sergeant, Infantry
E—Ordnance Sergeant, Artillery
F—First Sergeant, Artillery
G—Sergeant, Cavalry
H—Corporal, Cavalry

Figures I to L deal with elements of the infantry drum corps or band:

I—Bugle, Infantry
J—Regimental Drum
K—Musician's Tunic Button
L—Musician's Tunic

Plate 3

VOLUNTEER REGIMENTS

The Eleventh Indiana Volunteer Regiment (Figure A) was formed from independent companies in central and southern portions of the state. The Wallace Zouaves, as they were called under their leader Colonel Lew Wallace, entered Union service on April 26, 1861, for a three-month call ending August 2, 1861. The regiment reorganized and volunteered for a three-year period starting August 31, 1861. Following its mustering out, the regiment again reenlisted January 4, 1864, and served until July 26, 1865.

After several reorganizations, the Eleventh became the One Hundred and Fifty-first Regiment, National Guard, in 1917. Its engagements included: Forts Henry and Donelson, Shiloh, Manassas, Antietam, Fredericksburg, Chancellorsville, Gettysburg, Vicksburg, Chickamauga, Chattanooga, Wilderness, Spotsylvania, Cold Harbor, Petersburg, and the Shenandoah campaign.

The Second New Hampshire Volunteer Militia (Figure B) served a three-year enlistment under Colonel Gilman Marston, who had replaced Colonel L. P. Pierce, the unit's organizer.

The regiment, which wore a distinctive tail coat with red piping, was assigned to Burnside's Brigade at Bull Run. The Second New Hampshire, although caught in the general rout of Union forces, was able to re-form apart from the rest of the scattered brigade and continue to advance. It was involved thereafter in every major engagement connected with the Army of the Potomac until its mustering out on December 19, 1865.

The Tenth Massachusetts Volunteer Regiment (Figure C) was mustered into federal service on June 20, 1861, for three-years' duty and mustered out on July 6, 1864. This unit had its origin in companies formed in 1662 in Hampshire County.

It served in the following major engagements: Peninsula, Antietam, Fredericksburg, Chancellorsville, Gettysburg, Wilderness, Spotsylvania, Cold Harbor, and Petersburg.

Figure D shows the regimental insignia of the One Hundred and Fifty-first Infantry Regiment which was an outgrowth of the Eleventh and other Indiana volunteer regiments.

The Sharps Carbine (Figure E) was a breech-loaded short rifle commonly used by cavalry troops. It was a .52 calibre weapon about 39 inches long. The Confederate copies of this gun, made in Richmond, Model 1862, were 37¾ inches long.

The Second Massachusetts, or One Hundred and Fourth Infantry Regiment, whose insignia is shown in Figure F, was the regiment redesignated from the original Tenth Massachusetts.

Figures G to I show the artillery, infantry, and cavalry insignias worn on the forage cap and dress hat. When the dress hat ("Jeff Davis" or "Hardee" type) was worn, the insignia appeared in the front-center area. When the forage cap was used, the insignia appeared either in front or on top of the crown, at the discretion of unit commanders. If the corps patch also was worn on the forage cap, this symbol appeared at the top of the crown. Where a soft, wide-brim hat was worn it was attached front-center, as in the "Jeff Davis" hat.

Plate 4

VOLUNTEER REGIMENT AND U.S. MARINES

The First Rhode Island Detached Militia was organized in Providence and surrounding towns under Colonel Ambrose E. Burnside. The regiment left Rhode Island on April 20, 1861, to serve a three-month enlistment ending August 2, 1861. It was assigned to Hunter's Division in McDowell's Army of Northeast Virginia upon its arrival in Washington, D.C.

The First Rhode Island fought well in the early action at Bull Run, but the constant heat and heavy combat caused it to disorganize and become ineffective after a few hours. It used two types of uniform blouse. One was a style often referred to as a hunting jacket. This had a pleated front and wide collar as seen in Figure A. The other blouse, in the same length, had a double-breasted, buttoned flap in the chest. This conceivably could have been inspired by the volunteer fireman's shirt of that time since many volunteer militia groups were formed from these fire-fighting companies.

A distinctive feature of the Rhode Islanders' paraphernalia was their bright-red blanket which, slit in the center to allow the head to slip through, served as a poncho. When not in use, this blanket was tightly rolled and worn diagonally across the shoulder.

One of the regiment's officers and sixteen enlisted men were killed in combat; eight enlisted men died of diseases.

The United States Marine Corps performed many valuable but little-heralded services during the war. Their first duty consisted of securing ungarrisoned Federal forts in the Washington defense area. Along with this, they guarded the various naval yards against sabotage. Upon arrival of army troops, the Marines were relieved of garrison duty in these forts.

These amphibious soldiers were standing by on board a steamer in Charleston Harbor ready to reinforce Major Anderson when fighting broke out at Fort Sumter. Confederate bat-

teries, however, kept them at a distance until the surrender of the fort. The Marines, with 100 men, also held the Norfolk naval yard against superior forces in April, 1861. When, on April 20, 1861, it became apparent that their position was hopeless, they succeeded in rendering much of the cannon and barracks useless by burning them.

Under Major John G. Reynolds, 348 Marines took part in the flanking attack on the Confederates at Bull Run. The diversionary frontal assault failed to trick the Southern defenders and the Confederates concentrated their full strength on their endangered flank. The ensuing Confederate rally made difficult the Marine detachment's retreat across the Potomac bridge.

From this point on, the Marines served capably as naval gun crews and landing parties in assaults on Confederate coastal batteries. They saw successful action on the *Monitor*, on the *Kearsage*, and with Admiral Farragut at Mobile Bay. A force of 180 Marines also helped suppress the New York City draft riot in 1863.

The total strength of the Corps in 1864 was 64 officers and 3,075 enlisted men.

The Springfield Musket, Model 1861, was the chief Union weapon of the Civil War. It was a .58 calibre gun copied by the Richmond arsenal for Confederate use. The North manufactured 801,997 of these muskets during the war. Figure C illustrates this weapon, which was 55¾ inches long and weighed 8 pounds 14 ounces.

Figure E shows another popular arm, the Burnside carbine. This gun, invented by General A. E. Burnside, was the first to use a metallic shell cartridge. The Union Army purchased 56,000 of these 39-inch-long, .54 calibre rifles.

Figures D and F illustrate the tunic buttons worn by the First Rhode Island Detached Militia and Marines respectively.

Plate 5

ZOUAVE VOLUNTEER REGIMENTS

The U.S. Zouave Cadets (Figure A) were officially Company D of the Nineteenth Illinois Volunteer Infantry Regiment. They were better known as the Ellsworth Zouaves, after their colonel, Elmer E. Ellsworth, the first officer to lose his life in the service of the Union Army. He personally removed a Confederate flag from the roof of the Marshall House in Alexandria, Virginia, and so incited the pro-Southern hotel proprietor that he fired a deadly shotgun blast into Ellsworth as he descended the stairway. Sergeant Brownell, who in turn killed the proprietor, was awarded the Congressional Medal of Honor.

This crack Zouave unit was recognized throughout the country for its precision drill formations. It traveled about in the years immediately before the war, giving exhibitions of its training. This company, no doubt, further popularized the Zouave uniform among both Northern and Southern volunteer companies. The Nineteenth Illinois, of which the Zouaves were Company D, became the One Hundred and Thirty-second Infantry, N.G. (Ill.), in 1917.

During its three-year enlistment, June 17, 1861, to July 9, 1864, the regiment lost four officers and sixty enlisted men who were killed in combat and four officers and 101 enlisted men who died of diseases.

Engagements participated in by the Nineteenth Illinois Infantry included: Tennessee, 1862; Alabama, 1862; Murfreesboro, Chickamauga, Chattanooga, and Atlanta.

The One Hundred and Fourteenth Infantry Regiment (Figure B) was called the Collis Zouaves after Colonel Charles H. T. Collis, its organizer. The regiment was an enlargement or outgrowth of the Zouaves d'Afrique, a company also formed by Collis while he was a captain.

The Zouaves d'Afrique actually contained many Frenchmen who had served as Zouaves in French campaigns. The Corps d'Afrique was mustered in August 17, 1861, expressly to serve as a bodyguard to General N. P. Banks. The general was so impressed with the unit that Captain Collis was sent back to Philadelphia as a colonel to recruit a full regiment.

The uniform of the smaller company was adopted by this new One Hundred and Fourteenth Infantry Regiment, and the Corps d'Afrique became its Company A. Many of the veterans of the original Afrique Company became regimental leaders. The Collis and Ellsworth Zouaves were two of the outstanding units of this French type, as were Baxter's Fire Zouaves and the Birney Zouaves in Philadelphia; Wilson's, Bendix's, Duryea's and Hawkins' in New York; and Wallace's in Indiana.

The One Hundred and Fourteenth Infantry lost seven officers and sixty-six enlisted men in combat and one officer and thirty-seven men through disease. The engagements in which it participated included: Middletown, Cedar Mountain, Antietam, Fredericksburg, Chancellorsville, Gettysburg, Mine Run, Wilderness, and Petersburg.

The regimental insignia of the One Hundred and Thirty-second Illinois, which grew from the Nineteenth, is shown in Figure C. The Corps d'Afrique originally was associated with the Eighteenth Pennsylvania, which became the One Hundred and Eleventh Infantry in 1921. The One Hundred and Eleventh Infantry is represented in Figure D by its regimental insignia.

Figure E shows the waist belt buckle worn by most Union enlisted men.

Figure F is the regulation sword for staff officers. This sword is essentially the same type as the regimental officer's sword except for the fact that the "filigree" in the counter-guard of the sword hilt illustrated is a bit wider and slightly more ornamental than that of the regimental issue.

Figure G shows the distinctive brass eagle disc worn by enlisted men to secure the leather belts which crossed their shoulders. It is therefore known as a cross-belt plate.

Plate 6

NEW YORK REGIMENTS

Considering the large number of regiments New York contributed to the Union service, depicting three uniforms from a cross-section of these units is a small recognition of their part in the war. Certainly many New York regiments not mentioned served as valorously as those units represented here.

The distinctive regimental insignias shown around the main figures are limited to those New York units in existence today that served during the Civil War. They will be further defined below.

The Seventy-ninth New York Regiment (Cameron Rifle Highlanders) was named after an eighteenth-century Scottish Regiment.

The clan tartan was designed in the late 1700's by Colonel Cameron's mother and has been identified as Cameron of Erracht. The plaid trousers are considered a part of the undress uniform which was worn when they were mustered in, May 29, 1861. Their dress outfit called for kilts, glengarries (caps), and sporrans (pouches). The group began a three-year voluntary service under Lieutenant Colonel Samuel McKenzie Elliott. On May 17, 1864, all men with unexpired terms of service formed new companies, A and B, which, in March, 1865, joined with two others to form the New Cameron Highlanders.

The Seventy-ninth's engagements included: Bull Run, Pope's Campaign, Kelly's Ford, Chantilly, Antietam, Fredericksburg, Vicksburg, Wilderness, Spotsylvania, and Petersburg.

The regiment lost 358 officers and men.

The Ninth New York Volunteer Infantry was also known as Hawkins' Zouaves, so named for its leader, Rush C. Hawkins. Colonel Hawkins was originally the president of the military club formed in 1860 from which the regiment was recruited.

The enrollment, mostly New Yorkers, included recruits from Albany, Brooklyn, Hyde Park, Mt. Vernon, Staten Island, Connecticut, New Jersey, and Canada. The Ninth was mustered out on May 20, 1863.

Its engagements included: the Maryland Campaign, South Mountain, Antietam, and Eastern Virginia area.

The regiment lost 366 officers and men.

The Seventh Infantry Regiment, N.G., was mustered into service on April 26, 1861, under Colonel Marshall Lefferts. It served three short enlistments between that date and July 16, 1863.

The regiment participated in no major engagements but was part of the Union advance into Virginia in 1861 and helped subdue the New York City draft riot on July 16, 1863.

It was notable in that its membership listed some of the most prominent New York families of the day. The regiment is further reputed to have influenced the Confederate States Army to adopt cadet gray as their official color because of the impression the Seventh New York made while in Richmond before the war.

The Seventy-first New York N.G. (Figure D), also known as the American Guard, began Federal service on April 21, 1861. After three short terms of enlistment, its service ended on July 22, 1863. In September, 1863, several separate units reorganized for a three-year enlistment as the One Hundred and Twenty-fourth Volunteers under Colonel A. Van Horne Ellis.

The regiment's engagements included: Bull Run, Fredericksburg, Chancellorsville, Gettysburg, Wilderness, Spotsylvania, Cold Harbor, Petersburg, and Appomattox.

It lost 567 officers and men.

The Fourteenth Regiment Militia (Figure E), also called the Brooklyn Phalanx, was a volunteer regiment recruited by Colonel Alfred M. Wood in 1861 and mustered into Federal service by the year's end. Its record was one of the most distinguished of all Union regiments; its high casualty list of 716 men is evidence of this. The regiment served at Bull Run, Antietam, Fredericksburg, Chancellorsville, Gettysburg, Wilderness, and Spotsylvania. It is now the One Hundred and Eighty-seventh Field Artillery.

The Twenty-third Infantry, New York N.G. (Figure F), was also a Brooklyn regiment. It served a three-month enlistment, during which it participated in the battle of Gettysburg. It became the One Hundred and Sixth Infantry in 1921.

The Seventy-fourth New York (Figure G) was organized in Buffalo as New York State Militia in 1854. Some of its units later formed the Twenty-first New York Volunteer Regiment in 1861. The remaining group became the Seventy-fourth New York N.G. in 1862 and saw federal service during most of 1863. The two later re-consolidated to re-form the Seventy-fourth New York Regiment.

The Seventy-fourth's engagements were at Manassas, Antietam, and Gettysburg.

The Sixty-ninth's New York State Militia (Figure H) became the One Hundred and Sixty-fifth Infantry New York, N.G. It probably is New York City's most famous, partly due to its World War I reputation as the "Fighting Sixty-ninth" of the Forty-second "Rainbow" Division. During the Civil War it was an element of the renowned "Irish Brigade." Like the Fourteenth Brooklyn, it has a long list of engagements: Bull Run, Peninsula, Antietam, Fredericksburg, Chancellorsville, Wilderness, Spotsylvania, Cold Harbor, and Petersburg.

Plate 7

NAVAL UNIFORMS AND INSIGNIA

The naval officer depicted in Figure A suggests Farragut as he appeared holding the rank of commodore. This grade was re-created in 1862 by act of Congress along with the ranks of admiral and lieutenant commander to accommodate the wartime need for more officers.

Until 1862, only three grades existed in the U.S. Navy: captain, commander, and lieutenant. The uniform of the lieutenant denoted his rank with a ¾-inch gold stripe. The commander wore two and the captain three ¾-inch stripes. When the new grades were established, this system of rank identification had to be discarded.

One reason, of course, was that provision had to be made for the rank of lieutenant commander between the one stripe of lieutenant and the two of commander. Further, under the old system, adding one ¾-inch stripe for each rise in grade would have made an admiral's sleeve a little farcical in its bottom heavy appearance.

Thus, in 1863 a new series of rank insignia was devised. The gold "lace" was reduced in width to ¼ inch for each stripe; an admiral's sleeve was to show the maximum eight narrow rows of gold. Since Farragut's cuff shows six alternate widths, it appears that temporary identifications were in effect between the 1862 creation of his commodore rank and the new 1863 regulations governing rank insignia.

Figures C to E and I to K show the corresponding shoulder bars worn by the then expanded naval staff.

Figure L shows the cap device worn by engineer officers, and Figure N shows the cap insignia worn by captains and commanders. Junior officers wore a simple anchor motif on their cap fronts.

Figure M is the typical officer's buckle.

Figures F and H show the cutlass carried by officers and enlisted men respectively. The stenciled cut-out "U.S.N." identifies the Figure F weapon as an officer's.

The naval cannon marked Figure G is a Dahlgren gun named after its inventor, Admiral J. B. Dahlgren. It was popularly known as the "pop bottle."

The Navy Colt and Remington revolvers (not illustrated) were the commonly used naval side arms. It was the U.S. Navy Colt that was copied by the Confederates and used as an army weapon (see Plate 17).

The seaman holding the signal flag appears to be an apprentice since he does not wear the white collar and cuff stripes as does the first class seaman of the modern navy.

Important naval engagements of the Civil War included the famous meeting of the ironclads, the *Monitor* and *Merrimac*, on March 9, 1862, and the French coastal duel between the U.S.S. *Kearsage* and the C.S.S. *Alabama*, on June 19, 1864. The Battle of Mobile Bay, August, 1864, won by the Union steamer fleet of Admiral David Farragut, led to the surrender of New Orleans. The torpedoing of the Confederate ironclad *Albemarle* by Lieutenant Cushing on October 27, 1864, also contributed to the successful blockade of Southern ports.

Prominent Union naval officers were Admirals David Farragut, David Porter, Samuel Dupont, John Dahlgren, and Andrew Foote; and Captains John Rodgers, John Winslow, and Lieutenant William B. Cushing.

Plate 8

CORPS FLAGS AND BRANCH INSIGNIA

This color plate is the first of three on flags and badges of the many Union Army units. It is a difficult subject to cover in depth; but an attempt is made to do so by giving nearly complete corps headquarters coverage and then examples of division and brigade flags, which could guide an interested reader into deducing the pattern which the other divisional units followed.

The first group includes all the corps headquarters flags designed in the swallow-tail (guidon) style. This was the flag shape that prevailed in two-thirds of the corps headquarters. Figures A to L show them according to the numerical order of the corps involved. The smaller group of corps that used *rectangular* flags are represented in Plate 9.

The various symbols of these corps headquarters were repeated in most of the flags of the lower levels of command (division and brigade). In the case of the rectangular-shaped corps flags, a different system of denoting related divisions was used. In the corps using the flags depicted here, color changes alone separated the identity of one division in the corps from another.

In certain cases where corps used a box-shaped flag the following system of changes applied for divisions. The first division used a symbol or design *once* on the flag background or field. The second division repeated this symbol *twice* within the field, and the third division showed the symbol *three* times. An example of this was Eighteenth Corps. The First Division used one large star in the center, the Second Division

two stars, and the Third, three stars. The Tenth and Twenty-first Corps were other units whose divisions carried this star pattern (see Plate 9).

The First, Third, Eleventh, Twelfth, and Twentieth, though corps with the swallow-tail flag, used the divisional system found in the Tenth, Eighteenth, and Twenty-first Corps, which used a rectangular flag. In Plate 10, the first and most prevalent divisional flag system is illustrated and explained.

Certain numbered corps did not adopt an official flag until after the war; these corps are bypassed because it is uncertain whether the flags saw war service.

The three cavalry flags (Figures M to O) show the army to which each cavalry group was assigned. The cavalry corps itself had a headquarters flag, shown in Plate 10. This flag probably came into existence later in the war when the need for extensive independent cavalry command became apparent.

Figure P illustrates the standard artillery regimental flag. The artillery brigade flag is shown in Plate 10.

Figure Q illustrates what was known as a uniform badge; this one is that of the Signal Corps. Its symbol was probably incorporated in a unit flag as well. These service badges were small, palm-sized metallic insignia worn on the cap or jacket.

Figure R is the Corps of Engineers' version of the metal badge.

Plate 9

CORPS FLAGS

Plate 9 shows the rectangular or square-shaped corps head-quarters flags mentioned in the text accompanying Plate 8. Why they varied from the predominant guidon type will remain a mystery to this writer. Confusingly enough, it has given them the appearance of the standard rectangular division flag shown in Plate 10.

The Fourth, Fourteenth, Fifteenth, and Twenty-third Corps retained their corps symbols in their division flags and except for the corps headquarters flags themselves followed the di-vision pattern shown in Plate 10 that was used by the corps with guidon-type corps flags.

Figures H to J show additional examples of the metallic badges seen in Plate 8. These, however, are identified not with the various service branches but with elite units which dis-tinguished themselves in battle.

A list of the more prominent corps leaders may give more meaning to this survey of flags at the corps level:

UNIT	LEADERS (in order of command)
First Corps	McDowell, Hooker, Meade, Wadsworth, Reynolds, Doubleday
Second Corps	Sumner, Couch, Sedgwick, Howard, Hancock, Warren, Birney, Humphreys, Barlow, Gibbon, Hays
Third Corps	Sickles, Heintzelman
Fourth Corps (Army of Potomac)	Keyes
Fourth Corps (Army of Cumberland)	Granger, Howard
Fifth Corps	Porter, Hooker, Butterfield, Meade, Griffin, Humphreys, Warren
Sixth Corps	Franklin, Sedgwick, Wright
Seventh Corps	Dix, Naglee
Seventh Corps (Dept. of Arkansas)	Steele, Reynolds (This corps succeeded the previous Seventh Corps discontinued August 1, 1863.)
Eighth Corps	Schenck, Wallace
Ninth Corps	Burnside, Sedgwick, Willcox
Tenth Corps	A. H. Terry, Gillmore, Birney
Eleventh Corps	Sigel, Howard
Twelfth Corps	Mansfield, Slocum, Williams

UNIT	LEADERS (in order of command)
Thirteenth Corps	Sherman, Morgan, McClernand, Ord, Granger
Fourteenth Corps	Rosecrans, Thomas, J. C. Davis
Fifteenth Corps	Sherman, Blair, Logan, Osterhaus, Hazen
Sixteenth Corps	S. A. Hurlbut
Seventeenth Corps	McPherson, Blair, Mower, Belknap
Eighteenth Corps	Foster, Palmer, Butler, Ord, Gibbon, Weitzel
Nineteenth Corps	Banks, Franklin, Reynolds
Twentieth Corps	A. McD. McCook, Hooker, Slocum, Mower, Williams
Twenty-first Corps	Crittenden, Palmer
Twenty-second Corps	Heintzelman, Augur
Twenty-third Corps	Stoneman, Schofield
Twenty-fourth Corps	Ord, Terry, Devens, Gibbon
Cavalry—Division of the Mississippi	Wilson
Cavalry—Dept. of the Cumberland	D. S. Stanley
Cavalry—Army of the Potomac	Stoneman, Pleasonton, Sheridan, Torbert, Merritt, Stoneman, Gregg

Plate 10

DIVISION, BRIGADE, AND ARMY FLAGS

The derivation of brigade and divisional flags from corps headquarters flags is illustrated in Plate 10.

The Second Corps is used as an example. Its forked-tail headquarters flag (Figure A) has a clover-leaf symbol which is retained in the division flags. However, to establish these division flags (Figures B, C, and D) as belonging to a lower level of command, their outer shape becomes rectangular. It also becomes necessary, since there are three or more divisions, to separate one division from the other. This is done by varying the background (field) color as well as the symbol color in each. The First Division used a white field with a red symbol. The Second Division used a blue field with a white symbol. The Third Division used a white field, as in the First, but with a blue symbol.

This was the standard color rule for all corps using the guidon or swallow-tail flag, the type used in the majority of corps headquarters. Plate 8 illustrates all of these corps flags in numerical order.

While each corps had three basic divisions, each division showed three brigades or more. We now use the First Division of our example, the Second Corps, to illustrate the flags at the brigade level. The First Division (Figure B) has a white field and a red symbol. This color scheme and the clover leaf symbol are both retained for all the infantry brigades of the First Division.

The change takes place this time in the brigade flag shape to distinguish this step-lower echelon of command. The facing or trim done in blue on each of the four infantry brigades (Figures G to J) separates one brigade from the other by its successive contour variations. Figures E and F show further changes in color since they represent artillery and quartermaster brigades apart from the infantry brigades just described.

Thus a military observer could see a brigade banner and trace its division and corps lineage from the one flag alone.

Figure K shows the battle flag of Sheridan's cavalry corps. Figure L is the official headquarters flag of the entire cavalry corps itself.

Figures M to O show higher levels of command encompassing several corps. These are army flags—specifically, the Army of the Tennessee, Army of the Mississippi, and Army of the Potomac, in the order mentioned.

Plate 11

UNIFORM REGULATIONS OF THE CONFEDERATE ARMY

In 1862, uniform regulations for the Army of the Confederate States were issued in Richmond, Virginia. This was an extensive document, covering all details of attire.

The uniform coat was to be cadet gray for officers and enlisted men. The regimental officer's tunic was to have a double-breasted front with two rows of seven buttons each; the enlisted man's was to be the same. The brigadier general's frock coat was to be double-breasted but contain eight buttons in each row with each two buttons paired together.

The trousers were to be light blue for officers and enlisted men and dark blue for generals. The trouser stripes for general officers were to be two stripes of gold lace on the outer seam, ⅝ inch in width and ⅛ inch apart. Regimental officers were to have one stripe in the color of their service 1¼ inches in width. The staff officers' stripe would also be 1¼ inches in width but in the same gold lace as the general officers'.

The buff silk sash of the general officer went twice around the waist and tied at the left hip; the hanging ends were not to extend more than eighteen inches below this tie. Lower ranking officers' red silk sashes went once around the waist but followed the general's sash in the other specifics. Noncommissioned officers were to wear worsted sashes in the color of their service, tying twice around the waist and hanging as the others (see Figure R).

The forage caps of the enlisted men were to follow the service color in the entire crown and have a dark blue band around the bottom (see Figures C to H). The same color system applied to officers' caps, with the addition of thin gold lace running vertically to the top of the crown from the band on each side, front, and back area as well. The number of rows of lace to be used depended on rank (one braid for lieutenants, two for captains, three for majors and colonels, and four for generals). Figures A and B show this system, using the rank of captain as an example.

The cuffs of tunics also indicated rank and service by number of braids in a scroll design above a cuff-facing in the color of the service (Figures P, Q, S, T).

The collar, again, gave rank and service. The devices in Figures I to O are self-explanatory.

Because these rules were never strictly enforced, many depictions of C.S.A. officers' trousers show them to be exclusively flat gray when, as this plate indicates, many were a grayish blue. As was prescribed, the general's trouser-blue was fairly dark, to distinguish it from the lower ranks.

Returning to the waist sash, Figure R features the red silk sash representing all of the regimental officers. In a worsted material, its color was regulation wear for infantry and artillery sergeants. The colors in small boxes below the sash are the sash colors for officers of other services.

Official Confederate records compiled by General Marcus J. Wright give interesting statistics on the cost of an enlisted man's uniform. On October 8, 1862, the Confederate Congress passed a bill calling for the following articles and expenditures.

	Indiv. Cost	No. of Articles per Year	Total Cost
Cap	$ 2.00	2	$ 4.00
Oilskin Cover	.38	1	.38
Jacket	12.00	2	24.00
Trousers	9.00	3	27.00
Shirt	3.00	3	9.00
Drawers	3.00	3	9.00
Socks	1.00	4	4.00
Shoes	6.00	4	24.00
Great Coat	25.00	1	25.00
Blanket	7.50	1	7.50
Grand Total (per year)			$133.88

Plate 12

GENERAL OFFICERS

The general officers of Figures A and B display an elegance to be found among the higher ranking Confederate officers early in the war.

The lack of supplies and industrial facilities available to the South quickly frustrated any hopes of uniformity of dress among Confederate troops. However, all will agree that those officers who were able to outfit themselves as prescribed did create a magnificent military figure.

It is true that each Confederate state provided militia whose dress uniforms were visually excellent; but these had to be discarded as impractical or battle-worn, much like many of the Union volunteer regiments' regalia. As the reader runs the gamut of these color plates, he will be struck with the odd fact that the "blue and gray" interchanged itself many times between both armies.

Returning to the general officers, the reader will note that there is an overall compliance with the official uniform regulations for both Union and Confederate officers.

"Jeb" Stuart, depicted in Figure B, took some liberty with his jacket as did cavalry officers on both sides. The jacket, showing the earlier dragoon influence in its short cut, was obviously adopted for comfort in the saddle. Interestingly, Stuart has transformed it into a single-breasted garb by folding back the front edges and buttoning each on its own side.

His "Cavalier" hat shows the plume distinctive to the First Virginia Cavalry (although their feather was usually black). The saber he carries is shown close up in Figure F. This was generally the type both cavalries used.

His trousers are in the prescribed dark blue with the proper striping or lace for his rank. His boots, though not the ankle or Jefferson boot mentioned in regulations, are still of a type that was common in the higher ranks. The gloves come under the color restrictions to white or buff.

Figure A shows an older Confederate general. (The average age of all four Confederate ranks of general was only forty-one!) But among the senior officers in this group, many looked like General Sibley (portrayed here)—the inventor of the Sibley tent used by both armies.

The sword in Figure E is a type General Sibley may have carried. The belt to which it would be attached is properly illustrated in the uniform study. Generals usually wore the gold belts and line officers, black leather sword belts.

Figure C is a rare naval officer's sword modeled after the Union naval sword except for the dolphin-like head on the pommel. Note the rope effect on the sheath. This weapon was captured on the Confederate ship *Florida*.

Figure D is a C.S. Navy cutlass obviously influenced in the grip and guillon by the regulation foot artillery sword of the U.S. Army. Since the grip texture could be taken for eagle feathers as well as fish scales, the scaled grip was also used for the Confederate version of the foot artilleryman's sword.

Of the 429 generals who served with the Confederate States Army, 146 were West Point graduates. The Virginia Military Institute provided seventeen more and the South Carolina Military Academy four officers. At least two other generals were trained at Southern military schools.

The last surviving Confederate general was Felix H. Robertson, who lived until April 20, 1928.

Plate 13

SERGEANT AND CAPTAIN

The sergeant shown in Plate 13 is typical of the enlisted man early in the war. Even at this more successful period in Confederate affairs, the enlisted man's garb varied noticeably from the 1862 C.S.A. uniform regulations. The double-breasted frock coat prescribed for enlisted men in Article 47, Section 1470, was rarely seen. Most wore short, single-breasted jackets similar to the infantryman's shown here. Note the non-regulation sleeve detail.

Noncommissioned officers were supposed to wear a trouser stripe 1¼ inch wide in the color of their service (infantry, blue; cavalry, yellow; artillery, red). These stripes were to be of cotton webbing as described in Section 1470 of regulations.

The artillery captain (Figure B) is well outfitted and adhering strictly to standards. The uniform color, cut, and facings are proper, as are rank insignia. Plate 11 deals with the various officers' rank notations, which also apply to the captain shown here. The black leather belt, 1½ to 2 inches wide, follows specifications in Section 1511.

On the subject of belts, Figures C and E compare enlisted men's belt buckles with the officers' buckles (Figure D). Regulations called for a rectangular belt for regimental officers; but many, especially general officers, wore the circular type illustrated.

Figures F to M show the variations in tunic buttons denoting service branches. They are as follows:

F. Rifleman
G. Infantry
H. Corps of Engineers
I. General Officer (note shield or badge)
J. Staff Officer (no shield)
K. Navy
L. Artillery
M. Cavalry

Plate 14

VOLUNTEER COMPANIES AND INSIGNIA

The Washington Artillery of New Orleans, which began its Civil War service on May 26, 1861, was organized in 1838 as a volunteer militia company. The Fifth Company, represented here by a lieutenant (Figure A), was the last unit to be added to the regiment—on May 27, 1861, following the four-company muster of the day before.

Under the leadership of Captain W. I. Hodgson, the Fifth Company served with distinction at Shiloh just two months later. At that time it was assigned to J. P. Anderson's brigade in Braggs Corps.

An interesting note is that the New Orleans citizens as well as troops themselves provided for the outfitting of the entire regiment.

The First Virginia Cavalry (Figure B) was formed early in 1861 from several independent companies. It was placed under the leadership of Major J. E. B. Stuart, a West Point graduate, who, as Colonel Robert E. Lee's aide in 1859, participated in the capture of John Brown at Harper's Ferry.

By the summer of 1861 the First Virginia's roster had increased from four to ten companies with "Jeb" Stuart now holding the rank of Colonel. This cavalry regiment was closely allied with the Army of Northern Virginia throughout the war, performing valuable reconnaissance duty as well as daring raids.

Ironically, one such raid kept Stuart's Virginia cavalry away from Gettysburg until the second day of battle. It is conceivable that had Stuart been available for intelligence service, the battle might never have taken place where it did.

The First Virginia Cavalry participated at the First and Second Manassas, Fredericksburg, Chancellorsville, Brandy Station, and at Yellow Tavern, where Stuart met his death.

The Charleston Zouave (Figure C) has been noted in at least two publications: *The Photographic History of the Civil War* and *Pictorial Battles of the Civil War*. Little seems to be known about the specific origin of these, the McClellan Zouaves. In all likelihood, they are akin to the Zouave Cadets (Chichester's) who garrisoned Castle Pickney when it held Union prisoners from Bull Run. The uniform conforms in detail to the winter uniform of Chichester Zouaves Cadets who wore the leggings shown here.

Figures D to P show some of the various state regimental tunic buttons worn by Confederate soldiers. Note that two of the three border states who contributed troops to both sides are represented. Only Maryland has been omitted. They are as follows:

D—Arkansas	J—South Carolina
E—Kentucky	K—Georgia
F—Missouri	L—Alabama
G—Florida	M—Mississippi
H—Tennessee	N—Louisiana
I—Texas	O—North Carolina
	P—Virginia

These buttons were not the only ones to represent each individual state. Most buttons adopted the state insignia. The Florida button (Figure G) is one example where the state symbol was not incorporated in its design. However, this does not preclude the fact that such a button certainly existed.

Plate 15

VOLUNTEERS, FLAGS, AND AMMUNITION

The Clinch Rifles (Figure A) of Macon became Company A of the Fifth Georgia Volunteer Infantry Regiment on May 11, 1861. The company strength at that time was ninety-five officers and men. Earlier in the year on January 24, 1861, these Clinch Rifles took part in the capture of the Augusta arsenal.

The Fifth Georgia was sent to garrison Pensacola, Florida, under the command of General Braxton Bragg. The ten companies that formed this regiment varied so much in their elegant uniform style and color that Bragg nicknamed it the "Pound Cake Regiment." The unit saw action at Murfreesboro, Chickamauga, and Missionary Ridge. It suffered staggering losses at Chickamauga (Indian name for "River of Death"), where 55 per cent of its personnel were casualties. Despite these losses the regiment held out after Appomattox under the command of General E. Kirby-Smith. It was surrendered at Greensboro, North Carolina, on April 26, 1865.

The uniform of the Clinch Rifles is quite similar to that of a brother company, the Republican Blues of the First Georgia. This Savannah unit wore the white uniform trim shown in Figure A; and while available black and white photographs do not establish this trim specifically to be white in the Clinch Rifle uniform, the geographic proximity of the other regiment and the very light value of the trim in the photographs' "gray scale" make white the probable color.

The First Tennessee Light Artillery contained a unit from Nashville known as Rutledge's Battery (Figure B). This group became Battery A after its muster late in May, 1861. Captain Arthur M. Rutledge, the leader of this company of artillerymen, later was assigned to the staff of General Polk as an artillery major. The Rutledge Battery supplied its own cannon: four six-pound smooth-bore guns and two twelve-pound howitzers, cast in a Nashville foundry.

This unit saw action at Mill Springs and Shiloh. Because of heavy losses in the latter engagement, it was necessary to merge the battery with McClure's battery.

The first "national" flag of the Confederate States (Figure C) was adopted March 14, 1861. The battle flag (Figure D) was personally chosen by General Joseph E. Johnston in September, 1861, after the battle of Fairfax Courthouse. The second flag of the Confederate States (Figure E), was adopted May 1, 1863, but was found to be unsatisfactory because it resembled a flag of truce when it was folded over. The final banner of the Confederacy (Figure F), adopted in March, 1865, was never used; the war ended the following month. The red vertical bar at the edge of the white field was meant to correct the fault of the previous flag.

The four basic types of rifle ammunition used during the war are shown in Figures G to J:

  G—.69 calibre Buck and Ball
  H—.58 calibre Buckshot
  I—.69 calibre Ball
  J—.69 calibre "Minie" Ball

The bullet and powder were encased in a linen wrapper which had an appendage at the powder end, which the rifleman usually tore off by gripping it between his teeth and tugging away with one hand. This process was necessary to load the gun properly.

Plate 16

DRUM MAJOR AND ARMY SURGEON

Figures A and B introduce phases of the Confederate Army services that are less well known to the student of the period. The drum major was lost in shadows, so to speak, because such luxuries were short-lived in the Southern army. The army surgeon, as is the lot of his profession, was little noticed because of his passive role in the war.

Figure A is a representation of Sergeant Major Pohle of the First Virginia Volunteer Infantry. The sergeant came from a Richmond militia company known as the Virginia Rifles; before the war he had been a member of the U.S. Navy Band.

The Drum Corps led by Drum Major Pohle included fourteen boys, sixteen years or older; the band itself numbered thirteen pieces. A year later, when the regiment reorganized, both groups were disbanded.

The surgeon presented a colorful yet dignified appearance in full dress. The green, gray, black, and gold are mixed in ideal proportions. A Confederate army doctor held the rank of major although those who served in important administrative roles could and did receive higher rank.

It has been recorded that due to the limited knowledge of antiseptics at that time plus ever-present materiel limitations, unsterilized bandages and surgical tools further infected many wounds. The high-calibre bullets had a shattering effect as well. Add these factors and you will see with what the army surgeon of that time had to contend.

The Chimborazo Hospital in Richmond was a vast series of buildings on a high bluff, expressly constructed to handle the overflow of Confederate wounded. In addition, many wounded were individually nursed in private homes. During a soldier's convalescence the women of the house often repaired or replaced his torn uniform.

Plate 17

CONFEDERATE PISTOLS

The pistols represented here are typical of the many varieties of hand weapons used by the Confederates. Of the three shown here, the revolver marked Figure B was the most common and popular type. The gun was copied from the .36 calibre Colts used by the U.S. Navy prior to the war. The gun illustrated here is one of the late models manufactured by Griswold and Gunnison in Griswoldsville, Georgia. This company was active in gun-making from 1862 to 1864.

Only four other gun companies were very active in revolver manufacturing for the South. They were Leech and Rigdon, Rigdon-Ansley, Spiller and Burr, and the Columbus Fire Arms Manufacturing Company.

The pistol marked Figure A is a Palmetto pistol manufactured by Wm. Glaze and Company in Columbia, South Carolina, 1852/53. It is a single-shot, .54 calibre gun. The story connected with this gun is that it was first produced in South Carolina in 1850, obviously years before the war, along with many thousands of other weapons including rifles, muskets, cavalry sabers, and swords in anticipation of hostilities. South Carolina was the state independently involved in this manufacture and was the only state to remedy the lack of gun manufacturing facilities existing in the South at that time.

The Le Mat revolver (Figure C), was a .42 calibre, nine-shot pistol. Patented by a Dr. Jean A. F. Le Mat of New Orleans, it was rated a very lethal weapon. Besides its load of nine bullets it had an extra barrel which fired .50 calibre grapeshot.

Unfortunately for the Confereracy, Southerners lacked the special equipment to manufacture this gun. Le Mat, of French descent, was able, however, to leave for Paris, where he produced 3,000 of these revolvers. While the Union naval blockade did cut down on the number of guns delivered to the Confederates, many Le Mats were received.

Plate 18
PRESENT-DAY REGIMENTAL INSIGNIA

Figures A to F are the regimental coats of arms for present-day National Guard units that can be traced to the Confederate States Army. The original regiments or companies were organized at the time of the War or just before it (some states anticipated the hostilities and organized volunteer groups in advance).

The First Louisiana (Figure A) now the One Hundred and Fifty-sixth Infantry N.G. (La.), was originally the Second and Third Louisiana Volunteer Infantry, organized and mustered in Confederate service on May 9 and 17, 1861, respectively. Its components served until Appomattox. In 1896 the two regiments were consolidated to form the First Louisiana.

A reorganization two years later found some elements eventually forming the One Hundred and Fifty-sixth Infantry (1922). The others, through a long series of reorganizations, formed what was to become the One Hundred and Ninety-ninth Infantry in 1946 (Figure C).

The Second and Third Louisiana had the following battle credits: Peninsula Campaign, Second Manassas, Antietam, Fredericksburg, Chancellorsville, Gettysburg, Vicksburg, Wilderness, Spotsylvania, Cold Harbor, Petersburg, Shenandoah, and Appomattox.

The Stonewall Brigade (Figure B), now the One Hundred and Sixteenth N.G. (Va.), was organized as the First Brigade, Army of the Shenandoah, under Stonewall Jackson. It was comprised of the Second, Fourth, Fifth, Twenty-seventh, and Thirty-third Virginia Infantry Regiments. Reorganized in 1881, it was consolidated to form the Second and Third Regiments. In 1917 it joined with the First and Fourth Virginia Infantry Regiments to become the One Hundred and Sixteenth Infantry Regiment. Its engagements included: Bull Run, Peninsula, Second Manassas, Sharpsburg, Fredericksburg, Chancellorsville, Gettysburg, Wilderness, Spotsylvania, Cold Harbor, Petersburg, Shenandoah, and Appomattox.

The Second North Carolina Regiment, now the One Hundred and Nineteenth Regiment N.G. (N.C.), was originally the First North Carolina Volunteers. It was composed of militia from eight towns in the state. It became the Second North Carolina in 1898 and the One Hundred and Nineteenth on July 25, 1917. Its engagements included: Bethel, Gettysburg, Wilderness, Spotsylvania, Petersburg, and Appomattox.

The Second Georgia Regiment, now the One Hundred and Twenty-first Regiment N.G. (Ga.), was originally the Second Battalion Georgia Infantry, which entered C.S.A. service on April 20, 1861, with four companies from the Macon area. It consolidated with the First and Fourth Georgia Regiments in 1898 as part of the First Georgia Volunteer Infantry Regiment and was redesignated the One Hundred and Twenty-first Infantry Regiment in April, 1924. Its engagements included: Bethel, Gettysburg, Wilderness, Spotsylvania, Petersburg, and Appomattox.

The Third North Carolina (Figure F), now the One Hundred and Twentieth Infantry Regiment, was a part of the First North Carolina Volunteers. In the course of the many post-Civil War consolidations and reorganizations, elements branched off to become the Third North Carolina as others had become the Second North Carolina. The Third Regiment, with which we are presently concerned, was redesignated part of the One Hundred and Nineteenth Infantry Regiment in September, 1917.

In a regimental vein, Figures G and H illustrate two flags that were carried by volunteer troops. Figure G shows the state colors of Virginia, faded and worn from battle use. Figure H is the flag of the Florida Independent Blues.

Isolated companies that carry Civil War histories later merged into postwar regiments. All insignia illustrated here represent those units with complete regimental enlistments during the war.

Plate 19

PRESENT-DAY REGIMENTAL INSIGNIA

The regiments represented by the coat of arms in Figures A to F are National Guard units, originally formed as state militia well before the Civil War. All served in the Mexican War, and one regiment predates the Revolutionary War.

The Palmetto Regiment (Figure A), now the One Hundred and Eighteenth Infantry Regiment N.G. (S.C.), was organized in November, 1846. It was reorganized as the Second Regiment South Carolina Volunteers on April 9, 1861. It was directly or indirectly connected with the famous Charleston units (the Zouave Cadets, the Washington Light Infantry, and the Hampton Legion). It was redesignated the One Hundred and Eighteenth Infantry Regiment on December 19, 1921. The regiment's engagements included: Sumter, Bull Run, Peninsula, Second Bull Run, Antietam, Fredericksburg, Chancellorsville, Gettysburg, and Chickamauga.

The First Alabama Infantry (Figure B), now the Two Hundredth Infantry Regiment N.G. (Ala.), was organized in May, 1846, as the First Regiment Alabama Volunteers. It reorganized from 1846 until the Civil War, when it was mustered into Confederate Service as the Third Alabama Infantry. It was reorganized as the First Infantry Regiment during 1898 and 1899 and redesignated the Two Hundredth Infantry Regiment on December 2, 1946. Its engagements included: Peninsula, Antietam, Fredericksburg, Chancellorsville, Wilderness, Spotsylvania, Shenandoah, and Appomattox.

The First Missouri Regiment (Figure C), now the One Hundred and Thirty-eighth Infantry Regiment N.G. (Mo.), was organized in 1832 as the famous St. Louis Grays, a volunteer militia. Along with ten other companies, it became the nucleus of the First Missouri Regiment in 1852 and the following year became a separate battalion attached to the Second Missouri.

When this regiment was captured early in May, 1861, by Union forces at Camp Jackson, it was demobilized. On June 22, 1861, elements of this regiment and the First Missouri Regiment reformed as the First Missouri Infantry, C.S.A. It consolidated with the Fourth Missouri but kept its separate numerical designation until its surrender on April 9, 1865. It was redesignated the One Hundred and Thirty-eighth Infantry on October 1, 1917. The unit's engagements included: Shiloh, Vicksburg, Atlanta, and Nashville.

The First Mississippi (Figure D), now the One Hundred and Fifty-fifth Infantry Regiment, N.G. (Miss.), was formed originally in 1798 as Legions of Militia, Mississippi Territory. At the time of the War of 1812 it was mustered into service as the First Regiment, Mississippi Territory Volunteers. In June, 1846, it saw service under Colonel Jefferson Davis as the First Mississippi Infantry Regiment.

The First Regiment was organized for Confederate service on September 10, 1861. It surrendered to Union forces on February 16, 1862, but, after prisoner exchange, was reorganized and consolidated with the Thirty-ninth Mississippi in General Beall's Brigade until its surrender as a garrison force at Port Hudson on July 8, 1863. After parole, it reorganized again with the Twenty-second and Thirty-third Mississippi Infantry and the First Mississippi Sharpshooter Battalion to form the Twenty-second Mississippi Infantry Regiment, which surrendered on April 26, 1865, near Durham, North Carolina. In 1876 it was redesignated the First Infantry Regiment; and on September 27, 1917, it was redesignated the One Hundred and Fifty-fifth Infantry. Civil War engagements included: Forts Henry and Donelson, Franklin, Nashville, and North Carolina, 1865.

The First Virginia (Figure E), now the One Hundred and Seventy-sixth Infantry Regiment N.G. (Va.), was organized in 1652 as colonial militia for Charles City and Henrico County. It served in the three wars prior to 1861. Reorganized in 1851 as the First Virginia Volunteer Regiment, it was composed of eleven companies from Richmond. The regiment was mustered into Confederate service on July 1, 1861, and fought until Appomattox.

Its designation changed when it was merged with the Stonewall Brigade elements in 1917 to become the One Hundred and Sixteenth Infantry. After reverting to its First Infantry Regiment identity in 1920, it became the One Hundred and Eighty-third in 1922 and finally the One Hundred and Seventy-sixth on January 1, 1941.

The Second Alabama (Figure F), now the One Hundred and Sixty-seventh Infantry Regiment N.G. (Ala.), was organized as the Alabama Militia in 1836. It became the First Alabama Regiment during the Mexican War. Mustered into Confederate service as the Fourth Regiment in 1861, it served until the Appomattox Court House surrender.

It reverted to its First Regiment designation in 1875 and became the Second Regiment months later. It became the Third and eventually the Fourth Infantry Regiment in 1911. On August 5, 1917, its final designation as the One Hundred and Sixty-seventh Infantry became a part of regimental history.

The flag in Figure G is an early South Carolina flag discarded about the time of the Fort Sumter bombardment. This early flag appears to have influenced the later design of the official Confederate battle flag in the matter of the stars within the two crossed bars. The crossed bars variation used on the battle flag was known as the Swiss saltire.

On later South Carolina flags the crescent and palmetto tree appeared first on a solid red field (adopted January 9, 1861), and finally on a blue field (adopted January 28, 1861).

Figure H, the regimental flag of North Carolina troops, is close to the present state flag in design. Many Confederate units incorporated state symbols into their regimental flags (as in their tunic buttons).

Plate 20

UNION AND CONFEDERATE DRESS HATS

A bright spot in the dismal war picture was the pomp and circumstance connected with a military parade or ceremony. Most companies in both armies were specially outfitted with dress uniforms for these colorful but infrequent affairs. In the majority of cases, the dress hat was the focal point of the entire uniform. A selection of eight of these hats was made for this special color plate.

Figure A shows one of the most lavish of the "shako" hats in existence during the war. It was the dress hat of the U.S. artilleryman, the last semblance of the Napoleonic grandeur found in American uniforms. The black plume was made of horsehair, as were most plumes.

The Duryea Zouaves, officially the Fifth New York Volunteer Infantry Regiment, wore a bright red cap with a huge gold tassel (Figure B) both in combat and in parade. This regiment was mustered into service on May 9, 1861, for a two-year call.

Its engagements were Yorktown, Hanover Court House, Seven Days' Battle, Gaines Mill, Second Bull Run, Antietam, Fredericksburg, and Chancellorsville. Regimental losses were 6 officers and 171 enlisted men through combat wounds and 34 men from disease.

The horsehair plume appears again on the helmet of the Charleston Light Dragoons (Figure C). This cavalry was a part of the Confederate Fourth Brigade, recruited entirely from independent volunteer companies in Charleston, South Carolina. The palmetto tree, which is the state symbol, was stamped in brass on both sides and the front of the leather helmet.

The "glengarry" of the Seventy-ninth New York (Figure D) featured a silver heather pin above the regimental numbers. The regiment's history is given with Plate 6.

The Bersaglieri hat of the Thirty-ninth New York Volunteer Infantry was the most distinctive among the New York volunteers. Figure E shows this hat worn by this unit, which also carried the name Garibaldi Guard. The regiment, named after a famous Italian patriot, was actually composed of ten companies, each with a different European extraction. The Garibaldi Guard was mustered in May 28, 1861, and two months later served at Bull Run. The regiment was captured at Harpers Ferry on September 15, 1862, but after a prisoner exchange served the rest of a four-year enlistment. It saw action at Gettysburg, the Wilderness, Spotsylvania, and Petersburg. The regiment lost 8 officers and 107 enlisted men in battle and 1 officer and 158 men to disease.

The Seventh New York wore the shako depicted in Figure F. The regimental numeral appeared in the large brass sunburst, while the New York National Guard insignia was affixed below the white pompon. This regiment is mentioned at length with Plate 6.

United States naval officers were identified with the *chapeaux de bras* of Figure G. This hat bore a ribbon cockade much like the tricorn hats of American Revolutionary officers. Gold tassel braid extended from each hat-tip worn *front and back,* unlike Napoleon's hat of similar proportions, which was worn with the tips extending to the sides.

The Woodis Rifles of Norfolk, Virginia, (Figure H) were organized in March, 1858. They derived their name from a former mayor of Norfolk, Hunter Woodis. They were mustered into service on April 18, 1861, and remained in until the end of the war. Designated Company C of the Sixth Virginia Regiment, they were commanded by William Mahone. The Sixth Virginia saw action continuously from the Seven Days' Battle until the surrender at Appomattox.

PLATE 1
THE GENERAL OFFICER

OFFICER'S BELT BUCKLE

OFFICER'S HAT INSIGNIA

LIEUTENANT GENERAL

MAJOR GENERAL

BRIGADIER GENERAL

GENERAL OFFICER, U.S.A.

SWORD AND SASH
GENERAL OFFICER

COLONEL, ARTILLERY

LIEUTENANT COLONEL
STAFF

MAJOR, ARTILLERY

CAPTAIN, INFANTRY

FIRST LIEUTENANT
CAVALRY

SECOND LIEUTENANT
INFANTRY

SERGEANT MAJOR

QUARTERMASTER
SERGEANT

ORDNANCE SERGEANT

FIRST SERGEANT

SERGEANT, CAVALRY
(early issue)

CORPORAL, CAVALRY
(late issue)

PLATE 2
VOLUNTEER REGIMENTS

PRIVATE, 4th MICHIGAN
VOLUNTEER
INFANTRY REGIMENT

SERGEANT, 6th PENNSYLVANIA
VOLUNTEER
CAVALRY REGIMENT

BUGLE, U.S. INFANTRY

REGIMENTAL DRUM, U.S.A.

MUSICIAN'S
TUNIC BUTTON

MUSICIAN'S TUNIC

SHARPS CARBINE

PLATE 3

VOLUNTEER REGIMENTS

1st INDIANA
(151st INFANTRY
REGIMENT)

2nd MASSACHUSETTS
(104th INFANTRY
REGIMENT)

11th INDIANA VOLUNTEER
INFANTRY REGIMENT
(WALLACE ZOUAVES)

2nd NEW HAMPSHIRE
VOLUNTEER
INFANTRY REGIMENT

10th MASSACHUSETTS
VOLUNTEER
INFANTRY REGIMENT

ARTILLERY INSIGNIA

INFANTRY
INSIGNIA

CAVALRY INSIGNIA

MODEL 1861 SPRINGFIELD RIFLE

PLATE 4

VOLUNTEER REGIMENT AND U.S. MARINES

COLONEL, 1st RHODE ISLAND
MILITIA

PRIVATE, U.S. MARINES

RHODE ISLAND
BUTTON

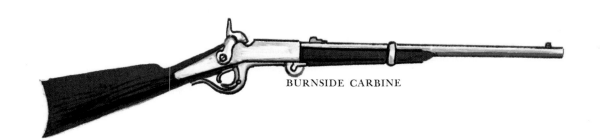

BURNSIDE CARBINE

MARINE CORPS
TUNIC BUTTON

MODEL 1861 SPRINGFIELD RIFLE

PLATE 4

VOLUNTEER REGIMENT AND U.S. MARINES

COLONEL, 1st RHODE ISLAND
MILITIA

PRIVATE, U.S. MARINES

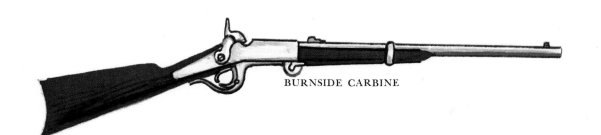

BURNSIDE CARBINE

ISLAND
TTON

MARINE CORPS
TUNIC BUTTON

PLATE 5
ZOUAVE VOLUNTEER REGIMENTS

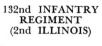

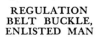

U.S. ZOUAVE CADET
(ELLSWORTH ZOUAVES)

114th PENNSYLVANIA
VOLUNTEER INFANTRY
REGIMENT (COLLIS ZOUAVES)

REGULATION
BELT BUCKLE,
ENLISTED MAN

REGULATION
CROSSBELT PLATE,
U.S.A.

REGULATION STAFF OFFICER'S SWORD

71st NEW YORK
REGIMENT (THE
AMERICAN GUARD)

14th NEW YORK
REGIMENT (THE
AMERICAN GUARD)

BAPTIZED BY FIRE

23rd NEW YORK
REGIMENT (106th NEW
YORK NATIONAL GUARD)

FIDELIS ET CONSTANS

79th NEW YORK
VOLUNTEER
INFANTRY
REGIMENT
(CAMERON RIFLE
HIGHLANDERS)

7th NEW YORK
STATE MILITIA

74th NEW YORK
REGIMENT (174th NEW
YORK NATIONAL GUARD)

PLATE 6
NEW YORK REGIMENTS

9th NEW YORK
VOLUNTEER
INFANTRY
REGIMENT (HAWKINS'
ZOUAVES)

69th NEW YORK
REGIMENT (165th NEW
YORK NATIONAL GUARD)

NAVAL ENGINEER'S
CAP INSIGNIA

NAVAL ENGINEER'S
BELT BUCKLE

JUNIOR OFFICER'S
CAP INSIGNIA

PLATE 7
NAVAL UNIFORMS
AND INSIGNIA

REAR ADMIRAL

COMMANDER

COMMODORE

LIEUTENANT

CAPTAIN

ENSIGN

COMMODORE, U.S.N.

SEAMAN, U.S.N.

NAVAL OFFICER'S
CUTLASS

DAHLGREN NAVAL GUN

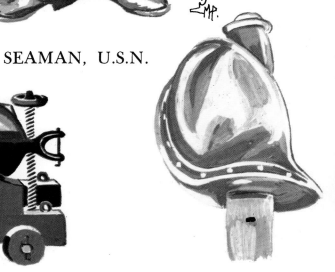

ENLISTED MAN'S
CUTLASS

PLATE 8
CORPS FLAGS AND BRANCH INSIGNIA

1st CORPS

2nd CORPS

3rd CORPS

5th CORPS

6th CORPS

9th CORPS

11th CORPS

12th CORPS

19th CORPS

20th CORPS

24th CORPS

25th CORPS

CAVALRY, ARMY OF
THE MISSISSIPPI

CAVALRY, ARMY OF
THE CUMBERLAND

CAVALRY, ARMY OF
THE POTOMAC

ARTILLERY REGIMENTAL
FLAG

SIGNAL CORPS INSIGNIA

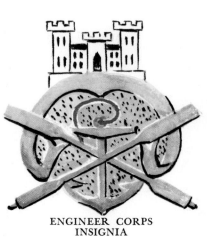

ENGINEER CORPS
INSIGNIA

PLATE 9
CORPS FLAGS

4th CORPS

10th CORPS

14th CORPS

15th CORPS

18th CORPS

23rd CORPS

21st CORPS

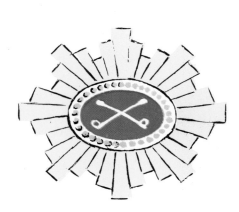

HANCOCK'S CORPS

SHERIDAN'S CORPS

WILSON'S CORPS

PLATE 10

DIVISION, BRIGADE, AND ARMY FLAGS

HEADQUARTERS
2nd CORPS

1st DIVISION
2nd CORPS

2nd DIVISION
2nd CORPS

3rd DIVISION
2nd CORPS

ARTILLERY BRIGADE
1st DIVISION

CHIEF QUARTERMASTER
1st DIVISION

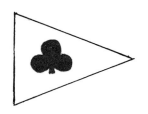

1st BRIGADE
1st DIVISION

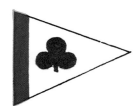

2nd BRIGADE
1st DIVISION

3rd BRIGADE
1st DIVISION

4th BRIGADE
1st DIVISION

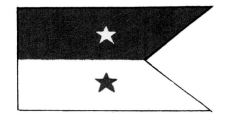

SHERIDAN'S
BATTLE FLAG

CAVALRY CORPS

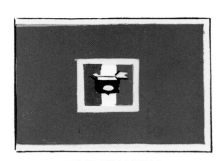

HEADQUARTERS
ARMY OF THE
TENNESSEE

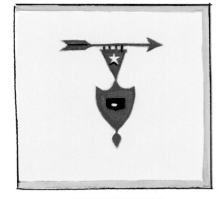

HEADQUARTERS
ARMY OF THE
MISSISSIPPI

HEADQUARTERS
ARMY OF THE
POTOMAC

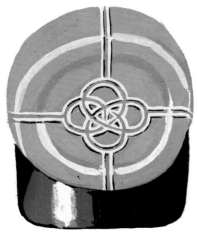

(top view)

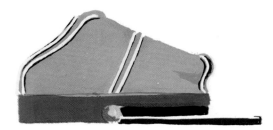

OFFICER'S CAP
(side view)
Two rows of gold lace
indicate rank of captain

ARTILLERY   CAVALRY

ENGINEERS   MEDICAL

GENERAL   REGIMENTAL
AND STAFF

PLATE 11

UNIFORM REGULATIONS OF THE
CONFEDERATE ARMY

COLLAR INSIGNIA

SECOND LIEUTENANT,
ARTILLERY

FIRST LIEUTENANT,
CAVALRY

CAPTAIN, INFANTRY

GENERAL OFFICER

MAJOR, MEDICAL CORPS

LIEUTENANT COLONEL,
ENGINEERS

COLONEL, INFANTRY

LIEUTENANT,
INFANTRY

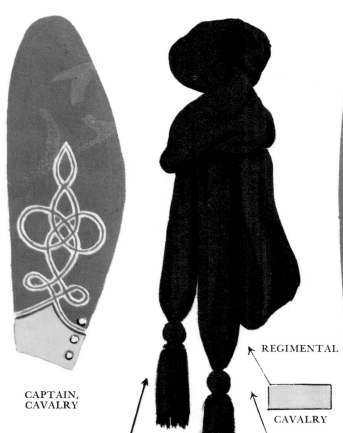

CAPTAIN,
CAVALRY

REGIMENTAL

CAVALRY

GENERAL   MEDICAL

OFFICER'S SASH

MAJOR,
LIEUTENANT COLONEL,
AND COLONEL,
ARTILLERY

GENERAL
OFFICER

(top view)

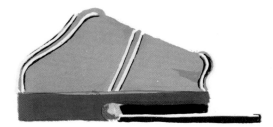

OFFICER'S CAP
(side view)
Two rows of gold lace
indicate rank of captain

ARTILLERY   CAVALRY

ENGINEERS   MEDICAL

GENERAL
AND STAFF   REGIMENTAL

PLATE 11

UNIFORM REGULATIONS OF THE
CONFEDERATE ARMY

COLLAR INSIGNIA

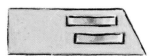
SECOND LIEUTENANT,
ARTILLERY

FIRST LIEUTENANT,
CAVALRY

CAPTAIN, INFANTRY

GENERAL OFFICER

MAJOR, MEDICAL CORPS

LIEUTENANT COLONEL,
ENGINEERS

COLONEL, INFANTRY

LIEUTENANT,
INFANTRY

CAPTAIN,
CAVALRY

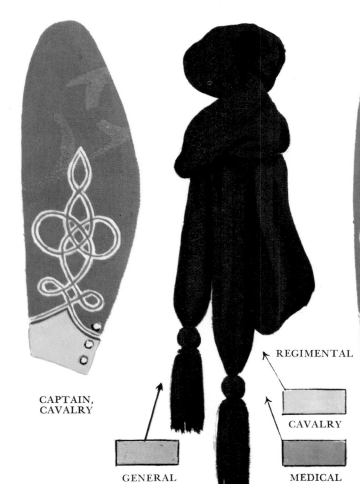

REGIMENTAL

CAVALRY

GENERAL

MEDICAL

OFFICER'S SASH

MAJOR,
LIEUTENANT COLONEL,
AND COLONEL,
ARTILLERY

GENERAL
OFFICER

PLATE 12

GENERAL OFFICERS

OFFICER'S SWORD, C.S.N.

CUTLASS, C.S.N.

GENERAL OFFICER
C.S.A.

CAVALRY OFFICER
C.S.A.

FOOT OFFICER'S
SWORD, C.S.A.

CAVALRY OFFICER'S
SWORD, C.S.A.

ENLISTED MAN'S
BELT BUCKLE

OFFICER'S
BELT BUCKLE

PLATE 13
SERGEANT AND CAPTAIN

ENLISTED MAN'S
BELT BUCKLE

INFANTRY SERGEANT, C.S.A.

ARTILLERY CAPTAIN, C.S.A.

RIFLEMAN

INFANTRY

CORPS OF
ENGINEERS

GENERAL
OFFICER

STAFF OFFICER

NAVY

ARTILLERY

CAVALRY

ARKANSAS　　KENTUCKY　　MISSOURI　　FLORIDA　　TENNESSEE　　TEXAS

TUNIC BUTTONS
PLATE 14
VOLUNTEER COMPANIES
AND INSIGNIA

LIEUTENANT
WASHINGTON ARTILLERY
NEW ORLEANS

TROOPER
1st VIRGINIA
CAVALRY

CHARLESTON ZOUAVE
(McCLELLAN'S)

SOUTH CAROLINA　　GEORGIA　　ALABAMA　　MISSISSIPPI　　LOUISIANA　　NORTH CAROLINA　　VIRGINIA

FIRST
CONFEDERATE STATES FLAG

BATTLE FLAG, C.S.A.

SECOND
CONFEDERATE STATES FLAG

THIRD
CONFEDERATE STATES FLAG

PLATE 15

VOLUNTEERS, FLAGS, AND AMMUNITION

OFFICER,
RUTLEDGE'S BATTERY
(1st TENNESSEE
LIGHT ARTILLERY)

SERGEANT CLINCH RIFLES
(5th GEORGIA INFANTRY)

BUCK AND BALL AMMUNITION

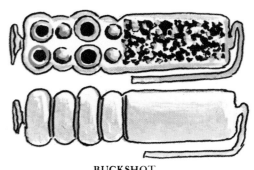

BUCKSHOT

BALL AMMUNITION

MINIE BALL

PLATE 16
DRUM MAJOR AND ARMY SURGEON

DRUM MAJOR
1st VIRGINIA INFANTRY REGIMENT

SURGEON, MEDICAL CORPS
C.S.A.

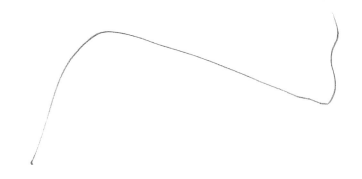

PLATE 17
CONFEDERATE PISTOLS

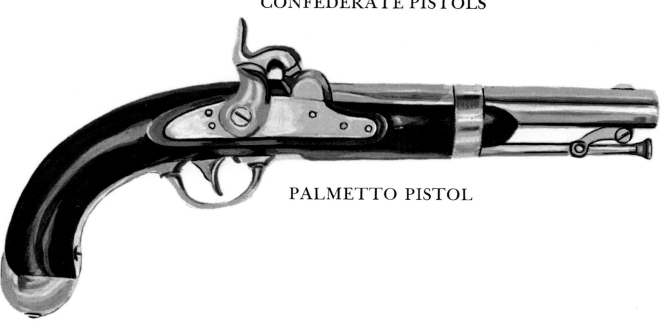

PALMETTO PISTOL

GRISWOLD AND GUNNISON PISTOL
(CONFEDERATE COLT)

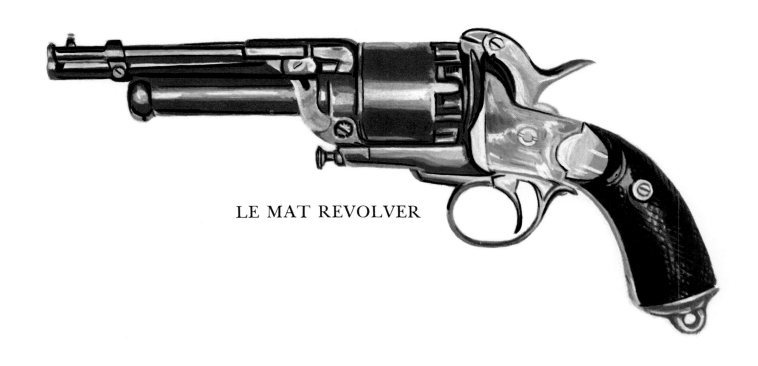

LE MAT REVOLVER

PLATE 18
PRESENT-DAY REGIMENTAL INSIGNIA

1st LOUISIANA
(156th INFANTRY REGIMENT)

STONEWALL BRIGADE
(116th INFANTRY REGIMENT)

2nd AND 3rd LOUISIANA
(199th INFANTRY REGIMENT)

2nd NORTH CAROLINA
(119th INFANTRY REGIMENT)

2nd GEORGIA
(121st INFANTRY REGIMENT)

3rd NORTH CAROLINA
(120th INFANTRY REGIMENT)

REGIMENTAL FLAG
INDEPENDENT VIRGINIA REGIMENTS

REGIMENTAL OR COMPANY FLAG
FLORIDA INDEPENDENT BLUES

PLATE 19
PRESENT-DAY REGIMENTAL INSIGNIA

PALMETTO REGIMENT
(118th INFANTRY REGIMENT)

1st ALABAMA
(200th INFANTRY REGIMENT)

1st MISSOURI
(138th INFANTRY REGIMENT)

1st MISSISSIPPI
(155th INFANTRY REGIMENT)

1st VIRGINIA
(176th INFANTRY REGIMENT)

2nd ALABAMA
(167th INFANTRY REGIMENT)

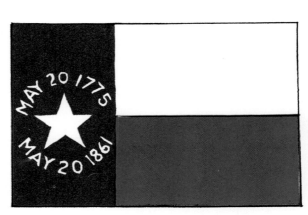

REGIMENTAL FLAG, 1860-61, SOUTH CAROLINA

REGIMENTAL FLAG, NORTH CAROLINA

PLATE 20
UNION AND CONFEDERATE DRESS HATS

ARTILLERY CORPS, U.S.A.

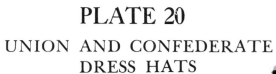

5th NEW YORK
VOLUNTEER INFANTRY REGIMENT
(DURYEA'S ZOUAVES)

79th NEW YORK VOLUNTEER
INFANTRY REGIMENT

CHARLESTON
LIGHT DRAGOONS

39th NEW YORK VOLUNTEER
INFANTRY REGIMENT

7th NEW YORK STATE MILITIA

OFFICER, U.S.N.

WOODIS RIFLES, NORFOLK, VIRGINIA

COMMAND ROSTER

Abraham Lincoln.

Jefferson Davis

Edward Porter Alexander

When Lee met Meade on the famous battlefield of Gettysburg, Edward Porter Alexander was in command of the Confederate artillery on Seminary Ridge. On Lee's orders, early in the afternoon of July 3, 1863, he opened fire on the Union forces on Cemetery Ridge with 160 guns and poured on an intense artillery barrage in preparation for Pickett's thrust against the Union center. Hancock met this attack with a counter massed-artillery attack that cut the oncoming rebels to ribbons. Alexander remained with Longstreet's Corps; and by the close of the war, he was one of the few veteran officers with Lee at Appomattox.

Graduated from West Point in 1857, Alexander was brevetted lieutenant of engineers and assigned to duty as an instructor at the Academy. During this tour of duty he developed the flag signal system used by both sides in the Civil War. In 1860 he was ordered to Washington Territory and the following year was transferred to Alcatraz Island, San Francisco, on an engineering project. He resigned his commission when Georgia seceded, hastened to the South, and was commissioned captain of engineers in the Confederate Army on June 3, 1861.

Appointed chief of ordnance in Beauregard's command the following month, he was later sent to a similar assignment with the Army of Northern Virginia. As colonel of artillery he performed brilliantly at Fredericksburg, his batteries on Marye's Heights shattering every Union charge.

This colorful Confederate rose to chief of artillery under Lee in the last days of the Confederacy and covered Lee's retreat from Richmond in 1865 with his artillery. He bitterly opposed any surrender, but Lee dissuaded him from any further resistance even though he wanted to fight on after Appomattox.

After the war Alexander achieved a distinguished career in education, industry, and public service. He was professor of engineering at the University of South Carolina from 1866 to 1869, when he resigned to become president of the Columbia Oil Company. Later he engaged in railroading and from 1887 to 1893 was president of the Georgia Railroad and Banking Company.

During the early 1890's he purchased North and South Islands off the South Carolina coast, where he developed rice planting. He served on a number of state and federal commissions and from 1885 to 1887 was a director of the Union Pacific Railroad. He published *Railway Practice* (1887) and *Military Memoirs of a Confederate* (1907), a critical study of the operations of the Army of Northern Virginia throughout the war and of the Army of the Tennessee during the war's final stages. Alexander died in Savannah, Georgia, on April 28, 1910.

ƒ V Alexandri

Robert Anderson

Robert Anderson is most noted for his valiant defense against the attacks on Fort Sumter—the immediate cause of the War Between the States.

The Major was born in 1805 near Louisville, Kentucky, and took the usual military academic training at West Point, graduating in 1825.

In the twenty-five years that followed, he saw active service in the Black Hawk, Seminole, and Mexican Wars. By 1857 he earned his promotion to major; and three years later he took command of Fort Sumter in the harbor of Charleston, South Carolina.

The government of the Confederacy, intent on a separate national existence, undertook, as an initial step, the seizure of the United States arsenals, custom-houses, and forts. The authorities in South Carolina were determined to capture Fort Sumter. They had seen the President fail in his attempt in January to relieve the fort by an unarmed merchant steamer, the *Star of the West*, laden with supplies. In the same month the *Charleston Mercury* had stated "let us be ready for war. . . . Border Southern States will never join us until we have indicated our power to free ourselves—until we have proven that a garrison of seventy men cannot hold the portal of our commerce. The fate of the Southern Confederacy hangs by the ensign balliards of Fort Sumter."

Lincoln had received messages from Major Anderson indicating that the food supply at the fort would not last beyond six weeks. The shift of the Major's garrison of eighty-two men from Fort Moultrie to the more secure Sumter had angered the secessionists of Charleston. Lincoln's cabinet members, in fact, voted five to two to give up the fort.

The Confederate government at Montgomery advised General G. T. Beauregard, who had resigned his commission in the Corps of Engineers of the United States Army in February, 1861, to take action. In addition, this government sent three commissioners to Washington to communicate with the Secretary of State, present their credentials, and state clearly the objectives of their mission. The Secretary of State refused to consider them as diplomatic agents.

The government at Washington was resolved to provision the garrison at Fort Sumter. By April 5, General Beauregard had deprived the fort of any daily supply of food from Charleston. A messenger, Lieutenant Talbot, was sent to Governor Pickens of South Carolina to inform him of the government's intentions. When General Beauregard learned of the message, he informed Mr. L. P. Walker, the Secretary of War of the Confederate States at Montgomery, that "provisions will be sent to Fort Sumter peacefully, or otherwise by force." Mr. Walker replied, "If you have no doubt of the authorized character of the agent who communicated to you the intention of the Washington Government, to supply Fort Sumter by force, you will at once demand its evacuation, and if this is refused, proceed in such a manner as you may determine to reduce it: Answer." Word was sent back, "the demand will be made tomorrow at twelve o'clock."

General Beauregard, in the name of the Confederate government, offered Major Anderson the following terms: "all proper facilities for the removal of yourself and command, together with company arms and property, and all private property, to any port in the United States which you may elect. The flag which you have upheld so long and with so much fortitude, under the most trying circumstances, may be saluted by you on taking it down."

Two aides of the General received a reply from Major Anderson stating that "it is a demand with which I regret my sense of honor and of my obligation to my Government prevent my compliance."

Anderson was appointed brigadier general in the regular army on May 15, 1861, and for a short time commanded in Kentucky, where he helped to save that state for the Union. When his health gave way, he was relieved in October, 1861. He never completely recovered and performed little duty between that time and the date of his retirement from active service on October 27, 1863. He was brevetted major-general of the volunteers in 1865 and was sent to raise the flag over Fort Sumter on April 14, four years from the date he lowered it. He died at Nice on October 26, 1871. He was an excellent officer and a just and popular commander. Though not brilliant, he was industrious, had a high sense of duty, and was deeply religious and considerate and kindly in his relations with all.

Robert Anderson

Nathaniel P. Banks

Nathaniel Prentiss Banks, a politician of many shades and a controversial soldier, was born at Waltham, Massachusetts, on January 30, 1816, the eldest son of a local cotton mill superintendent. He edited a weekly paper at Waltham, studied law, and was admitted to the bar. As a Free Soiler he served in the Massachusetts House of Representatives from 1849 to 1853, and was Speaker in 1851 and 1852.

In 1853 Banks became president of the state constitutional convention and, in the same year, was elected to Congress as a coalition candidate of Democrats and Free Soilers. Although reelected in 1854 as an American or "Know-Nothing," he soon left this party. In 1855 he presided over a Republican convention in Massachusetts.

At the opening of the Thirty-fourth Congress, the anti-Nebraska men gradually united in supporting Banks for Speaker; and after one of the bitterest and most protracted speakership contests in the history of Congress, lasting from December 3, 1855, to February 2, 1856, he was chosen on the one hundred and thirty-third ballot. Banks was reelected in 1856 as a Republican but resigned his seat in December, 1857, and became governor of Massachusetts from 1858 to 1861.

In 1861 he succeeded George D. McClellan as president of the Illinois Central Railway. When Sumter fell, Banks was quick to offer his services to his country; and Abraham Lincoln appointed him major general of volunteers. In the spring of 1862 Banks was ordered to move against Jackson in the Shenandoah Valley. With superior forces, the latter defeated him at Winchester, Virginia, on May 25 and forced him back to the Potomac River.

On August 9, 1862, Banks again encountered Jackson at Cedar Mountain and, though greatly outnumbered, succeeded in holding his ground after a sanguinary battle. In November he sailed from New York with a strong force to replace General B. F. Butler at New Orleans as commander of the Department of the Gulf. Ordered to cooperate with General U. S. Grant, who was then before Vicksburg, he investigated the defenses of Port Hudson in May, 1863. After three attempts to carry these works by storm, he began a regular siege. The garrison finally surrendered to Banks on July 9, 1863.

In the autumn of 1863 Banks organized the Red River expedition to Texas, chiefly for the purpose of preventing the French in Mexico from aiding the Confederates. He secured possession of the region near the mouths of the Nueces and the Rio Grande.

The second Red River expedition (March–May, 1864) was a complete failure. It brought on an investigation and a minority report censure. Banks was superseded by General Canby; and in August, 1865, he was mustered out of the service. He returned home and from 1865 to 1873 was once again a member of Congress, serving as chairman of the committee on foreign affairs. A personal quarrel with President Grant in 1872 caused him to join the Liberal-Republican revolt. He supported Horace Greeley as the Liberal-Republican and Democratic candidate. In 1874 he was successful as a Democratic candidate, serving one term in Congress. Having rejoined the Republican party in 1876, he served as United States Marshal for Massachusetts from 1879 to 1888. In that year he was elected to Congress for the ninth time. His health failing, he retired at the close of his term (1891) and died at Waltham on September 1, 1894. A statue to his memory was erected on the grounds of the State House in 1908.

Banks in many ways was a highly interesting figure. He was a self-made man who faced youthful poverty and frustration and the denial of a decent early education. His ambition and talents proved him capable of growing from a mill-hand in youth to a state and federal public official and major general in the Civil War.

Though successful as a state and federal politician, he was but one example of several incompetent military commanders who hindered the successful prosecution of the war by professionals.

N. P. Banks

William F. Barry

William F. Barry, a famous Union artillery expert, was born in New York City on August 18, 1818. He attended the public schools of that city and entered West Point in 1838; he graduated seventeenth in a class of forty-five cadets. Like so many other young graduates from this famous academy, Barry saw service on the frontier and in the Mexican War.

During the bloody days in Kansas before the Civil War Barry was stationed at Fort Leavenworth. He helped Major Ringgold organize the first battery of light artillery in the Army. As major of the Fifth Artillery, he served in the defense of Fort Pickens, Florida, and was General McDowell's chief of artillery in the First Battle of Bull Run. He was made a brigadier general of United States volunteers in August, 1861, and was later promoted to chief of artillery during the Peninsular Campaign.

Barry fought at Yorktown, Gaines Mill, Mechanicsville, Malvern Hill, and Harrison Landing. From September, 1862, to March, 1864, he acted as chief of artillery in the defense of Washington against Confederate attacks.

Early in March, 1864, he was assigned to General Sherman's army as chief of artillery. His knowledge of accurate artillery fire was fully appreciated at Rocky Face Ridge, Resaca, Casswell, Kenesaw Mountain, Peach Tree Creek, Atlanta, Jonesboro, and in the "March to the Sea." For his work in these campaigns he was brevetted major general of volunteers in September, 1864. Within a year he won the coveted promotions of brigadier general and major general in the regular army.

Barry was anxious to participate in active service to the end of the conflict. He witnessed Johnston's surrender to Sherman.

After the close of the war he continued in the regular army. From 1867 to 1877 he organized and directed the Army's artillery school at Fortress Monroe, Virginia. His health became impaired, and he was assigned to Fort McHenry. He died on July 18, 1879.

William F. Finny

Pierre G. T. Beauregard

Pierre G. T. Beauregard, a general in the Confederate Army, was born in 1818 at St. Bernard Parish near New Orleans, Louisiana. He received his early education there and in New York City and was graduated from West Point in 1838, second in his class. Among his classmates was Irwin McDowell, who was destined to fight him in the bloody Battle of Bull Run.

After graduation he became lieutenant of engineers. He was employed on fortification work, chiefly in Louisiana, until 1846, when the Mexican War was declared. As an engineer on General Scott's staff, Beauregard was present at the siege of Vera Cruz and fought in the battles of Cerro Gordo and Contreras. He received a brevet on August 20, 1847, for gallant conduct in the latter engagement. He suffered wounds and earned another brevet on September 13, 1847. When the war was over, he served as chief engineer for three years, 1858–61, drafting the site for New Orleans.

In 1860 he was appointed to the post of Superintendent of West Point; but openly expressing his desire to go with his native state if it seceded, he kept the post for only five days, resigning in February to become a brigadier general in the Confederate Army. Sent to Charleston, it was he who gave the command to fire on Fort Sumter. He won great popularity and was given a high post as commander of a Confederate army.

In July, 1861, under General Joseph Johnston, he fought at the great Battle of Bull Run. The following year he won a promotion to full generalship for his services and was sent to the West. There he took over A. S. Johnston's command when the latter met his death in the battle of Shiloh.

Beauregard next became the commander of the Army of the Tennessee. His tactics were to delay the Union forces, but he was forced to retreat more than once when faced by General Halleck's superior forces. He finally relinquished his command to General Bragg because of ill health. When he recovered, Beauregard was sent to defend the South Carolina and Georgia coasts. He did remarkably well in defending Charleston, and at Petersburg he won the admiration of the South by holding back General Grant's forces on June 15 until the arrival of Lee. Once again, in the fall of 1864, he took over an administrative command in the West.

Before the war came to an end, he was made second in command of the Confederate forces. He continued fighting in the Carolinas until the surrender at Appomattox.

His career in the postwar years began with his appointment as president of the New Orleans, Jackson, and Mississippi Railway. He later managed the Louisiana state lottery and for a time was state adjutant general. He died in 1893.

G. T. Beauregard

David B. Birney

David Bell Birney was an example of an army officer who could acquit himself commendably as a brigade commander but who fell short of the necessary talents of a good corps commander.

Birney was born in Huntsville, Alabama, on May 29, 1825, the son of James Gillespie Birney. He studied law in Cincinnati in 1848 and began his career as a practicing lawyer in Philadelphia.

At the outbreak of the Civil War he joined the Union cause and rendered creditable service in the fighting at Yorktown and Williamsburg in McClellan's first Peninsular Campaign and in the bitter fighting under Burnside and Hooker in the battles of Fredericksburg and Chancellorsville.

Birney's brigade had a taste of fighting Lee's Army of Northern Virginia in the desperate battle of Gettysburg, where the Birney forces were actively engaged in fierce fighting at Peach Orchard. When Sickles was wounded in the fighting, Birney succeeded him as commander of the Third Corps.

In the important battle of Petersburg, Birney served as senior division commander of the Second Corps under Hancock. He was slow in getting his corps into action; and when Meade and other Union commanders failed to grasp fully the opportunity to take the Petersburg forts, Lee rushed in to aid General Beauregard. The attack by Birney and the other Union forces was thus repulsed.

In the final assault on the forts and trenches at Petersburg, Birney sent green artillery troops into the fighting and suffered the loss of some 6,000 men in a few minutes.

D. B. Birney

Braxton Bragg

General Braxton Bragg is noted in Southern history as the hero of Chickamauga, where he soundly defeated the large Union Army under Rosecrans.

This Confederate general was born in 1817 in Warrenton County, North Carolina. Along with other famous soldiers, he made a name for himself at West Point, where he graduated in 1837. He distinguished himself in the fierce Seminole War and fought valiantly in the Mexican War at Buena Vista, earning a promotion to lieutenant colonel. He remained a soldier until 1856.

Plantation life in his beloved Louisiana attracted him sufficiently to cause him to offer his resignation. He developed his sugar plantation until the outbreak of the Civil War, when he was offered a commission in the Confederate Army as brigadier general.

Bragg's first assignment was the protection of the long coastline from Pensacola to Mobile. In February, 1862, he was promoted to major general and given the opportunity to command the Second Corps under General Albert S. Johnston. When the latter was killed in action at Shiloh, Bragg became a full general.

In June, 1862, Beauregard was relieved of his command of the Army of the Tennessee; and Bragg assumed responsibility. He took the initiative quickly by invading Kentucky, believing that this state ultimately would join the Confederacy. However, when Union general D. C. Buell cleverly united his forces and gave battle at Perryville, Bragg was forced to retreat to Tennessee. General Rosecrans was sent against him with a new Union army. Bragg stood his ground at Murfreesboro on December 31, 1862, and won a partial victory. His failure to follow through and force Rosecrans to surrender his army caused criticism of the conduct of this campaign in the South.

On September 19, 1863, Bragg achieved his greatest victory, at Chickamauga. He forced the Union Army back to Chattanooga and there laid siege until Grant forced him to give up and retreat back into Georgia.

On December 2, 1863, he asked to be relieved of his command; and General Joseph E. Johnston took over his army. President Jefferson Davis put Bragg on his staff as military advisor with the nominal rank of commander in chief of the Confederate armies. In this position he clashed with General Joseph E. Johnston, then following a policy of retreat, and scorched earth in his losing campaign against Sherman.

When Lee, in a desperate last effort to avoid surrender, assumed command of all Confederate field forces, he induced Johnston to resume command again and put Bragg in charge of one of the divisions aiding Johnston. But Bragg also failed in his activity against Sherman, and "Joe" Johnston finally surrendered his skeleton army to "Billy" Sherman a few weeks after Lee had surrendered at Appomattox. After the war Bragg's only public service was acting as chief engineer of Alabama. He died in 1876, not yet sixty years of age.

John Cabell Breckenridge

John Cabell Breckenridge, soldier, statesman, and politician, was born near Lexington, Kentucky, on January 15, 1821, a descendant of a distinguished Scotch-Irish family.

After graduation from Center College, Kentucky, he entered the practice of law, interrupting it long enough to see service in the war against Mexico. Upon his return home, he was elected first to the state legislature and then to Congress in 1851, where he served two terms.

When the Democratic Party became hopelessly divided over the question of the extension of slavery, the Northern wing supported Stephen A. Douglas as its presidential candidate in 1860. The Southern wing selected Breckenridge as its Democratic standard-bearer. His selection, however, while one of desperation and bitterness, was not one of recklessness; for Breckenridge had served as Vice-President under President James Buchanan.

Abraham Lincoln resolved the Douglas-Breckenridge conflict by defeating them both in the presidential election of 1860. Breckenridge, however, remained undaunted, becoming United States Senator from his home state in 1861. His tenure was short because he resigned his Senate seat and followed his native state into the Confederacy.

Breckenridge was a man of considerable ability and served with credit as a major general, especially under Bragg in the bitter fighting at Shiloh, Stone River, Murfreesboro, Chickamauga, Chattanooga, and Cold Harbor.

In the bitter fighting along the Tennessee River and around Shiloh Church, Breckenridge served under General Albert S. Johnston, later joining Bragg to crush the Union general Prentiss at Shiloh. With the death of Johnston, Beauregard took charge of the battered Confederate Army and broke off the bloody battle with Grant, Sherman, and the other Union generals.

When Bragg succeeded to the command of the Confederate forces in Tennessee, Breckenridge became one of his corps commanders.

In December, 1862, when Rosecrans decided to engage Bragg, the two forces met along the winding Stone River with Murfreesboro to the rear of Bragg's forces. The rival commanders both hit upon the same plan of attack, a sort of reversal of what had been attempted at Shiloh. Rosecrans hoped to roll up the rebel flank along the Stone River and get behind Bragg at Murfreesboro. Bragg, however, had heavily reinforced his left flank and attacked the Union right in an effort to force it back. Breckenridge was given the difficult task of taking a high hill along the right bank of Stone River, with the intention of fortifying it with artillery in order to shell the Union forces.

Breckenridge opened the attack at dawn on a cold January 2 morning only to discover, to his horror, that on the hill were massed some fifty-eight guns under the veteran Van Cleve. The Union artillery opened fire, and the brave forces under Breckenridge were torn to pieces.

Negley and Palmer had come to the aid of Van Cleve; and as a result Bragg, badly mauled, called off his forces and retreated along the road to Chattanooga. Rosecrans was not slow to exult over the victory. However, a second and final chapter in the Bragg-Rosecrans struggle found them again locked in deadly conflict at Chickamauga in hilly Tennessee. Once more Breckenridge faced Negley and shattered the Union forces. However Baird, who was behind some small fortifications, held off the Confederates and protected the Union flank. The Union forces were shattered by Bragg's attack; only Thomas held the line in one of the fiercest and bloodiest battles of the war. This attack forced Rosecrans to rush his defeated Army into Chattanooga. Rosecrans was humiliated; but Bragg paid for his victory with the loss of 23,000 men killed and wounded— a terrible butchery.

Breckenridge later returned east and saw service at Cold Harbor. He was entrusted with the escape of the Confederate forces in the fall of Richmond, and it was he who ordered all bridges burned upon the evacuation of that city.

From January to April, 1865, Breckenridge served as Secretary of War under Jefferson Davis. After the close of the war he journeyed to Europe and, returning home in 1868, resumed his law practice. He died in Lexington, Kentucky, in 1875.

Wm C Buckinunji

Simon Bolivar Buckner

Simon Bolivar Buckner, soldier and political leader, was born in Hart County, Kentucky, on April 1, 1823. He had a strong desire to go to the Academy at West Point. He achieved his goal and proved a good student. When he graduated from the Point in 1844, he was offered an opportunity to teach there; and for one year, 1845/46, he became assistant professor of geography, history, and ethics.

When the Mexican War broke out, Buckner saw real action at Churnbusco. He was brevetted first lieutenant for gallantry and later became a captain.

In 1848–50 he served again at West Point, this time as an assistant instructor of infantry tactics. He left to serve on the frontier and in 1855 resigned from the army.

When Governor Beriah Magoffin attempted to keep Kentucky neutral at the outbreak of the Civil War, Buckner was given command of the State Guard.

However, Buckner turned toward the Confederate cause, in which he finally achieved the rank of lieutenant general. He became third in command of Fort Donelson. He served under Floyd in the campaign that resulted in the surrender of the important fort on the Cumberland, with its garrison of 21,000 men. Floyd, who was the former Secretary of War under President Buchanan, took command of the fort. He was considered a timid man who feared that any mistake made by him would result in his hanging by the Southern leaders.

Grant attacked this fort but was repulsed. Floyd, in turn, took the offensive and flung 8,000 of his men against General McClernand, rolling back the Union line. General Wallace came to McClernand's aid, and the enemy attack was checked. Grant then ordered General Smith to attack Floyd and try to cut off any escape. The latter was flung back into his defenses; and when Grant's forces were ready to attack, the Confederate leader lost his courage and, after turning his command over to General Pillow, fled. This general, in turn, also fled.

The command then fell to Buckner, who, in turn, asked Grant what terms he would give if he surrendered. Grant made his now-famous reply of "Unconditional Surrender."

Bragg, in an angry note to Grant, turned over the fort and 17,000 men. Grant thus became prominent and his star was definitely on the rise.

Buckner was exchanged in August, 1862, and subsequently fought hard under Bragg in the campaign of Chickamauga. He and his division aided Cheatham and Hardee in the attack on Sheridan's hill position, only to be repulsed.

In 1887–91, Buckner became the governor of Kentucky. Five years later he was chosen candidate of the "Gold" Democrats for Vice-President of the United States. He died on January 8, 1914, at Munfordville, Kentucky.

Don Carlos Buell

The Civil War produced many generals who were very successful as brigade commanders but who were, at best, only mediocre army corps leaders. This was especially true of Don Carlos Buell.

Buell was born in Lowell, Ohio, on March 23, 1818. His parents provided for his elementary education, and he eventually entered West Point.

When he graduated from the Academy in 1841, he was commissioned a second lieutenant. In the war with Mexico he saw service but made no outstanding record for himself.

At the beginning of the Civil War Buell served as an adjutant general in the regular army and soon earned a promotion to brigadier general, attached to the Army of the Potomac. He was sent west for military service in the Ohio, Cumberland, and Tennessee areas.

When Halleck became commander of all Union forces in Kentucky and Tennessee, Buell was assigned to the Army of the Cumberland. He was extremely rigid on the matter of army regulations and was a strict disciplinarian. When it came to rendering decisions, however, he, like other generals on both sides, was very slow and indecisive.

Halleck's battle plan called for clearing out the Confederate forces in the Kentucky-Tennessee areas. He was to cooperate with Grant in cutting the Confederate supply line near Corinth. When Grant got into difficulty at Shiloh, Buell aided him by rushing Nelson's brigade to the battle. Later Buell's three divisions took part in the campaign around Shiloh.

When Halleck decided to capture Memphis, he sent Buell with 40,000 men to smash into Chattanooga and hold that important railroad and supply center. Buell had to build a railroad in order to draw his supplies from St. Louis through Corinth. The active Confederates raided his lines and slowed up his lumbering advance. Halleck sent him more aid, but even that did not prevent the wily Bragg from getting to Chattanooga first.

When Halleck went east as the military advisor to Lincoln and Pope followed to "supplant" McClellan, Grant was given the overall command of the forces in the area. Buell expected Bragg to attack Nashville and concentrated his forces near Murfreesboro. When it became apparent that Bragg was instead aiming for Louisville, Buell followed him, thus draining Grant's forces when they were desperately needed.

One of Bragg's divisions under Kirby-Smith entered Covington, and the populace prepared for an attack. Buell left three divisions at Nashville under George Thomas, but Bragg again changed plans and now, with a larger army, prepared to meet Buell.

Grant sent aid to Buell, and Bragg retreated, thus leaving Louisville to the Federal troops; but Governor O. P. Morton of Indiana got into a three-way controversy with Buell and General Nelson. Morton demanded that "Buell must go."

Lincoln, aware of Morton's political influence, agreed, and offered Buell's command to General Thomas. When Thomas refused, Buell was restored to his position. At Perryville he came to grips with Braggs' forces. It was here that young "Phil" Sheridan won great fame by repeatedly hurling back the Confederate attack. Bragg was forced to retire hastily into the hill country of Tennessee.

Governor Morton now asked Lincoln to replace Buell with Rosecrans. The President did so, and Buell's career as a commander ended. He retired from the volunteer service, and in 1865 he resigned from the regular army. On November 19, 1898, he died near Rockport, Kentucky.

D. C. Buell

John Buford

John Buford is regarded by many as one of the finest cavalry officers of the Civil War. His coolness, courage, and judgment were outstanding.

Born in 1826, Buford went through the usual academic training and attended West Point. After graduation in 1848, he was appointed to the Second Dragoons. He served efficiently in the great Sioux expedition of 1857, in the Kansas disturbances of that year, and in the Utah expedition of 1857/58. In November, 1861, he was appointed a major in the Inspector General's Corps and was attached to General Pope's staff the following year.

When Pope succeeded McClellan as commander of the Army of Virginia, he appointed Buford to reorganize the cavalry.

Pope prepared to meet the enemy at Gordonsville—a railway junction controlling the Confederate route from Richmond to the Shenandoah Valley. Buford warned Pope of the advance of Stonewall Jackson with 25,000 men, ready to strike. He also alerted him to the fact that Lee and his army were approaching. This gave Pope a welcome opportunity to make a stand on the Rappahannock while Buford was hounding Jackson and his men.

In the days preceding the battle of Gettysburg, Buford, Gregg, and Kilpatrick engaged Stuart along the valleys of Pennsylvania. At Gettysburg, Buford fought a delaying skirmish with Ewell's corps until Howard arrived on the battlefield and concentrated on Culp's Hill. Lee turned down Longstreet's plan to try flank attacks on the Union forces at Gettysburg because without Stuart present the Confederate infantry could be turned by the cavalry divisions of Buford and Kilpatrick.

Buford took part in several bloody engagements—Antietam, Fredericksburg, and South Mountain. He made a brilliant record in his attacks at Round Top in the Gettysburg area. Following the engagement at Culpeper, he pursued the enemy across the Rapidan, cutting the way to rejoin the Union Army north of the Rappahannock.

Buford fell ill and died in Washington in December, 1863. He was buried at West Point.

Jno Buford

Ambrose E. Burnside

Union general Ambrose E. Burnside is best known for his invention of a breech-loading rifle and for his valiant aid to Grant in the Wilderness and Cold Harbor campaigns.

At the age of eighteen Burnside was apprenticed to a tailor; but a year later, in 1843, he abandoned this trade and became a cadet at West Point. Four years later, with the Mexican War almost over, he graduated from the Academy. For seven years his only service was garrison duty.

In October, 1853, Burnside resigned his commission as first lieutenant and became engaged in the manufacture of fire arms at Bristol, Rhode Island. He formed a company for the purpose of manufacturing the rifle he had invented. His poor financial backing caused the company to fail, and his creditors took over the venture in 1857.

When the Civil War broke out, Burnside became commander of a Rhode Island regiment of militia men. He took part in the relief of the national capital and in the First Battle of Bull Run served as a colonel of the Rhode Island volunteers, commanding a brigade.

By August, 1861, he was commissioned brigadier general of volunteers and placed at the head of a vital expeditionary force. In 1862 he took Roanoke Island, Newbern, and Fort Macon, and became commander of the Department of North Carolina. For this he won another promotion, being raised to the rank of major general of volunteers. Subsequently his troops became part of the famous Ninth Army Corps.

After the Second Battle of Bull Run, Burnside was offered the command of the Army of Virginia; but he declined. It was his wish instead to serve with the Ninth Corps under General George McClellan. There he revealed his military ability, especially in the bloody battles of South Mountain and Antietam. In November, 1862, Lincoln turned over McClellan's command of the Army of the Potomac to him. The choice was a mistake, for Burnside attacked Lee near Fredericksburg and was badly repulsed with a loss of 10,000 men. Burnside in turn was replaced by Hooker.

In March, 1863, Burnside was transferred to the Department of Ohio. He made the headlines by his arrest and court-martial of Clement L. Vallandigham, a Democratic member of Congress who had made an allegedly disloyal speech. The General also aroused bitter criticism among civilians because he forced newspapers to suppress editorial and news items not in favor of the army. On the other hand, he gained ample praise when he helped crush Morgan's Ohio raids.

In November, 1863, he captured Knoxville and held firm even though Confederate general James Longstreet, with a superior force, laid siege to the town.

When Grant assumed command of the Army of the Potomac in 1864 and reorganized it into several army corps under Hancock, Warren, Sedgwick, and Sheridan, Burnside was given command of the Ninth Corps. He rendered good service to Grant in the battles of the Wilderness and Cold Harbor. However, he committed a terrible blunder before Petersburg when he attempted to capture Cemetery Hill, the high ground that dominated the city. He had ordered his troops to mine the area, and they were soon trapped in the mine crater where they were cut down by Confederate guns on Cemetery Hill.

This marked the end of Burnside's career as a soldier. He received a "leave" and came north, never again to rejoin the army. After the war he entered business and politics and was connected with several railroad enterprises. He served as governor of Rhode Island from 1866 to 1869, and from 1875 to his death in 1881 he was United States Senator from Rhode Island.

A. E. Burnside.

Benjamin Franklin Butler

Benjamin Franklin Butler, a notorious politician and a controversial soldier, was born in Deerfield, New Hampshire, on November 5, 1818. He graduated from Waterville (now Colby) College in 1838, was admitted to the Massachusetts bar in 1840, and began practice in Lowell, Massachusetts. He quickly attained distinction as a lawyer, particularly in the field of criminal law. Entering politics as a Democrat, he was elected to the Massachusetts House of Representatives in 1853 and to the State Senate in 1859. He was a delegate to the Democratic national convention from 1848 to 1860. In the Democratic national convention of 1860 at Charleston, he supported the party movement that nominated Breckenridge and divided the Democratic party.

After the outbreak of the Civil War, Butler was commissioned in the Union Army and soon took possession of Baltimore without bloodshed. While in command at Fortress Monroe, he agreed to return a group of fugitive slaves to their owner on the condition that the owner, a Virginia colonel, take an oath of allegiance to the United States. In commenting on the decision the action was defended on the grounds that Negroes were "contraband of war," thus originating the phrase "contraband" as applied to Southern Negroes during the war. In the conduct of tactical operations Butler was almost uniformly unsuccessful; and his first action at Big Bethel, Virginia, was a humiliating defeat for the Union forces.

In 1862 he was assigned command of the Federal force that occupied New Orleans. In the administration of that city he showed firmness and severity. He opposed the use of Negroes as troops in that area. Many of his acts, however, gave great offense, particularly his seizure of $800,000 which had been deposited in the office of the Dutch Consul and his order that any woman who insulted or showed contempt for any officer or soldier of the Union Army should be treated as a woman of the town plying her vocation. This order provoked a storm of protest and increased the Confederates' hatred of him.

Butler showed indecision and lack of leadership while commanding forces near Fortress Monroe. He failed to threaten Richmond and to keep Lee busy and instead became bottled up at Bermuda Hundreds. Grant and Halleck wanted to retire him but were advised not to provoke party division on the eve of the presidential election of 1864. When Lincoln was reelected, Grant fired Butler; and Lincoln supported Grant's action. Discredited and bitter, Butler returned to Massachusetts. He died in Washington, D.C., on January 11, 1893.

Benj. F. Butler

Edward R. S. Canby

Edward R. S. Canby was born in Kentucky in August, 1817. He covered many theaters during the Civil War and held many posts. He made a brilliant record as a Union commander and had a colorful career.

In 1835 Canby entered West Point and was commissioned four years later as a second lieutenant in the Second Infantry. He saw action in the Seminole War and by 1847 had achieved the rank of captain. In that capacity he accompanied General Scott's army, fighting with Riley's Brigade when it entered Mexico. He witnessed the siege of Vera Cruz and participated in the capture of Mexico City. On two occasions he won honors on the field of battle.

Following the Mexican War he was stationed in San Francisco and later in Washington, remaining there until 1855. In that year he became a major with the Tenth Infantry, fighting at various posts along the frontier.

When the Civil War broke out, Canby was at Fort Defiance, New Mexico. In May, 1861, he took over the command of the Department of New Mexico. It was a dreary area, far from the great theaters of the war but nevertheless very important to the Union cause. The Confederates, under General Sibley, had planned to push an expedition into New Mexico, not to occupy the territory but to overtake the Union forces and then move on towards California. The Confederacy wanted the gold that state offered, and they hoped to obtain help from Southern sympathizers in California. The Union's occupation of California meant a heavy drainage of gold, sorely needed by the Confederacy.

Canby had only a small force of unreliable volunteers from the local territory. He tested these troops in combat in January, 1862, and was defeated. Thereafter it was necessary to avoid combat and utilize the weapons of hunger, thirst, and heat. These reduced General Sibley's forces by almost 50 per cent. His men could no longer fight and began to retreat to Texas.

As a result of this campaign, General Canby gained national prominence. He was promoted to brigadier general in March, 1862, and was ordered east, where he was given a routine job as assistant adjutant general in Washington. Again he made the headlines when he was assigned to suppress the July, 1863, draft riots in New York City. He remained there for four months and carried out the regulations of the draft.

In May, 1864, he earned the title of major general of volunteers and was put in command of the military division of West Mississippi, covering the Gulf States and Southwest. In November of that year he suffered severe wounds when he was attacked by guerillas. However, he recovered sufficiently to take command again and lay siege to Mobile, which surrendered on April 12, 1865.

Following the Appomattox Court House surrender, Confederate generals Taylor and Kirby continued to fight. It was to General Canby that these men surrendered on May 4 and May 26, respectively.

He saw considerable service after the war fighting Indian tribes on the Pacific coast, and was killed by the Modoc Indians on April 11, 1873.

Ed M Canby

Benjamin F. Cheatham

Benjamin F. Cheatham was born in Nashville, Tennessee, on October 20, 1820. He served first as a captain of Tennessee volunteers in the War with Mexico and became a colonel when Mexico City was attacked.

In the Civil War he commanded the Tennessee volunteer militia and became a brigadier general in the Confederate Army in July, 1861. He commanded a division of General Polk's army in the fighting around Belmont, Shiloh, and Perryville.

As one of Bragg's division commanders at Chickamauga, he first tried to turn the Union left flank under McCook; and then along with Hardee, he attacked the Union right center. This center was under the commands of Generals Dodge, Reynolds, and Schofield. Generals Thomas and Sheridan, however, checked the attack.

In 1864 Cheatham was assigned as one of the main corps commanders of General Hood's army. He took a part in the bitter fighting around Atlanta and Nashville, and in the Atlanta campaign he was in charge of the inner defense of the city.

Cheatham succeeded Hardee as one of Hood's key corps commanders; and during Hood's bitter fighting against Thomas, a heated argument arose between Cheatham and Hood. Cheatham charged that Hood had not been specific in his order to attack Schofield's corps at Atlanta. On the other hand, Hood charged that Cheatham had spent more time dancing with the ladies than paying complete attention to military business.

Cheatham was transferred to the army of Joseph E. Johnston, which later surrendered to General Sherman.

After the war Cheatham entered politics, becoming State Superintendent of Prisons and later postmaster of Nashville, Tennessee, where he died on August 4, 1886.

B F Cheatham

Patrick R. Cleburne

Patrick R. Cleburne, a colorful Confederate officer, was an example of an immigrant who, despite the adversities of life, achieved a modest niche in the history of his adopted country.

Born in County Cork, Ireland, the son of a physician and farmer, Cleburne was educated by tutors in a private school. At the age of eighteen he apprenticed himself to a druggist. He failed in classical languages and in French and was unable to pass an important examination given to qualifying apothecaries. To hide his chagrin over failure, he enlisted in the Forty-first Regiment, British Infantry.

After three years of service he purchased his army discharge with money obtained from his father's estate. Setting out with his sister and a half-brother, he landed at New Orleans in 1849 and moved on to Cincinnati, where he became a druggist's clerk.

After six months in this job he moved to Helena, Arkansas, to take up a similar position. Here he made his home amidst pleasant surroundings and genial friends. He studied law, was admitted to the bar in 1856, and continued in practice until the outbreak of the Civil War.

In 1860 Cleburne organized a rifle company; and when the war broke out, his group volunteered for service. He became a captain and was soon a colonel with the Arkansas Fifteenth Infantry Regiment.

Early in 1862 he was promoted to brigadier general and served with skill and daring at Shiloh and in the battle of Perryville. In December of the same year, he became a major general and served with distinction in the fighting around Murfreesboro and Chattanooga. His men fought with great courage at Chickamauga. His resolute action at Ringgold Gap saved Bragg's artillery and wagon trains from capture. For this action he received a vote of thanks from the Confederate Congress.

Cleburne was able, also, to get most of his men to re-enlist for service at a time when the Confederate forces were being rapidly depleted.

He urged that slaves be offered freedom in exchange for service in the Confederate Army. While many officers favored this plan, General Joseph Johnston, who had succeeded Bragg, refused to send it to Richmond, stating that the idea was more political than military. A fellow officer, however, took it upon himself to send it to Jefferson Davis, who declared that he appreciated the patriotic motives that had prompted the idea. However, he deemed it unwise to publish it at that time.

Cleburne had been warned that writing this paper would cost him further promotion. This proved to be true; Hood succeeded Johnston in the Atlanta campaign. Cleburne was by-passed and ordered to serve under the new commander. He fought well in the bitter fighting against Sherman and followed Hood in the fierce sorties in Tennessee. In fact, the reckless Hood goaded Cleburne for not revealing enough fierceness in the attacks. Cleburne earned the title among his colleagues of "Ney of the Confederacy—the bravest of the Brave."

When Hood recklessly attacked the forces under Thomas at Franklin in the Nashville campaign, Cleburne led his troops in a fierce attack on the Union lines and was killed. Hood paid dearly for this folly. He lost six generals killed in action, two severely wounded, and a total of 6,000 men killed. Hood was forced to retreat in confusion, his army no longer a fighting force.

Cleburne was also known as the Stonewall Jackson of the West. General Lee compared him to a "meteor shooting from a clouded sky." Though he was not as intensely religious as Jackson, he was scrupulously honest, modest, retiring, a strict disciplinarian, possessed of the confidence of his men.

P R Cleburne

George Crook

The ablest and most experienced Indian fighter in our history, according to some military experts, was not the showy Custer but George Crook. He was feared, trusted, and respected by some of the fiercest tribes west of the Mississippi.

Crook was born near Dayton, Ohio, on September 23, 1829, of Scotch-German ancestry. Entering West Point in 1848, he graduated four years later and was commissioned a second lieutenant of infantry.

Until the outbreak of the Civil War, Crook served in the Northwest, protecting the settlers from periodic Indian raids. In the fall of 1861 he was made colonel of the Thirty-sixth Ohio Infantry and sent to West Virginia. In the spring of 1862 he was brevetted major in the regular army in reward for his defeating an enemy force under General Heth at Lewisburg. Later in the same year he was made a brigadier general of volunteers and his brigade was sent east.

He saw action in the battles of South Mountain and Antietam. In 1863 he returned west, commanding a cavalry division in the Army of the Cumberland. He took part in the Chickamauga campaign. For this successful engagement against General Joseph Wheeler's cavalry at Farmington, Tennessee, he was again promoted.

In the spring of 1864 he was active again in West Virginia, where he destroyed a number of bridges and depots and cut rebel communications between Lynchburg and the West.

When Sheridan formed his Army of the Shenandoah, Crook was given command of the Eighth Army Corps, superseding the discredited Hunter. He took part in the battles of Winchester, Fisher's Hill, and Cedar Creek, where his corps was badly beaten.

When Sheridan joined Grant in the Petersburg campaign in the spring of 1865, Crook was assigned to one of Sheridan's cavalry divisions. Here his division took part in the final battles of the war—Dinwiddie Court House, Sailor's Creek, Farmville, and Appomattox.

After the war, Crook was given command of the Twenty-third Infantry and assigned to the District of Boise, Idaho. Here he spent three years fighting in southern Oregon, Idaho, and northern California before defeating the Indians in that region. For this he was publicly commended by the Oregon Legislature and the War Department.

In 1871 he was sent by President Grant to subdue the wild Apaches in Arizona. He performed this mission so skillfully that once again he was publicly commended and promoted to brigadier general in the regular army.

In 1876 he was placed in command of the Department of the Platte, where he was faced with the problem of subduing the warlike Sioux and Cheyennes, tribes on the warpath against the white settlers seeking gold in the Black Hills of Dakota. Here Crook took part in the great Sioux campaign of 1876 and helped crush that uprising.

In 1882 he was transferred back to Arizona, where he fought an outlaw band of Apaches led by their chief, Geronimo.

In 1886 Crook was again given command of the Department of the Platte. Two years later he was made a major general with headquarters at Chicago. He was later assigned to the Department of Missouri, and there he remained until his death on March 21, 1890.

George Crook

William Barker Cushing

William Barker Cushing was born on November 4, 1842, at Delafield, Wisconsin. At the age of fourteen he became a page in the House of Representatives at Washington. In 1857 he entered the Naval Academy, but his lack of discipline and his flair for fun and frolic alienated his professors. In his senior year he was recommended for dismissal. On March 23, 1861, he resigned from the Academy; however, his friends were able to secure for him the warrant rank of acting master's mate on the U.S.S. *Minnesota.*

In May, 1861, as prize master, he took the captured crew of the vessel *Pioneer* and sailed her to New York. It was a dangerous task and earned him the rank of acting midshipman. He was promptly restored to the navy in October, 1861, and given duty in the North Atlantic Squadron.

Almost a year later, in July, 1862, he became a lieutenant at the early age of nineteen. A few months later, in October, 1862, he proved his bravery and courage when the ship *Commodore Perry* jammed her bow into an embankment and was clearly exposed to the enemy. Cushing, disregarding personal risk, used a field piece, shot point blank at the enemy, routed them, and gave his superiors a chance to save the ship from capture.

Soon afterward he was given command of a steamer, the *Ellis.* He destroyed several salt works and captured an enemy ship, the *Adelaide.* He shelled a town, destroyed a Confederate camp, and captured two prizes. When his own boat, the *Ellis,* was run aground and exposed to heavy enemy fire, he destroyed her and occupied one of the prizes. This incident disturbed him sufficiently to ask for a court of inquiry. They understood his mission and praised his valiant efforts.

On September 5, 1863, he obtained the command of the ship *Monticello* after commanding the *Commodore Barney* and the *Shokokon.* He undertook various successful missions with this ship, including an endeavor to capture high officers of the Confederate army.

Cushing was a man of ideas. He convinced his superiors that it was vitally necessary to build quick torpedo boats in order to destroy the devastating Confederate ram *Albemarle.* After carefully planning a surprise attack, he succeeded in exploding a torpedo into the hull of the vessel, which was destroyed. He was, in turn, rewarded with the rank of lieutenant commander. The Navy Department gave him a personal commendation, and Lincoln requested Congress to give him a formal thanks.

On November 22, 1864, Cushing was given his own flagship, the *Malvern,* a vessel of the North Atlantic Squadron. He was shortly transferred to his own ship, the *Monticello;* and on January 15, 1865, he led a fiery and successful attack on Fort Fisher.

After the Civil War Cushing served in the Pacific and Asiatic Squadrons. In 1870 he became ordnance officer at the Boston Navy Yard and on January 31, 1872, was made commander of the yard. He died on December 17, 1874.

W. B. Cushing

George Armstrong Custer

George Armstrong Custer stands out not only for his exploits as a fine cavalryman on the Western plains but also for his valiant service during the Civil War.

Custer was born at New Rumbey, Ohio, on December 5, 1839. In 1861, having finished his vigorous military training at West Point, he joined the Second Cavalry and soon saw action in the bloody First Battle of Bull Run.

Through his daring cavalry raids, Custer became a valuable member of General George B. McClellan's staff. At the end of the great Peninsula campaign in June, 1863, he was made brigadier general of volunteers and was put in full command of a brigade of Michigan cavalry. He was the youngest general in the Union Army at the time. He soon became even more noted for his daring on the field of battle and for his colorful dress uniforms.

At Gettysburg he made a valuable contribution toward the great victory by his leadership of the gallant cavalry brigade which curbed the fierce onslaughts of the Confederates.

By 1864 he had become a national figure. He assisted General Sheridan with numerous cavalry charges at the battle of Yellow Tavern. The famous Shenandoah Valley campaign brought him up to brevet rank with the command of a division.

General Jubal A. Early felt Custer's sting so severely at Waynesboro that the Confederate general actually saw his army disintegrate on March 2, 1865. By April 9, General Custer was in full pursuit of Early's army, which was just beyond Richmond. He helped cut off this retreat, and it was he who received Lee's flag of truce—a towel! Afterwards, General Sheridan gave this towel to his colleague as a memento of the battle.

When Lee surrendered at Appomattox Court House, Custer witnessed the signing of the necessary papers. By this time he had become a major general of volunteers and had attained a spectacular record in the Civil War. He reverted to a peace-time rank of lieutenant colonel.

With the coming of peace Custer turned his attention to other fields of fame and glory. Still a very young man, enjoying a great reputation for his daring in warfare, he moved into the rough, wild country of the West.

The rush of gold prospectors to the Black Hills of South Dakota brought on a bitter clash with the warlike Sioux Indians. The situation became critical when the Sioux warriors, under their able chief, Sitting Bull, carried on raids on a wide scale. It was finally decided to send General Custer and the Seventh Cavalry to crush the uprising.

Custer, by this time, had acquired great renown as an Indian fighter; but his end came when the Sioux, three thousand strong, fell upon Custer's men at the battle of the Little Big Horn on June 25, 1876. Custer and most of his men were killed in the bloody hand-to-hand combat.

G H Custer

John A. Dahlgren

One of the most famous naval officers of the Civil War, John A. Dahlgren, was born in Philadelphia on November 13, 1809. He got his early education in a Quaker school in the same city. His teachers found him an excellent classical student.

It was his early ambition to enter the United States Navy. When he applied for entrance, he was rejected; but he retained his determination to go to sea. An opportunity came when he shipped on the brig *Mary Beckett* bound for Trinidad.

On February 1, 1826, he was appointed acting midshipman in the navy and made his first cruise on the frigate *Macedonian* under the command of Captain James Barron. Several years later he was assigned to the brig *Ontario* of the Mediterranean squadron, serving on this ship from 1829 to 1831.

In 1833 he was assigned to the famous United States Naval Station. During all that time he pursued the study of law.

In 1834 he went to the Coast Survey, where his keen ability to solve mathematical problems was discovered. As a result of this display of talent, he was promoted to lieutenant on March 8, 1837. He worked so hard that he almost went blind, but a famous oculist saved his eyesight.

In 1847 he entered a field that made him world renowned—ordnance. He studied at Washington and spent sixteen years in this field, reaching the highest position in the field—chief of the Bureau of Ordnance. In this post he introduced the Hale System of rockets, which was eventually adopted. There was a great demand for his services in other quarters, and he was transferred to Annapolis to teach gunnery.

In the great Washington Navy Yard, he built up an efficient cannon foundry, gun carriage shops, and experimental batteries.

When the Civil War broke out, Dahlgren was one of three officers at the Yard who did not resign because of Confederate sympathies. His rank at the time was commander, and command of the Yard could be held only by a captain. President Lincoln, however, was so impressed with Dahlgren's work that he insisted on retaining him and a special act of Congress gave him legal qualification to hold the command. In 1863 he was elevated to rear admiral. He remained on duty until his death on July 2, 1870.

Jno A Dahlgren

Jubal A. Early

Jubal A. Early was born in Franklin County, Virginia, in 1816. He made a good record at West Point and graduated from there in 1837. The following year he saw action against the Seminoles in Florida. After contemplation, however, he decided to resign from the army; and within a few years, he became a lawyer and developed a practice in the little town of Rocky Mount, Virginia.

When the Mexican War broke out, he once again saw military action. When this war was over, he entered politics; and at the Virginia convention in the year 1861 he bravely voted against secession. However, when Virginia seceded and called for volunteers, he joined the ranks as colonel. He made a brilliant record in his share of the conflict in the First Battle of Bull Run and was rewarded with a promotion to brigadier general in July, 1861.

For two years he fought in all of the campaigns of the Army of Northern Virginia, including the battles of Antietam and Chancellorsville. However, it was in the Gettysburg campaign that he made a name for himself for his audacity and bravery in helping to defeat Howard's attack on Ewell's right flank.

In 1864 a temporary but important command was given to him when he took over General A. P. Hill's forces, who were fighting in the Wilderness campaign. Soon afterwards, he was transferred to the Second Army Corps and became its commander after General Ewell left the army.

At Lynchburg, Early was given the important assignment of defeating the Union general David Hunter. Early looked upon this assignment as one which must not fail. It was, in fact, so well done that not only did he defeat General Hunter but also swept his forces right through the Shenandoah Valley and across the Potomac River, threatening Washington. The Union forces under General Lew Wallace met him at Monocacy on July 9, 1864, and were defeated in combat.

Washington was in a dangerous situation. Grant was called upon to send considerable numbers of his troops to check Early's mad rush toward the capital. Only a great deal of hard fighting forced Early and his troops to retreat back to Virginia. However, he did a lot of serious damage. He even raided Chambersburg, Pennsylvania, demanding a ransom of $500,000. When the mayor could not raise the sum, Early gave orders to burn the town. This act of reprisal angered the North. Lincoln was determined that this should not happen again and that the Shenandoah Valley should be rendered useless to the South by ravaging it from end to end.

Grant selected the dashing Sheridan and placed him in full command of a new Army of the Shenandoah. This army was composed of the army divisions of Generals Wright, Emory, Crook, and three divisions of cavalry led by General Torbert aided by Custer, Meritt, Devin, and Wilson. Lee was aware of this new threat and sent Early two divisions from Longstreet's corps. After a lull of a month, the Shenandoah blazed forth in furious conflict. When Grant again moved toward Petersburg, he wired Sheridan: "Go in."

By 3:00 on the morning of September 10, 1864, Sheridan's forces were on the march. Sheridan took Early's fortified ravine near Berryville and drove Early's forces before him. Though Wright's slowness allowed Early a respite, Wilson, Torbert, and Custer routed the rebel forces. Congress gave Sheridan a gold medal, and Lincoln wired "God bless you." But Sheridan kept on after Early's forces with the order to follow them to the death. Early reached Strasburg and fortified its strongest point by nightfall; but his flank was turned, and the Confederates fled in wild confusion. The North went wild with joy, and Grant and Sherman each fired a one hundred-gun salute to Sheridan's army.

October 18 found Sheridan's forces camped by a brooklet called Cedar Creek near the battlefield of Fisher's Hill.

With additional reinforcements sent by Lee, Early made a dawn attack on the sleeping forces of Sheridan and drove them in confusion. Sheridan awoke to the danger and raced to the battlefield, turning his men back as he came. The Union forces rallied and routed the enemy. Early lost even the twenty guns he had captured that morning, his army was crushed, and the valley was cleared forever of a Confederate threat.

Following his defeat at Waynesboro on March 2, 1865, Early was widely denounced by the South, and his removal was demanded. General Lee yielded to this demand and removed him from active command. This action so embittered Early that he went to Canada but returned home in 1867 to resume the practice of law. He died in Lynchburg, Virginia, in 1894.

Jubal Early was rated next to Lee and Jackson in ability in the Confederate Army. He was the terror of the Shenandoah Valley. He was at the outskirts of Washington, and yet he ended his army career in defeat and disgrace.

J A Early

Richard S. Ewell

Richard S. Ewell was born on February 8, 1817, in Georgetown, North Carolina. He graduated from West Point, and was commissioned as a lieutenant of dragoons.

During the Mexican War, Lieutenant Ewell was brevetted for gallantry in several fierce battles. In 1849 he won his promotion to captain and held this rank until 1861. He won further distinction in fighting the Apaches in New Mexico in 1857.

Like many other Southern colleagues he had to decide whether to join the colors of his native state, Virginia, when the Civil War broke out. He resigned his commission on May 7, 1861, and was readily appointed colonel in the Confederate Army. It was his duty to act as a cavalry instructor. By June 17 he earned another promotion to brigadier general.

General Beauregard gave Ewell command of the Second Brigade, but he saw no fighting. By October, 1861, he was made head of a division under "Stonewall" Jackson, promoted to major general, and given an opportunity to use his military skill against Union general Banks at Winchester. The latter was utterly defeated on the battlefield.

In the bloody Seven Days' Battle before Richmond, Ewell gave a good account of himself. A short time later he lost a leg in a fierce battle at Groveton; but by May, 1863, he had won another promotion to lieutenant general. When he recuperated, he showed dauntless courage and demanded full participation in the thick of battle. Very often he was lifted into the saddle and strapped there.

After Chancellorsville Ewell was recommended for the command of the Second Corps. His job was to clear the Federals out of the Shenandoah Valley. It took initiative for Ewell to advance boldly into Pennsylvania, reaching as far as the town of Carlisle. At Gettysburg he took his position on the Confederate left and pressed until he captured the town. Under orders from General Lee he held on until the Union right flank attacked on Culp's Hill, from which he was driven on July 3.

When Ewell faced Grant in the Wilderness campaign, the latter realized he had a very skillful, powerful adversary. Ewell's corps fought bitterly at Spotsylvania Court House and checked for a time the advance of the Federal troops. When he was injured in a fall from his horse, he was removed from active combat and put in command of the Department of Henrico and the defenses of Richmond. But the fortunes of war turned against him. On April 5, surrounded by Union forces, he surrendered his army corps of 8,000 men at Sailor's Creek. This was the signal for Lee that the end was close at hand.

Ewell was held prisoner until the end of the war, after which he returned to his farm and died of pneumonia in 1872.

R. S. Ewell

David Glasgow Farragut

David Glasgow Farragut, the first admiral of the United States Navy, was the son of George Farragut, a Spaniard from the Island of Minorca who came to America in 1776. The elder Farragut was active in the Revolutionary War and soon after George married a woman of Scotch descent and settled near Knoxville, Tennessee. On July 5, 1801, David was born. At the age of nine he entered the navy under the protection of Captain David Porter, after whom he was named.

Two years later, David Farragut became a midshipman on the *Essex,* which cruised the Atlantic under the command of Captain Porter. He saw action during the War of 1812 and played a gallant part in the battle between the *Essex* and two English ships, *Cherub* and *Phoebe,* in March, 1814, in the harbor of Valparaiso. After the capture of the *Essex,* David served on the *Washington,* which carried the broad pennant of Commodore Chauncy in the Mediterranean.

Farragut pursued his professional studies under the guidance of the ship's chaplain, Mr. Folsom, with whom he formed a long friendship. When Folsom was appointed United States Consul at Tunis, he obtained leave for his pupil to pay him a visit, in the course of which he became familiar with the Arabic and Turkish languages. In later years David acquired a knowledge of all the principal European languages, which he was said to have spoken fluently. This may have been an exaggeration, though; his heritage of Spanish from his father may have helped him learn French and Italian. This visit to European waters with Mr. Folsom was the only one he made during his career.

While serving in the navy yard at Norfolk, Virginia, Farragut was promoted to the rank of lieutenant. He served in this capacity from his appointment in 1825 until 1832, when he was assigned to a commission on the coast of Brazil. He later commanded the *Saratoga* during the Mexican War, maintaining a blockade of Tuxpan. He was sent to San Francisco to supervise the construction of a navy yard and several years later

was given command of a sloop of war, the *Brooklyn,* which he held until the outbreak of the Civil War.

When the war of secession began in 1861, the citizens of Norfolk counted on David to throw in his lot with the South because he was a Southerner by birth and marriage. His professional pride and the love he had for the flag which he had served with courage and fidelity for more than fifty years caused him to remain loyal and true to his allegiance. He passionately rejected the proposals of townsmen. Under the circumstances, it was regarded as very dangerous for him to remain at Norfolk; so he left the city and offered his services to the government at Washington.

When his services were accepted, he was required to sit on the Naval Retirement Board, whose function it was to clear the navy of unfit or disloyal officers. After several months of this he was appointed to command the Western Gulf Blockading Squadron with the rank of flag officer and was ordered to proceed forthwith to the Gulf of Mexico. With the *Hartford* as his flagship, Farragut collected seventeen vessels to blockade the Gulf. One of the most brilliant achievements in naval history was his daring run of the *Hartford* past the forts in the Mississippi River, which resulted in the destruction of fifteen Confederate ships and the surrender of New Orleans.

Farragut gave valuable assistance to Grant in the capture of Vicksburg; this brought the Mississippi River under Union control. After a terrific battle in which he lost his ship, the *Tecumseh,* he destroyed the forts in Mobile Bay and captured the city of Mobile. Because of ill health, he withdrew from active life in December, 1864, with the rank of rear admiral. In 1866 Congress created the rank of admiral, which they bestowed on him. In the sixty-nine years of his life, 1801–1870, David G. Farragut proved himself worthy of the respect he had gained as a gentleman, scholar, and military leader. He was one of the stars in the American banner of freedom and democracy.

D. E. Farragut

Andrew Hull Foote

Andrew Hull Foote, a great admiral, was born at New Haven, Connecticut, on September 2, 1806. His father, Samuel Augustus Foote, was a prominent lawyer and Whig politician who, as United States Senator, drew up the "Foote's Resolution" in 1829. It resulted in the famous discussions during which Daniel Webster made his reply to Robert Hayne.

Andrew Foote joined the U.S. Navy in 1822 and eight years later was a commissioned lieutenant. After cruising around the world for three years on the *John Adams*, he was assigned to the Philadelphia naval base and later (1846–48) the Boston Navy Yard. In 1849 he was made commander of the *Portsmouth*, serving on the East Indian Station under commander James Armstrong. The nation applauded his capture of the Barrier Forts near Canton.

From October, 1858, to the outbreak of the Civil War, Foote was in charge of the Brooklyn Navy Yard. In August, 1861, he was assigned to the command "of the Naval operations upon the western waters." His brilliant deed in capturing Fort Henry on February 6, 1862, won him high praise, since he had received no cooperation from General Grant's land forces, which had not arrived in time. It was a brilliant success.

In March and April, Foote cooperated in the capture of New Madrid and Island No. 10. In June he retired; and in July he was promoted to rear admiral, later being made chief of equipment and recruiting. He died in New York City on June 26, 1863.

A H Foote

Nathan Bedford Forrest

Nathan B. Forrest was born near Chapel Hill, Tennessee, on July 13, 1821. He had no formal schooling but managed to teach himself. Mathematics became his favorite subject. As a young man he became a horse and cattle trader in Mississippi and by 1859 was quite wealthy. He next turned to cotton planting in northwestern Mississippi.

At the outbreak of the Civil War, Forrest volunteered as a private and raised a cavalry unit, of which he was made lieutenant colonel. In February he took part in the defense of Fort Donelson. Refusing to surrender with the rest of the Confederate forces, he forced his way out with his brave cavalrymen. As a result he was made a colonel and regimental commander. He fought at Shiloh with great gallantry. Again in July, 1862, he was promoted, this time to brigadier general.

At the head of a mounted brigade, he took a brilliant part in General Bragg's autumn campaign. In the winter of 1862/63, Forrest was continually active in raiding the enemy lines of communication. One of the most remarkable feats of his career was his capture of an entire cavalry brigade under Colonel A. D. Streight near Rome, Georgia, in April, 1863. He was made a major general in December, 1863.

On April 12, 1864, Forrest assaulted and captured Fort Pillow in Tennessee. Negro troops had formed a large part of the garrison, and it was said that many were massacred after the fort surrendered. This event has been the subject of much controversy, but there is conflicting testimony regarding it. Forrest himself was never implicated.

On June 10, 1864, Forrest decisively defeated another superior Federal force at Brige's Cross Roads, Mississippi. He was with the main Confederate Army of the West in Hood's disastrous campaign against Nashville and fought determined rear guard actions to cover the retreat of the broken Confederates.

In February, 1865, he was made a lieutenant general, though the struggle was almost at an end. General James H. Wilson rapidly forced back the few Confederates still under Forrest's command. The surrender of General Forrest and his whole command followed on May 9, 1865.

Following the war Forrest lived in Memphis. There, for some years, he was president of the Selma, Marion, and Memphis Railroad. He died at Memphis on October 29, 1877.

General Nathan B. Forrest was a bearded giant who looked like a pirate and gained fame with his well-known ungrammatical "I'll get there fustest with the mostest." It was his way to win battles.

N. B. Forrest

William Buel Franklin

William Buel Franklin was born in York, Pennsylvania, on February 27, 1823. He entered West Point and graduated in 1843 at the head of his class, which included Ulysses S. Grant.

When the Mexican War raised the need for engineers, he readily served under Zachary Taylor and became his topographical engineer, obtaining the rank of colonel. The Capitol dome at Washington was constructed under this supervision.

At the outbreak of the Civil War, he took over the command of a brigade. In May, 1861, he became brigadier general of volunteers and fought valiantly in the First Battle of Bull Run.

In the Peninsular campaign, Franklin fought under General McClellan. He served well under Burnside at Fredericksburg, where he commanded the left wing. He was, however, partially blamed for the defeat. General Burnside was so bitter that he ordered Franklin's dismissal. Franklin regained his command by March, 1865, and reached the rank of major general in the regular army.

After the war he became the vice-president of the Colt Automatic Firearms Manufacturing Company in Hartford, Connecticut. He died in 1903.

W.B. Franklin

John C. Frémont

John C. Frémont, a great explorer and soldier, was born in Savannah, Georgia, in 1813. He attended Charleston College. His ambition was to teach mathematics to naval cadets, but he also yearned to explore. Thanks to a friend, Joel R. Poinsett, he had a chance to assist Joseph N. Nicollet on a surveying expedition for three years, 1838–41.

When he married Jessie Benton, the daughter of Senator Thomas H. Benton, the latter secured for Frémont command of an expedition in the West to explore the Des Moines River. In 1842 he traveled with Kit Carson to the great Rocky Mountains, where he made the famous trip through Nevada country, crossed the great Sierras in that area, and reached California. His reports were a sensation and aroused interest in the wondrous West.

When the Mexican War began, Frémont was in California influencing Americans to revolt against the Mexican authorities. With his encouragement, the Bear Flag Republic was set up at Sonoma.

When Stephen W. Kearny came to California, Frémont refused to take orders from him. This meant his arrest and a court-martial, in which he was found guilty. The President remitted the verdict. However, Frémont, in anger, left the government service.

When gold was discovered on Frémont's estate in California, he became rich. He entered politics and served California in the United States Senate.

In 1856 the Republican party nominated Frémont for President. The nation, however, turned to James Buchanan.

In the Civil War Frémont was given command of the Western Department; but when he issued an order confiscating the property of Missouri rebels, he was immediately removed.

Placed under the command of General John Pope, Frémont resigned his commission. After the war he lost his great fortune, retaining only the loyalty of his wife. In 1878 he became the governor of the Arizona Territory and served in this post for four years. He died in 1890.

J.C. Fremont

John W. Geary

John W. Geary was born near Mount Pleasant, Pennsylvania, on December 30, 1819. He received an ordinary education but was sufficiently persistent in his efforts to become a student of Jefferson College, Canonsburg, Pennsylvania.

When his father died, Geary turned to school teaching to earn a living and, for a time, even clerked in a store. He finally decided to study civil engineering and law and turned toward land speculation to clear up his father's debts. When the Allegheny Postage Railroad needed an engineer, Geary was hired.

At the outbreak of the Mexican War, Geary became captain of the "American Highlanders." When these men joined the Second Pennsylvania Infantry at Pittsburgh, he became a lieutenant colonel. This group participated in Scott's landing at Vera Cruz in 1847 and in his advance on Mexico City.

Geary had an opportunity to replace temporarily his sick commander and make an assault on Chapultepec. This ended in the capture of the fortress; and when his commander, Roberts, died, he became the successor to the regiment command. In addition, he was promoted to colonel.

When President Polk needed a mail agent and postmaster at San Francisco, he was happy to appoint Geary. He prospered in that city, and in 1850 he became its first mayor. Unfortunately, Geary's wife became ill in 1852; and they were forced to return to their farm in Pennsylvania.

President Pierce urged Geary to become governor of Utah, but he declined. Instead he took over the governorship of the Kansas Territory. There he found, in 1856, a bloody feud between the proslavery militia and the antislavery abolitionists. Geary sent in Federal troops to maintain peace and order and to protect Kansas from both factions. By 1857 the proslavery elements were bold enough to actually become hostile toward the Governor. His life was threatened, and a host of complicated situations perplexed and embarrassed Geary sufficiently to cause him to resign his position.

The firing on Fort Sumter gave Geary the opportunity once again to see action. He immediately set up means to recruit men for service and in a short time became colonel of the Twenty-eighth Pennsylvania Regiment. On October 16, 1861, he fought at Bolivar Heights, where he was wounded in action. Almost a year later, after winning a promotion to brigadier general, he suffered severe wounds at Cedar Mountain. Even this did not stop him, for he recuperated sufficiently to command a division at Chancellorsville and at Gettysburg.

Geary and Hooker aided Grant in the Tennessee campaign. In this campaign Geary met with a personal tragedy when his son was killed in action.

Sherman employed Geary's ability in the famous "March to the Sea," and by the end of the war Geary was made a major general.

Politicians in Pennsylvania felt that Geary could easily be elected governor after the war was over. His popularity and military fame made his election an easy one. He served in this executive capacity for two terms, 1867–73. On February 8, 1873, he died.

He had made an enviable record as governor, advocating protection against accidents in the mines, regulation of insurance, and state control of gas companies.

Jno W Geary

Quincy Adams Gillmore

Quincy Adams Gillmore, a brilliant soldier, had an unusual career as an educator at West Point and as a military engineer.

Gillmore was born on February 28, 1825, at Beach River, Ohio. Young Quincy was educated in the fundamentals taught at elementary school and was then sent to the Norwalk Academy, where he made a name for himself as a student of mathematics. At the age of fifteen he was asked to teach school, and this he did for three years. At the same time he himself attended the Elyria High School for two summers.

In 1845 Gillmore received an appointment to West Point and graduated at the head of his class four years later. He was given a commission as second lieutenant of engineers. His duties were threefold. He helped construct the basic fortifications needed at Hampton Roads, Virginia; and in addition, he became both treasurer and quartermaster of the Academy. However, he most enjoyed his position as assistant instructor of practical military engineering. By August, 1861, he had achieved the rank of captain.

Gillmore's service as chief engineer to the Port Royal Expedition, 1861/62, was most brilliant. He helped to capture Fort Pulaski, Georgia, in April, 1862. For this he won the rank of lieutenant colonel. In the same month he received another promotion—brigadier general of volunteers, and for a year was given command of special areas in Kentucky and West Virginia.

When he met the forces of General Pelgram at Somerset, Kentucky, and defeated them in battle, he was rewarded by his superiors with a rank of colonel in the regular army.

In the latter half of 1863 he helped reduce Morris Island and made several offensives against Charleston, South Carolina, and Fort Sumter.

Next, Gillmore became major general of volunteers. He fought in the battle of Drury's Bluff and in the reconnaissance before Petersburg. In the summer of 1864 he was seriously injured when he fell from his horse. He was then removed to other duties including president of the board for testing wrought iron cannon, and inspection of fortifications along the Atlantic seaboard.

Early in 1865 Gillmore was given command of the Department of the South and made a major general in the regular army. He gained a great reputation as an artillerist. His use of a rifled cannon for breaching masonry walls at Fort Pulaski caused a sensation in military circles.

Gillmore died at Brooklyn, New York, on April 7, 1888.

Q A Gillmore

John Brown Gordon

One of the most colorful, capable, and courageous officers under "the Gray Fox," General Lee, was John B. Gordon. This Southerner was born February 6, 1832, in Upson County, Georgia. He had the usual schooling but persisted in his educational pursuits and finally graduated from the University of Georgia in 1852. Soon afterwards, he entered the practice of law.

At the outbreak of the Civil War Gordon joined the Confederate Army as captain of volunteers. By hard, determined effort, he successfully achieved the high rank of lieutenant general.

While General Gordon had served in several other campaigns, he became prominent as an infantry commander in the fighting between Sheridan and Early, especially at Cedar Creek. Sheridan was dispatched to Washington for a conference; and during his absence, Gordon worked around the Union left flank on October 19, 1864. The Union forces were thrown into confusion. Crook's corps quickly being put out of action, Sheridan hurried to the battlefield, restored order, and routed Early's forces.

In the closing days of the war, with Lee pinned down behind his fortifications, guarding Richmond, General Gordon was given a very crucial order to carry out. In one final desperate move, Lee planned an attack on the Union forces in the hope that in the momentary success he could rush his troops down the Donville Railroad into the Carolinas, join Johnston, and between them crush Sherman's army. This plan called for General Gordon to use a fast-moving column, pierce Grant's center, smash his base at City Point and, if possible, to capture the powerful Union stronghold, Fort Stedman.

On March 26, 1865, Gordon surprised Parke's Ninth Corps and entered Fort Stedman. However, Parke's artillery, stationed on a hill, blanketed the fort with shot and shell; and the trapped forces under Gordon were beaten with a loss of 6,000 men. Then Grant closed the gap on Lee with the forces of Ord, Warren, and Sheridan.

Gordon was next engaged at Sailor's Creek, escaping only with the loss of some 15,000 men. When Lee retreated from Richmond and fled to the West, Gordon was ordered to cover the rear guard.

In the council of war on April 8, 1865, Gordon approved Lee's surrender and even urged Longstreet to suggest this to him. However, the famous general refused to follow this suggestion, stating that Lee should well know what to do in this matter. When Custer came to Gordon and ordered him to surrender in the name of General Sheridan, the tall Georgian defied him. He did suggest to General Sheridan that hostilities cease in order to give Lee time to make up his mind.

At the time of the surrender at Appomattox, Gordon commanded one of the two corps of Lee's army. He made the last charge and was fighting against the Federal forces when news of Lee's surrender ended his actions.

Following the war, he settled in Atlanta, Georgia, soon entered politics, and was very active at the Democratic national conventions of 1868 and 1872. He went to the United States Senate in 1873 and achieved reelection twice, in 1879 and 1890. He also served one term as governor of the state.

In 1900 he became the commander in chief of the United Confederate Veterans. Four years later, on January 9, 1904, he died in Miami, Florida.

John B. Gordon

Gordon Granger

Gordon Granger was another gift of New York State to the Union cause. This gallant officer was born on November 6, 1822, at Jay in Wayne County, New York. His life's ambition was an army career. Entering West Point in 1841, he graduated from the Academy in 1845 with a commission as second lieutenant in the Second Infantry.

Like so many other famous army men, he served in General Scott's army in the Mexican War, especially in the siege of Vera Cruz, and in the great battle of Chapultepec and entered with Scott's army when Mexico City surrendered. Between 1848 and 1861 Granger saw service on the frontier fighting Indians, and during this interval he received two promotions to first lieutenant and captain.

Early in the Civil War he made a name for himself for bravery, earning the rank of colonel of the Second Michigan Cavalry. In the spring of 1862 he waged a series of operations against Island No. 10 and commanded a brigade at Corinth the same year. He commanded an army corps under Rosecrans in the campaign against Bragg in Tennessee and Kentucky.

When the bloody battle of Chickamauga was raging (September 19 and 20, 1863), Granger was in the thick of it, supporting Mitchell in the fighting near Shelbyville. When Rosecran's forces were defeated, he helped cover the retreat.

Thomas, however, held the Confederates in check in a desperate effort. At the opportune moment Granger, with two brigades, moved to the support of Thomas and helped drive the Confederate Army back on its heels. Almost 50 per cent of the men engaged died in battle. General Thomas, "the Rock," held his ground, thanks to the help of Granger. Granger also saw action with his men at bloody Missionary Ridge and at Chattanooga.

By 1865 Granger saw the surrender of Mobile and lived to witness the laying down of arms of the Confederate Army. At the end of the war he earned the rank of colonel of infantry in the regular army.

Goram Granger

Ulysses Simpson Grant

Ulysses Simpson Grant, the great commander in chief of the Union armies, hated war and openly stated it throughout his military career.

Grant was born on April 27, 1822. He was named Hiram Ulysses Grant. Although he had no desire to attend West Point, his father, through a friend, got him an appointment. According to the records of the academy, his academic ability was mediocre. He excelled only in mathematics. Grant did not like the strict discipline and rigid regulations enforced upon the cadets, but he felt it was better than working in his father's tannery at Galena.

Grant's name became Ulysses Simpson when Congressman Thomas L. Hamer of Ohio sent Grant's papers to West Point and penned the latter's name as Ulysses Simpson Grant, the middle name belonging to Grant's mother.

After graduating from West Point, Grant expressed a desire to become an instructor in mathematics at the Academy. He was disappointed when he learned there was no vacancy available to him. He had a strong dislike for the Mexican War, in which he was assigned to duty as quartermaster of his regiment. He was a good soldier, but he remained unknown.

On August 22, 1848, Grant married into a Southern family.

Six years later Grant gave up the army after a dismissal by his colonel. His father hastily wrote to Jefferson Davis, the Secretary of War, pleading with him to take Grant back into the army.

When the bombardment of Fort Sumter opened the Civil War, Grant wrote to his father, "My own opinion is that this war will be but of short duration. . . ."

Governor Yates of Springfield, Ohio, appointed Grant captain of a regiment. He made a great impression indirectly on President Lincoln by his proclamations to the people of Paducah, Kentucky, which his troops had occupied.

Soon afterward Grant learned through a statement printed in a newspaper that he had become a brigadier general. His congressman, Elihu B. Washbourne of Illinois, had insisted that since President Lincoln had given many promotions to military officers, some of those in Washbourne's district should receive higher rank. In this way Grant received his promotion.

In the siege of Fort Donelson Grant first made a name for himself. He had taken the Confederate outer trenches and ringed the fort with complete thoroughness.

Within the month Congress rewarded Grant by making him a major general in command of the Military Department of Western Tennessee. But Grant had enemies. His great rival was General Halleck, who hoped to oust him from the army. However, Lincoln and public opinion thwarted Halleck's plans. The shortcomings of Grant in the battle of Shiloh and Halleck's intrigues with politicians once again created heavy demand for the removal of Grant. However, Lincoln told one politician, a Republican, A. K. McClure, "No, I couldn't do it. I can't lose this man. He fights." The President was vindicated when Grant won the great victory of Vicksburg. Another promotion came to the General. This time he was titled major general of the regular army. When he won another battle at Missionary Ridge, Lincoln, highly elated, elevated him to the position of lieutenant general of all the Union armies on March 9, 1864.

On May 1, 1864, Grant put an effective plan into action to end the war: the greatest concentration of military strength necessary to check the Confederate armies, leading finally to the invasion of Georgia and to the destruction of railroads and resources.

The Wilderness campaign was the bloodiest of the war. Grant took the fight to Lee and inflicted very severe losses, forcing the latter to retreat almost in sight of Richmond. These head-on clashes with the Confederate armies resulted in very heavy casualties, especially in the battle of Cold Harbor. Heavy criticism fell on Grant. Politicians in Washington began to call him "the Butcher." Morale soon began to lower among the rank and file in the Union Army. Lincoln and Grant quickly realized that in the last year of the war Sherman's methods were effective although hard and cruel on the people of the South. In fact, Grant refused to exchange prisoners of war even though Northern prisoners at Andersonville were dying at a fast rate. In his mind a plan was engendered to break the back of the Confederacy at all costs and end the war.

On April 2, 1865, Lee sent a note to President Davis that the Confederate Army must abandon Richmond. In fact, from that day on Lee's army was hard pressed by Grant and Meade. Lee hoped to make a junction with Johnston but to no avail. There were no rations for either men or horses.

On April 7 Lee received a letter from Grant stating "the results of last week must convince you of the hopelessness of further resistance." Grant wanted to avoid any more bloodshed, and Lee wished to hear Grant's terms. For the next two days Meade, Sheridan, and Grant closed in and continued to destroy or capture Lee's men. He was down to 25,000 men on April 9 when Grant and his staff walked over to Appomattox Court House. When Lee asked Grant to put his terms in writing, the General took out a piece of paper and pencil and then wrote his terms: "All soldiers could depart to their homes after signing that they would no longer fight for the Confederacy. Also, no soldiers will be molested if they obey the law. Only public property will be taken by the Northern army. Officers may carry their sidearms and personal baggage."

Lee was pleased with the extremely magnanimous terms.

As he rose he told Grant that his men were starving. They had only parched corn for three days. Grant immediately offered 25,000 rations. Lee replied this was "plenty and abundance." He rode off, and the bloodiest war in history was over.

In April, 1867, President Johnson made Grant Secretary of War, replacing E. M. Stanton. Grant, however, did not accept the office when the Senate refused to remove Stanton.

In 1868 Grant was elected President after a bitter election in which his opponent was Horatio Seymour.

In 1872 Grant was renominated and reelected by the American people. In 1880 he retired and set up residence in New York City. He entered the private banking business and went bankrupt in two years. When he learned that it was necessary to provide sufficiently for his family, he began to write his personal *Memoirs* (2 vol., 1885, 1886). He suffered from cancer of the throat and died a few days after completing the manuscript. The General and his wife rest in peace in the magnificent Grant's Tomb in New York City.

U. S. Grant

David McMurtrie Gregg

David McMurtrie Gregg, the son of Matthew D. Gregg and Ellen McMurtrie, of Scotch-Irish ancestry, was born in Huntington, Pennsylvania, on April 10, 1833. He spent the early part of his life in Pennsylvania, where he attended private schools before entering Bucknell University. He was appointed a cadet at West Point in 1851 and after graduation began his career as a second lieutenant of cavalry. He spent six years of his early military life fighting against the Indians in the Far West.

At the outbreak of the Civil War Gregg was only a first lieutenant, but he was quickly promoted to captain and assigned to troops then protecting Washington. In January, 1862, he was made colonel of the Eighth Pennsylvania Cavalry and served under McClellan in the Army of the Potomac. He saw service in the Peninsular campaign, fighting at Fair Oaks, Seven Pines, and Glendale. His cavalry covered the movement of McClellan's Army of the Potomac from Harrison Landing to Yorktown. He led a cavalry division under Hooper in the fighting around Chancellorsville.

Gregg, along with Custer, was considered one of the bright, up-and-coming young cavalry officers in the army. He and Custer covered the right wing of the Union Army at Gettysburg, coming into conflict with the wide-ranging "Jeb" Stuart. Gregg helped check the Confederate attack under Ewell on Culps Hill.

In the mine-run campaign against Lee's army, Gregg supported the infantry movements under General French. He led the Second Cavalry in the last Peninsular campaign under Grant, and Gregg's "Raiders" were assigned the job of raiding the Weldon Railroad and disrupting Lee's wagon-train supply system. It was necessary for Lee to send forces under General A. P. Hill in order to protect his line of communication with Petersburg and Richmond. Gregg resigned from the army as a major general of volunteers early in the spring of 1865. He was later appointed American Consul at Prague but resigned that office to become Pennsylvania's auditor general. In 1907 he published *The Second Cavalry Division of the Army of the Potomac in the Gettysburg Campaign*. He died August 7, 1916, at the age of eighty-three.

D. M. M. Gregg.

Charles Griffin

Charles Griffin was born in Grandville, Ohio, on December 18, 1825. He wanted to enter the military service and prepared for West Point by the usual educational procedures. In 1843 he was accepted by the Academy and after four years of hard study was commissioned to the artillery.

Since the Mexican War was in progress, he was sent at once to Mexico to serve under General Patterson. He obtained a promotion to first lieutenant in 1849.

For eleven long years Griffin served on the frontier. In 1860 he instructed West Point cadets in tactics. When the war broke out he organized a light battery made up of men on duty at the Academy. It became known as the "West Point Battery" and showed distinguished service at the First Battle of Bull Run, even though it was almost annihilated by a Confederate regiment which had been mistaken as approaching Union soldiers. Griffin had been assured by his chief of artillery that the oncoming men were a body of Union troops.

Griffin, now made captain, was given a new battery and saw action in the early part of the Peninsular campaign. By 1862 he was a brigadier general of volunteers.

At the battle of Antietam he led a fighting brigade of the Fifth Corps. At the Second Battle of Bull Run his brigade saw no action though they were near at hand. When Griffin made severe criticisms of the general commanding the action on the battlefield he was relieved of his command. Nevertheless, his superiors felt he was worthy of an even higher command; and soon he was made head of a division that fought fiercely at Fredericksburg and Chancellorsville. Illness kept him from the field until the last day of fighting at Gettysburg. Griffin was attached to the army's Fifth Corps under General Warren in the final year of the war against Lee.

General Griffin was an excellent and fearless artillery officer. He took part with Warren in the battles of the Wilderness and Five Forks and was with Sheridan in the final days before Lee surrendered. When Warren was slow and late in the crucial battle of Five Forks, Sheridan, in a rage, fired him and appointed Griffin in his place as the commander of the Fifth Corps. This action caused some controversy, especially among Warren's defenders.

Griffin was one of the commissioners appointed to carry out the terms of Lee's surrender. In the middle of January, 1866, he was mustered out of the service. The following year he was put in charge of the military district of Texas during the great era of Reconstruction. When yellow fever broke out in Galveston, he refused to abandon his post there. He soon contracted the disease and died on September 5, 1867.

Chas Griffin

Henry Wager Halleck

One of the strangest and yet in many ways most talented generals of the Civil War was Henry Wager Halleck.

Halleck was born in Westernville, New York, on January 16, 1815. On his mother's side he was the grandson of Henry Wager, a personal friend of Baron Von Steuben. At an early age he ran away from his farm home and was adopted by his maternal grandfather. He was sent to the Hudson, New York, Academy and later to Union College. He graduated from Union in 1835.

Halleck entered West Point on July 1, 1835. His ability was soon recognized, and he became a cadet officer of high rank. He graduated from the Academy in 1839, standing third in a class of thirty-two.

Commissioned a second lieutenant, his first assignment was an engineering one, the fortifications of New York harbor. He went to France in 1844 and made an inspection of the fortifications of Provence. On his return home he wrote *A Report on the National Defense,* which was published by Congress. He delivered a series of lectures at Lowell Institute, Boston, which appeared in 1846 in a book called *Elements of Military Art and Science.*

Halleck resigned from the army in 1854 and went to California, where mining was one of his activities. Shortly after the Civil War began Halleck was sent West to replace Frémont as commanding officer in the Kentucky-Mississippi River area.

Halleck, like McClellan and others who fought "by the book," believed in a war of position rather than the war of movement favored by Grant. He was slow in action, overcautious in decision, and more inclined to defensive or holding tactics in fighting the enemy. He was in command of three armies in the Kentucky-Mississippi River campaign. His main armies were the Missouri under Pope, the Tennessee under Grant, and the Cumberland under Buell. Being a military perfectionist and a "book fighter," he opposed Grant's idea of storming Forts Henry and Donelson.

Halleck's plan called for sending Pope's division against Memphis while Grant and Buell were to go against Corinth. While Pope attacked Island No. 10, Grant opposed Johnston at Shiloh. The bitter fighting was really a drawn battle, with heavy losses of men on each side. When Johnston was killed in action, his successor, Beauregard, ordered a retreat.

When Bragg removed the Confederate Army to Chattanooga, Halleck sent Buell with 40,000 men to oppose him. At this juncture Lincoln called Halleck to Washington to serve as his military adviser. Halleck took Pope east with him. Halleck was opposed to Grant's plan to take Vicksburg and to Burnsides' plan of direct attack on Richmond by way of Fredericksburg. Despite some disheartening episodes, Grant had his way in conducting the campaign against Vicksburg. Halleck had given command of the "Army Virginia," virtually replacing McClellan, to Pope, in the hope that this veteran corps commander would repeat his exploits in the West. Yet Pope was badly beaten at the Second Battle of Bull Run, and McClellan was replaced a second time.

When Pope was badly beaten at Bull Run, the disappointed Halleck agreed to restore McClellan "for the good of the service." When McClellan was replaced a second time, it was proposed that Halleck take command; but he refused the honor unless he was made also commander in chief.

Lincoln, however, was not ready for such a decision because he was not completely satisfied with Halleck. While Lincoln deferred to the "military" judgment of Halleck, the President entertained a more aggressive concept of war. That Halleck suffered from the "slows" was amply shown after Gettysburg. Halleck wanted to hear from Meade after Gettysburg; but instead of going to the theater of action, he waited for a report from Meade. This indecision annoyed Lincoln—a man of bold decision, absolute action, and a man who put first things first. Grant, in the meantime, had been making a name for himself; and his reputation was enhanced when Vicksburg surrendered the day after the battle of Gettysburg. Lincoln now called Grant east to take command of all the field forces of the Union Army.

Grant came to Washington and was made a lieutenant general. Halleck was kept at his desk at Washington; and in order to soften the embarrassing problem of promoting Grant over Halleck, Lincoln made Halleck chief of staff. While Halleck and Meade were surprised by Grant's bold, aggressive plan, Lincoln was delighted by this man of action.

Halleck saw the terrible loss of life on both sides caused by Grant's relentless attack on Lee and after the bloody defeat at Cold Harbor suggested that the army take no chances and conduct only a siege to wear down the enemy. He told Grant that "we are receiving only one-half as many men as we are discharging" and that volunteering had ceased. Despite this situation and the fact that he was denounced as a "butcher" in some parts of the press, Grant favored a war of movement, a relentless war on the enemy.

Halleck, though generally opposed to using political generals in the army, overruled Grant's request to remove Butler as a general because of this general's reputed political influence. Halleck did tell Sherman that it was "little better than murder" to give command to such men as Butler, Banks, Siegel, McClernand, and Wallace. But when Halleck suggested that Sheridan be placed in command of the cavalry, Grant replied, "The very man."

Halleck had entertained fears that Washington would be attacked but insisted that Grant had the responsibility to protect it. With Stanton's consent Halleck refused to appoint General Franklin to defend Washington, because he was a "McClellan man."

When Early and his army appeared in the suburbs of Washington, Grant dispatched the veteran Sixth Corps to relieve McCook and his 4-F troops. Halleck had been made chief of staff on March 12, 1864, but was relieved of this position after April 19, 1865, and put in command of the Army of the James with headquarters at Richmond. On August 20, 1865, he was transferred to San Francisco to command the Division of the Pacific. In 1869 he was assigned the command of the Division of the South with headquarters at Louisville. He died in that city on January 9, 1872.

H. W. Halleck

Wade Hampton

Wade Hampton was born on March 28, 1818, in Columbia, South Carolina, the son of a wealthy planter. In 1836 he graduated from South Carolina College and prepared for a career in law.

He took part in politics in the state of Mississippi. He opposed the states' rights theory, but he espoused the Southern cause.

In 1861 he raised a mixed command known as Hampton's Legion, which he led at the First Battle of Bull Run. In the Army of Northern Virginia under General Lee he was given a command in Stuart's Cavalry Corps, where he served during part of the Civil War. The corps fought hard in the bloody battle of Gettysburg, and in 1864 Hampton assumed command of Lee's entire cavalry.

In 1865 Hampton led the cavalry of Joseph E. Johnston's army in an attempt to prevent Sherman's advance through the Carolinas. Kilpatrick's cavalry was too much for him, however, and drove off his attacks. When Columbia, South Carolina, fell, Hampton attempted to burn it. He failed in his attempt, but Union forces did it for him when they invaded the city.

After the war his attitude was conciliatory, and he recommended a frank acceptance by the South of the military and political consequences of defeat.

From 1876 to 1879 he was Governor of North Carolina; from 1879 to 1891, United States Senator; and from 1893 to 1897, United States Commissioner of Railroads. He died in 1902.

Wade Hampton

Winfield S. Hancock

Winfield S. Hancock was born on February 14, 1824, in Montgomery County, Pennsylvania. He graduated in 1844 from the Military Academy and was later brevetted first lieutenant for gallant and meritorious conduct in the Mexican War.

After serving in the West, in Florida, and elsewhere, Hancock married Miss Almira Russell of St. Louis. He became a first lieutenant in 1853 and assistant quartermaster with the rank of captain in 1855. At the outbreak of the Civil War he was ordered east at his own request and on September 23, 1861, was made brigadier general of volunteers and assigned to command a brigade in the Army of the Potomac. He took part in the Peninsular campaign; and the handling of his troops in the engagement at Williamsburg on May 5, 1862, was such that McClellan reported "Hancock was superb," an epithet always afterward applied to him. At Antietam he was placed in command of the First Division of the Second Corps.

In the Battle of Fredericksburg Hancock's division was among the troops that were ordered to storm Marye's Heights. Out of the 5,006 men in his division, 2,013 fell at Chancellorsville, where his troops received the brunt of the attack of Lee's main army. Soon after this battle he was appointed commander of the Second Corps.

In the battle of Gettysburg Hancock arrived on the field with orders from Meade to assume command and to decide whether to continue the fight there or to fall back.

He decided to stay and held Cemetery Ridge until the arrival of the main body of the Union Army. During the second day's battle he commanded the left center of the Union Army and, after General Sickles had been wounded, the whole of the left wing. In the third day's battle he commanded the left center with his Second Corps, upon which fell the full brunt of Pickett's charge, one of the most famous incidents of the war.

As the guns of the Confederate Army opened the attack on July 3, Hancock rode along the front of his line to show his soldiers that he shared the dangers of the cannonade with them. His corps lost 4,350 out of somewhat less than 10,000 fighting men, but it captured seven Confederate battle flags and as many prisoners as it had men when the fighting ceased. Hancock's intense artillery fire broke the back of Pickett's charge. Hancock himself was struck in the groin by a bullet but continued in command until the Confederate attack was repulsed.

Six months passed before Hancock resumed his command. In the battles of 1864 he commanded at the Wilderness and at Spotsylvania, where he had charge of the successful attack on the "salient." At Cold Harbor his corps formed the Union left wing facing the Confederate lines. His old wound troubling him, he obtained a short leave of absence, and General Birney took over his command. Hancock, however, was detailed to raise a new corps and later was placed in charge of Washington. It was under his command that Booth's accomplices were tried and executed. In July, 1866, he was placed in command of the Department of the Missouri and the following year assumed command of the Fifth Military Division, comprising Louisiana and Texas. His policy, however, of discountenancing military trials and conciliating the conquered territory did not meet with the approval of the "radicals" in Washington; and he was transferred at his own request.

Hancock had all his life been a Democrat. His war record and his personal popularity caused his name to be considered as a candidate for the Presidency. In 1880 he was nominated for that office by the Democrats but was defeated by his Republican opponent, General Garfield, by the small popular plurality of 7,000 votes. He died at Governor's Island near New York City on February 9, 1886.

Hancock was in many respects the ideal soldier of the Northern armies. He was quick, energetic, and resourceful, reckless of his own safety, a strict disciplinarian, a painstaking, hardworking officer, and a born commander of men. Grant said of him, "Hancock stands the most conspicuous figure of all the general officers who did not exercise a separate command. He commanded a corps longer than any other, and his name was never mentioned as having committed in battle a blunder for which he was responsible."

William Joseph Hardee

William Joseph Hardee, an able Confederate infantry general, was born in Savannah, Georgia, on October 12, 1815. After graduating from West Point in 1838, he had the opportunity to study for two years at the well-known French cavalry school at St. Maur.

When the United States went to war with Mexico, Hardee saw action, was taken prisoner, and soon afterward was exchanged in time to take part in the battles of Vera Cruz, Contreras, and Molino del Rey.

Two years after the end of the war he became the commander of West Point. While there he wrote and then published a textbook, *United States Rifle and Light Infantry Tactics,* which for years was the standard book on the subject.

When the Civil War broke out, Hardee resigned his commission and entered the Confederate forces. He soon created the famous "Hardee's Brigade" and became one of the corps commanders in General Bragg's invasion of Kentucky, the subsequent battles of Perryville and the Chattanooga campaign.

His reputation as a fighter was duly established when he attacked General McCook's forces in the battle of Perryville. He boldly engaged both Generals Sherman and Thomas in the bitter fighting at Stone River.

For a short time after the siege of Chattanooga, Bragg was blamed for the failure of the campaign. Hardee was made temporary commander of the Second Corps and in due time was succeeded by Joseph E. Johnston.

In the great battle of Chickamauga Hardee tested his military ability against General Rosecrans and his forces.

To meet the famous march of Sherman's army to crush the forces of Johnston operating in the South, Hardee was appointed one of three corps commanders. Polk and Hood were the others. All three men were used by General Johnston in the battles of Resaca and Atlanta and in the Carolinas.

On several occasions Hardee tasted defeat. He attacked the flank of General Thomas' forces at Cedar Creek and was repulsed. He joined with Stewart to attack Howard and Palmer at Peachtree Creek, but heavy artillery barrages repulsed him there.

Hardee made a great effort to stop Sherman at Jonesboro, but he once again tasted defeat with the loss of over 5,000 men.

It can be said that Hardee was one of the best fighters on either side of the conflict. Although rather austere in manner, he commanded respect. He died at Wytheville, Virginia, on November 6, 1873.

WHardee.

Samuel P. Heintzelman

Samuel P. Heintzelman made a name for himself in the eastern theater of the Civil War. He was born on September 30, 1805, at Manheim, Lancaster County, Pennsylvania. In 1822 he became a cadet at West Point and achieved the rank of second lieutenant in the Second Infantry soon after graduation in 1826. Two years later he became a captain.

He was another of those gallant officers who joined General Scott's expedition against Mexico City. There he was brevetted for gallantry and meritorious conduct at the battle of Huamantla. When the war was over, he remained in the army; and by 1855 he had been commissioned as a major and served with the First Infantry in California, fighting the Indians. His chief duty, however, was to clean the Rio Grande border of marauders. In addition, he founded Fort Yuma in Arizona.

When the Civil War broke out, he was called back to Washington as inspector of the forces. By May, 1861, he was appointed colonel of the Seventeenth Infantry and then rapidly reached the rank of brigadier general of volunteers. In this same month he captured Alexandria, Virginia, near Washington. As a result of this he was first in command of the Third Division of General McDowell's army. Both fought hard in the First Battle of Bull Run. General Heintzelman and his troops captured the Henry House, the key point of the battlefield. To hold this House the troops fought desperately, and even Heintzelman was seriously wounded. He recuperated sufficiently to take over the command of the Third Corps in General McClellan's army.

In the Peninsular campaign in the spring of 1862, Heintzelman advanced on Yorktown, initiating operations. Although he told General McClellan that this siege was impracticable, it was maintained until May 4, when the Confederate Army slipped away with Heintzelman and his troops in pursuit. The enemy was stopped near Williamsburg on May 8, and a great battle ensued; but the results were indecisive.

Heintzelman fought bravely in the famous battle of the Seven Pines, resisting the advancing enemy with his untiring troops. When plans were made to attack Richmond, on June 25, 1862, General Heintzelman was elected to lead the troops. This started the Seven Days' Battle. On July 4 he was promoted to the rank of major general of volunteers.

In August of the same year Heintzelman was ordered to send his troops to reenforce Pope's army in the Manassas campaign. On August 29 he met the great Stonewall Jackson and his army, primed for battle. Heintzelman attacked but suffered a severe repulse and had to withdraw his troops. Soon afterwards he was given the assignment of defending Washington. He remained there until October, 1863. The following year he was ordered to handle courts-martial, his assignment for the duration of the war. Retiring from the army in 1869, he lived in Washington until his death on May 7, 1880.

S. P. Heintzelman

Ambrose Hill

One of the most famous and dependable Confederate corps commanders under Lee was the veteran infantry general Ambrose Hill. Hill was born in Culpeper County, Virginia on November 9, 1825. He graduated from West Point in 1847 and was appointed to the First Artillery. He served in the Mexican and Seminole Wars and soon won promotion as first lieutenant in 1851. For five years, from 1855 to 1860, he was employed on the United States coast survey.

In March, 1861, just before the firing on Fort Sumter, Hill submitted his resignation as first lieutenant. When Virginia seceded, he became colonel of an infantry regiment. He soon earned on the battlefield the title of brigadier general. He fought bravely in the First Battle of Bull Run against the forces of General McClellan and became one of Lee's top infantry commanders.

In the Peninsular campaign of 1862 he gained further promotion to major general. His division formed part of Stonewall Jackson's corps. During the flank attack of Chancellorsville in May, 1863, he was severely wounded. After Jackson's death Hill became a lieutenant general and was placed in command of another corps of Lee's army. This time he led the corps in the historic Gettysburg campaign of 1863. He commanded part of Lee's left center in the fighting opposite Culp's Hill and Cemetery Ridge, though he failed to drive Hancock's forces from the ridge.

Later Hill took part in the famous Mine Run campaign, and became, along with "ole Pete" Longstreet, one of Lee's most trusted generals in the last phases of the war.

His corps fought against Meade's forces in the Wilderness campaign, being opposed particularly by the most famous Union infantry commander, Hancock, and the Second Corps.

Hill was heavily engaged against Warren in the defense of Petersburg and the protection of the Weldon Railroad. He held the Petersburg line from Fort Bragg to Burgess Mill.

After the defeat of Pickett at Five Forks and the resulting break in the Petersburg defenses, Hill fought on gallantly and recklessly. On April 2, 1865, he was shot and killed at point-blank range by a Union rifleman—Corporal John W. Mauk of Company F, Thirty-eighth Pennsylvania Infantry. Amidst the confusion in the evacuation of Richmond, a hearse containing Hill's body rattled into the city at one o'clock of the morning of April 3. He was buried by his nephew.

A. P. Hill

David Harvey Hill

David Harvey Hill was born in York, South Carolina, on July 12, 1821. He entered West Point in 1838, where he graduated twenty-eighth in a class of fifty-six cadets. He was assigned to the infantry and saw military service on the Maine border, in garrison work, and in the Mexican War.

Hill resigned from the army in 1849 to become first professor of mathematics at Davidson College and then director of the North Carolina Military Institute for ten years. His wife and Stonewall Jackson's wife were sisters.

At the beginning of the Civil War Hill was made colonel of a North Carolina regiment and saw action at Big Bethel. He tried to turn Porter's flank in the fighting around Gaines Mill. He later saw service at Seven Pines, South Mountain, Antietam, and during the Gettysburg campaign. He was advanced to brigadier general and by 1863 was a major general in the Confederate Army.

To aid Bragg, Hill was dispatched to Chickamauga. There both faced the Union general Rosecrans. Here Hill criticized Bragg and suggested that he should be replaced. President Davis, a friend of the latter, refused to do so but instead held up Hill's promotion. Soon afterwards Hill was sent south to join Johnston's army in the Atlanta campaign. He surrendered with Johnston in North Carolina in April, 1865.

After the war Hill published a magazine and became president of the University of Arkansas from 1877 to 1884. During the following five years he served as president of the Georgia Military Academy. On September 29, 1889, he died at Charlotte, North Carolina.

D H Hill

John B. Hood

John B. Hood was a soldier's general. He was born in 1831 at Owingsville, Kentucky. Like other famous officers he graduated from West Point in 1853. He soon saw action as a cavalry officer, fighting Indians in the West; and several years later he became cavalry instructor at the Academy.

When the Civil War erupted, Hood felt impelled to resign from the United States Army. He received a commission as a colonel in the Confederate Army. He proved his ability and earned a new commission with the famous Texas Brigade in the Army of Northern Virginia as brigadier general. He served throughout the campaign of 1862.

At Gettysburg Hood fought valiantly and lost an arm commanding one of the divisions in the corps of James Longstreet. Both these men soon joined the Army of the Tennessee. Tragically, at the bloody battle of Chickamauga, Hood was terribly wounded and had to have his leg amputated. He still remained in active duty after he recuperated; and, in fact, he replaced General J. E. Johnston as commander of the Army of the Tennessee.

General Hood was known as a fighting general. He fought hard around Atlanta, trying to force Sherman and his army to retreat northward. More than once he used bold strategy, making every effort to have Sherman's forces follow his corps away from Atlanta; but his methods failed. Sherman successfully completed his famous "March to the Sea," devastating the Southern countryside. Meanwhile General Thomas opposed Hood in battle at Franklin on November 30, 1864. A month later this Union army, under Thomas, almost annihilated Hood's forces in the battle of Nashville. Hood was relieved of his command at his own request on January 23, 1865. He died of yellow fever in New Orleans on August 30, 1879.

J B Hood

Joseph Hooker

The popular "Fighting Joe Hooker" was born in Hadley, Massachusetts, in 1814. He graduated from West Point in 1837 and as a lieutenant saw action in the Mexican War. There he had an opportunity to show his skill and bravery and earned the rank of lieutenant colonel for gallantry on the battlefield. In 1853 he retired from the army and devoted himself to farming and engineering.

In 1861 Hooker was appointed brigadier general of volunteers and in the following year attained the same rank in the regular army. His gallantry on the battlefield earned for him the nickname of "Fighting Joe."

Hooker fought brilliantly in the Peninsular campaign at South Mountain and at Antietam. In January, 1863, President Lincoln showed his confidence in Hooker by turning over full command of the Army of the Potomac. He did a good job of rehabilitation and organization, but he somehow lacked as a commanding general the leadership qualifications he had displayed as a corps and divisional commander.

The Battle of Chancellorsville, May 2–4, 1863, was lost because of Hooker's inability to cope with the constant surprise attacks made by the Confederate forces under Lee and Jackson. Hooker was so humiliated that he gave up his command of the Army of the Potomac, and Meade became his successor. Some believe he did this primarily so President Lincoln could avoid embarrassment.

Hooker made up for this defeat by fighting brilliantly with his new command, the Twentieth Corps, at the battle of Chattanooga and especially at the "Battle of the Clouds" on Lookout Mountain. President Lincoln was pleased, and Hooker was given the rank of major general in the regular army. He later became the head of the Department of the East, joining Sherman in Georgia to win fame in the attack on Atlanta.

Hooker suffered a stroke from overwork and had to retire from active service in 1864. However, he retained the full rank of major general in the regular army even after the war. He retired from the service in 1868 and died in 1879.

Joseph Hooker

Oliver Otis Howard

Oliver Otis Howard was born in Leeds, Maine, on November 18, 1830. He graduated from Bowdoin College in 1850 and from West Point in 1854. He was then assigned to the ordnance department of the regular army. When trouble broke out with the Seminole Indians, he served the army in the Florida campaign. Two years later he was appointed professor of mathematics at West Point, where he taught for four years.

At the outbreak of the Civil War, Howard entered the volunteer service as colonel of the Third Maine Regiment. In 1861 he fought in the First Battle of Bull Run and afterward was made brigadier general of volunteers. The following year he served in the Virginia campaign and fighting at the battle of Fair Oaks was wounded and had an arm amputated. He recovered sufficiently to be given a command at the battles of Antietam and Fredericksburg. In 1863 he was given command of the Eleventh Army Corps and led this group in the battle of Chancellorsville and at Gettysburg. Sherman thought Howard ought to command the Army of the Tennessee, which was the right wing of Sherman's army on his "March to the Sea."

In 1864 Howard was appointed brigadier general in the regular army. The following year he forced the surrender of General Joseph Eggleston Johnston and his men.

After the war Howard served as commissioner of the Bureau of Refugees and Freed Men and later became president of Harvard University. He always fought for the higher education of the Negro.

In 1874 he went back into the army service and conducted four campaigns against the Indians. During 1881/82, he served as superintendent of the United States Military Academy. He retired in 1895 and wrote an autobiography in 1907. He died on October 26, 1909.

O.O. Howard

Benjamin Huger

Benjamin Huger was born in Charleston, South Carolina, on November 22, 1805. It was his wish as a boy to enter West Point, which he did, graduating with a commission as second lieutenant of artillery. For three years he served in the topographical service and by 1832 was captain of ordnance. For the next few years, Huger was put in full command, respectively, of the arsenals in Harper's Ferry, Pikesville, and finally in his hometown, Charleston.

In 1840 he was sent abroad by the army to study European methods of warfare. He became an expert in ordnance and was appointed to the ordnance board of the War Department.

When the Mexican War broke out, he headed the ordnance bureau under General Winfield Scott. His military action at Vera Cruz and at Chapultepec earned him promotion from major to colonel.

When Fort Sumter fell, Colonel Huger resigned from the War Department and returned to Charleston. He was soon a brigadier general and later became a major general.

By May, 1861, he had taken over the Department of Norfolk as full commander. A year later he revealed his courage by outwitting General McClellan who threatened to take Norfolk. Huger dismantled the fortifications, set fire to the navy yard, blew up the *Merrimac,* and removed all stores.

When the first Peninsular campaign was in full swing, Huger was given the command of a division in General Johnston's army. He served well in the famous Battle of Seven Pines and at Malvern Hill. However, General James Longstreet criticized him severely for his dilatory movements at Seven Pines.

On July 12, 1862, he was relieved of his command and given an inspectorship in ordnance and artillery. Before the war was over he was sent to the Trans-Mississippi Army, where he fought on until the surrender of the Confederate forces at Appomattox.

David Hunter

David Hunter was a weak general with an irascible temper.

Hunter was born in Washington, D.C. Like so many other officers, he studied at West Point. He graduated in 1822 and served his country well until 1836. In that year he handed in his resignation in order to enter the business world.

When the Mexican War broke out, Hunter became a major under General Wood. He did not especially distinguish himself; however, in February, 1861, he was appointed as one of four generals to guard President Lincoln on his journey from Springfield, Illinois, to Washington, D.C.

After the fatal attack on Fort Sumter, Hunter won a commission as a brigadier general of Union volunteers. He served as commander of a division under General McDowell and fought against Beauregard's forces at the First Battle of Bull Run.

When Frémont was removed from command in Missouri, Hunter was placed at the head of a division. However, his work was so unsatisfactory that he was shelved and given few responsibilities. Hunter's peculiar habit of writing nasty letters of criticism attracted the attention of President Lincoln, who looked upon these letters as a matter of bad taste and irritation to the army.

When Hunter was given command of the Carolina coast, he again offended the President by prematurely proclaiming the freedom of the slaves under his jurisdiction before Lincoln had announced his Emancipation Proclamation. Hunter was taken off active service until 1864.

In that turbulent year he was given command of the Union forces in the Shenandoah Valley, with the approval of General Grant, who had been disappointed by Sigel's leadership at New Market.

Hunter made another blunder. This time he marched his forces up the valley to Staunton, Virginia, and scattered a small Confederate force. Grant wanted him to join forces with Sheridan at Charlottesville and then march on toward Richmond; but Hunter instead marched on Lynchburg and then came face to face with the redoubtable Early, who promptly cut Hunter's supply line.

It was necessary for Hunter to protect Washington by retreating toward Harper's Ferry. The general had his own plans and took his forces into West Virginia. This action angered Lincoln and Stanton and even disgusted Grant. Hunter began to blame everyone but himself for this blunder. In fact, after the war was over he even wrote to General Lee about the affair. Lee and the Southern leaders held him in special contempt because his troops had burned the Virginia Military Institute, the Governor's Mansion, and the surrounding area. General Grant, enraged by Hunter's blunders, met him and bluntly demanded that he give up his command in favor of Sheridan. Hunter, weary and tired and buffeted by ill fortune, complied with the request.

D. Hunter

Thomas Jonathan ("Stonewall") Jackson

"Stonewall" Jackson was born in 1824 at Clarksburg, Virginia. When he graduated from West Point in 1846, he was commissioned as a lieutenant and soon saw service in the Mexican War. He served under General Scott with great distinction and for ten years, 1851–61, taught at the Virginia Military Institute.

When the Civil War began, Jackson, as a colonel, was sent to Harpers Ferry by the Confederacy.

At the First Battle of Bull Run he was given a brigade and promoted to the rank of brigadier general. It was here that he earned the famous sobriquet "Stonewall." General Barnard Bee had observed the general standing like a stone wall amidst all the fierce fighting.

General Johnston now assigned Stonewall Jackson to take command in the Shenandoah Valley; and again the latter earned another promotion, this time to major general. His job was to divert large formations of Union troops so that it would become difficult for them to unite in the coming campaign against Richmond. Jackson attacked Shield's division at Kernstown on May 23, 1862. The diversion succeeded even though the attack was repulsed. Jackson struck again, falling upon General Banks and his army. General Lee hoped that this diversionary tactic would prevent McDowell's army from joining General McClellan. Jackson repeated his methods of attack on General Frémont's forces, which were part of General McDowell's army. Then he hurried back to the Shenandoah Valley and routed Bank's army at Front Royal and at Winchester.

The administration in Washington feared a possible advance on the capital by this courageous and daring Southern commander. Plans were hastily made to have Generals Shields and Frémont to use their forces to cut off Stonewall Jackson's army in the Shenandoah Valley. However, the latter eluded them successfully after checking them in heavy counterattacks.

Lee was happy to have Jackson on his side in the fierce Seven Days' Battle, though the fighting of the latter was less brilliant than in the Shenandoah campaign. At the Second Battle of Bull Run Jackson prepared the preliminaries through the rapid attacks made by his cavalry. As a result, the Confederates were able to win a crushing victory.

In the famous Antietam campaign Jackson rushed to the aid of Lee and also captured the garrison at Harpers Ferry. Lee had great confidence in Jackson's ability to win victories. When the great Army of Northern Virginia was reorganized by Lee, Stonewall Jackson was put in command of the Second Corps and also earned the rank of lieutenant general. Once again, Jackson used daring tactics to earn a victory in the bloody battle of Fredericksburg.

In the Second Battle of Bull Run, Lee and Jackson had used tactics which stunned the Union forces. Now, in the battle of Chancellorsville, these same tactics won them another victory. Jackson completely routed Hooker's right wing, but the victory was won at the price of a great tragedy. The fighting had continued into the night; and Jackson's own men had mistaken him for the enemy and fired upon him, mortally wounding the general. His death was a severe blow to the Confederate cause.

The men of the Confederate Army had great respect and affection for Jackson even though on many occasions they had a taste of his strict discipline. They admired his fighting ability and winning tactics.

Stonewall Jackson was a Confederate enigma. A man of puritanical origin, in fact, of Calvinistic attitudes, he fought like a fanatic. Though deeply religious, even carrying his prayer sessions onto the battlefield, he was possessed of a ruthless and consuming ambition. While lying mortally wounded at Chancellorsville, he received Lee's praise with the comment, "General Lee is very kind, but he should give his praise to God."

Jackson was a master of surprise, rapid movement, and flank attack. His foot soldiers moved almost with the speed of cavalry. Operating with Lee as a "one-two" punch, he made the Confederate leader look good—Lee with the frontal attack, Jackson with the flank and rear attack. Bull Run, Shenandoah, and Harpers Ferry only added to his greater fame at Fredericksburg. He received his greatest success at Chancellorsville, where his path to glory led "but to the grave." His death cut down the speed and striking power of the Confederate forces. No wonder Lee exclaimed "I have lost my right arm." Had he lived, Jackson no doubt would have been given a separate command—probably the Army of the West. One can imagine a Grant-Jackson duel on the Mississippi and then a Lee-Jackson combination opposing Grant in the Wilderness, Petersburg, and Richmond. Jackson was a corps commander and never had more than 30,000 men, yet his campaigns have been studied in army staff schools everywhere. Jackson remains today a legend in the South.

T. J. Jackson

Albert Sidney Johnston

Albert Sidney Johnston, one of the most promising Confederate generals, was killed in action before his full talents could be used.

He was born on February 2, 1803, and was educated first by private tutors and later attended school in western Virginia and at Transylvania University.

In 1822 Johnston was appointed to West Point, where he was highly popular. His best subject was mathematics. After his graduation in 1826 he was commissioned a second lieutenant. As a regimental adjutant he participated in the Black Hawk War of 1832. When his wife died two years later, he resigned his commission and took up farming in Texas.

However, Johnston soon gave up this occupation and joined the army in Texas as a private. General Rush was commander of this army, and he appointed Johnston adjutant general and later brigadier general of the Texan army. When Johnston became head of the army in place of General Felix Houston, this act caused much conflict between the two men. As a result Houston challenged Johnston to a duel, in which the latter received serious wounds. Johnston's command lasted until 1838, when he was made Secretary of War for the Republic of Texas.

A year later he led an expedition against the hostile Cherokee Indians and defeated them. When the Mexican War started, he was commissioned a colonel of the First Texas Rifle Volunteers and distinguished himself many times in battle. In 1849 he re-turned to the United States Army and was appointed paymaster by President Taylor.

In 1857, as a colonel, he led an expedition to quiet the Mormon controversy. He performed this dangerous mission successfully and without bloodshed and for his brilliant feat earned the new title of brevet major general.

When the war began, Leonidas Polk, the Right Reverend Episcopal Bishop of Louisiana, who had buckled the "sword over the gown," recommended his West Point roommate, Johnston, to President Jefferson Davis. Johnston was given the impressive title "General Commanding the Western Department of the Army of the Confederate States of America."

When Texas seceded from the Union in April, 1861, Johnston resigned his commission. He had planned to hold Fort Donelson but had to withdraw from the line of defense he had built during the year.

At Shiloh he fought valiantly against Grant and was killed in action. Over 100,000 men on both sides were engaged in this battle. Johnston's purpose was to surprise the invaders before they had time to concentrate large numbers. He wanted to destroy Grant's forces. In the midst of battle the general was struck by a fragment and bled to death. The South lost a great leader. Beauregard, his successor, continued the bloody battle until his men were exhausted and his ammunition almost gone. He has been blamed for the retreat by many Southern colleagues.

A. S. Johnston

Joseph E. Johnston

Joseph E. Johnston was born in Cherry Grove, Georgia, in 1807. His father was a judge, and his mother was a niece of Patrick Henry. Johnston graduated from West Point in 1829, a classmate of Robert E. Lee. During the war against the Seminole Indians, he was an aide to General Scott, winning the rank of brevet captain.

In the Mexican War he was wounded twice at the battle of Cerro Gordo. In 1855 he became colonel of the First United States Cavalry and by 1860 had risen to the rank of quartermaster general of the United States Army.

At the outbreak of the Civil War in 1861, he resigned from the army and offered his services to the Confederacy.

He was soon commissioned a brigadier general and was given a command in the Army of the Shenandoah. In the first real battle of the Civil War, Bull Run, in July, 1861, his force of 15,000 men stood at Manassas Junction, a key spot in the railroad to Richmond. He joined forces with General Beauregard and together with Stonewall Jackson and General Bee inflicted a defeat on the Union Army under General McDowell and forced it to retreat to Washington. He was given command of the Army of Virginia and opposed the clever General George B. McClellan in the First Peninsular campaign that had as its object the capture of Richmond.

Johnston was wounded at the battle of Fair Oaks on May 31, 1862; and as a result Robert E. Lee took command in his place.

Upon his quick recovery Johnston was given command of the Army of the Tennessee, superseding General Braxton Bragg, whose campaign against Chattanooga had caused considerable criticism in the South. Johnston occasioned some criticism for his campaign in the West against Grant and Sherman. He had a force of some 12,000 men at Jackson and was expected to join Pemberton's army of 50,000 in and around Vicksburg. However, the Confederate high command did not relish his plan of a combined attack on Grant's army. The result was that Grant moved between Johnston and Pemberton, and ultimately the latter was forced to surrender to Grant on July 4, 1863.

Johnston soon came east to engage in probably his greatest and most memorable campaign. Sherman had succeeded Grant in the West in 1864, when the latter went east to tackle Lee and to crush the rebellion.

Sherman's plan was to move east from Chattanooga, strike south into Georgia up through the Carolinas and come up behind Lee's rear and crush him with the aid of Grant in front.

Sherman's force consisted of 98,000 men commanded by such able generals as Thomas, Howard, McPherson, and Kilpatrick. Opposing him was "Old Joe" Johnston, wary and battlewise though fighting a hopeless cause. Johnston knew that if Sherman took Atlanta, Savannah, and Charleston, the defeat of the Confederacy was inevitable.

At the outset of the campaign Johnston's best-known corps commander was impulsive, aggressive, lion-hearted John B. Hood. Johnston adopted a plan of defensive positions, delaying actions, and retreat. He was dubbed "Fabius Cunctator," after the Roman general who was famous for his cautious delaying tactics against the enemy. His fortified line at Dalton was taken, and he was driven out of Resaca. He was continually forced to retreat with his forces.

Jefferson Davis and others felt that this policy was destroying rebel morale; and after Bragg went to Atlanta to make a personal inspection for Jefferson Davis, Johnston was removed from command and Hood put in his place.

Hood adopted a new plan of campaign. With a force of some 55,000 he turned north and west, hoping to draw off Sherman from Atlanta and also to cut his lines of supply.

Sherman sent Thomas to oppose Hood while he continued to march through Georgia. Thomas, despite threats of being replaced, prepared for battle, and in the furious engagement around Nashville destroyed Hood's army. An army of 55,000 men was now reduced to a crushed force of 9,000 men.

Consternation and fear gripped the South. General Lee assumed command of all rebel forces and recalled Johnston to the command of the Confederate forces left to face Sherman. Lee gave Johnston the two corps of Hardee and Bragg which, together with other forces, totaled 34,000 men.

Johnston desperately sought to save Augusta and Charleston. He put Hardee in Charleston and Bragg in Augusta while he set up headquarters at Columbia. It was a fine city, with homes made of wood. When the Union forces invaded the city they became roaring drunk and burned down the homes.

The loss of Columbia split the Confederate Army, and Hardee beat a retreat. Lee had sent him a letter stating, "if you are forced back from Raleigh and we are deprived of the supplies from eastern North Carolina I do not see how this army can be supported. The supplies in Virginia are exhausted."

Johnston was determined to stop Sherman, but the latter had Schofield and his Twenty-third Corps to help crush Johnston. General Logan and his Fifteenth Corps moved in to help. The rebels began to retreat since there were only 17,000 left to face an army of 90,000 Union troops. Johnston had lost Raleigh and Goldsbore. He had only one real alternative—surrender—but the South rejected Sherman's terms. However, Johnston was forced to surrender to Sherman on April 26, 1865.

After the war he entered politics and served in Congress. He died in Washington, D.C., on March 21, 1891.

J. E. Johnston

James Lawson Kemper

James Lawson Kemper was born on June 11, 1823, in Madison County, Virginia. He obtained a good elementary education and received a B.A. in 1842 from Washington College. He also had a grounding in military drill at the Virginia Military Institute. He won a commission as captain of volunteers in the Mexican War; but when he reached General Taylor's army, it was too late to participate in active service.

When the war was over Kemper married Cremona C. Cave, went into politics, and was elected to the House of Delegates of Virginia for five terms. He was chairman of the commission on military affairs, president of the Board of Visitors of the Virginia Military Institute, and Speaker of the House of Delegates from December, 1861, to March, 1862.

With the outbreak of the Civil War, Kemper joined the Confederate cause and was made colonel of the Seventh Virginia Regiment, with which he served at Bull Run, Williamsburg, and the bitter campaigns of Fredericksburg and Chancellorsville. At Williamsburg he led a famous charge under the keen observation of General A. P. Hill. Following this he was commissioned brigadier general.

At Gettysburg Kemper served along with Armistead, Garnett, and other generals in Pickett's Brigade. He courageously led his men in Pickett's charge against the Union Second Corps under Hancock and fell in battle just as his troops reached the crest of the Union lines. Though he was given charge of Pickett's right wing in this famous assault, even his courage could not save the day for Lee's defeated army. He was captured and held as a prisoner of war.

After the war Kemper returned to his law practice in Madison County, Virginia. Elected governor in 1873, he served for four years, urging civil rights and federal protection for Negroes.

He died in 1895 at the age of seventy-two.

J. L. Kemper

Erasmus Darwin Keyes

Erasmus Darwin Keyes was born on May 29, 1810, in Brimfield, Massachusetts. When the Keyes family moved to Kennebec County, Maine, he was assured by his family that they would approve his appointment to West Point if secured by him. He entered the Academy, was a good student, and graduated in 1832 as second lieutenant. He was stationed at Fort Monroe, Virginia, and then at Charleston, South Carolina.

On August 31, 1833, he was placed in the Third Artillery. He became the aide-de-camp to Winfield Scott four years later. Then, after seeing service in the West, he once again served as Scott's aide-de-camp.

By 1841 Keyes was promoted to the rank of captain, remaining with the Third Artillery. However, the following year he was sent to the barracks at New Orleans. From 1844 to 1848 he instructed West Point cadets in field artillery and cavalry tactics.

The next phase of his military career was in the West, particularly on the Pacific Coast. For nine years he fought Indians, playing a role in the famous Spokane Expedition of 1858. In that year he won recognition for his services and was promoted to the rank of major and placed in the First Artillery.

Once again, General Scott desired Keyes' invaluable services. This time he became Scott's military secretary and was elevated to the rank of lieutenant colonel in 1860.

When the Civil War broke out, Keyes was made colonel of the Eleventh Infantry. Soon afterward he was raised to brigadier general of volunteers and given a brigade to command under General Tyler. He fought hard at the First Battle of Bull Run.

Keyes' services were soon requested by General McClellan in the Peninsular campaign. Keyes commanded the Fourth Army Corps and on May 5, 1862, after going through many hard-fought battles, won another rank—major general of volunteers. His men had done a valuable service in helping protect the transfer of McClellan's men from the York to the James rivers.

In 1863 Keyes became involved in a serious controversy with General John Dix over his ineffective expeditions against West Point, Virginia. He insisted that an official investigation be made, but the request was rejected. A year later Keyes retired from the army.

After the war Keyes went into business and became president of the Maxwell Gold Mining Company. He was connected with business firms until his death in Nice, France.

He was buried at his beloved West Point on November 19, 1895.

E D Keyes.

Hugh Judson Kilpatrick

Hugh Judson Kilpatrick, soldier and diplomat, was born on January 14, 1836, near Deckertown, New Jersey, the son of a farmer. After a commonplace school education he entered West Point in 1856 as Judson Kilpatrick, graduating May 6, 1861—a month earlier than usual—as second lieutenant of artillery. He is said to have possessed more than ordinary ability—graduating seventeenth in a class of forty-five members. On the day of his graduation he married Alice Nailer of New York, and three days later he secured appointment as a captain with the Fifth New York Volunteers (Duryee's Zouaves). He left his regiment for Fort Monroe, Virginia, in time to participate in the battle of Big Bethel on June 10, 1861, in which he was severely wounded. His gallant service won for him an appointment as lieutenant colonel, Second New York Cavalry, and thereafter until the end of the Civil War he had almost continuous field service with the cavalry. When McClellan transferred the Army of the Potomac to the James River, Kilpatrick assisted in covering the defenses of Washington with his cavalry.

For two years Kilpatrick took an active part in cavalry operations of the Army of the Potomac, especially in the Northern Virginia campaign, where he was constantly and gallantly fighting Stuart's cavalry. At Beverly Ford he commanded a brigade and participated in the ill-fated Stoneman's River engagement, where he destroyed immense quantities of the enemy's stores and penetrated to within two miles of Richmond. He was promoted to brigadier general of volunteers on June 3, 1863, and shortly afterward commanded a cavalry division in the engagements of Aldie, Middleburg, and Upperville, Virginia. For gallant and meritorious services at Aldie he was brevetted major in the regular army. He took an active and successful part at Gettysburg in cavalry assaults upon the Confederate right flank around Round Top, in hot pursuit of the defeated enemy. In subsequent operations in central Virginia, he initiated the Kilpatrick raid on Richmond, with the object of releasing Federal prisoners in Libby Prison. Thereafter he was transferred to command the Third Cavalry Division assembling in northern Georgia for the campaign against Atlanta. For conspicuous service at the battle of Resaca, where he was again severely wounded, he was brevetted colonel in the regular army. He joined Sherman's march to the sea while still unable to ride a horse; and in the invasion of the Carolinas which followed, his cavalry division performed valuable service. He was brevetted brigadier general and major general, respectively, for gallant and meritorious services in the capture of Fayetteville, North Carolina, and in the campaign in the Carolinas.

After the war Kilpatrick resigned from the army and entered politics, receiving an appointment as United States Minister to Chile (1866–68). After Grant's second campaign for the Presidency, Kilpatrick was recalled. He joined the Democratic party to support Horace Greeley in 1872, but in 1876 he again returned to the Republican party. In 1880 while a director of the Union Pacific Railroad, he was nominated for Congress from his native state but was defeated. In the same year he was a delegate to the Republican national convention and in March, 1881, was reappointed by President Garfield as United States Minister to Chile. He became involved in a diplomatic controversy with Stephan A. Hurlbut, United States Minister to Peru (Chile and Peru being then at war). He died in 1881 at Santiago, Chile, of kidney trouble.

As a cavalry commander he was a brilliant leader, having originated the saying that "cavalry can fight anywhere except at sea." In political life he was an eloquent, magnetic, and forceful public speaker.

Evander McIvor Law

Evander McIvor Law, Confederate soldier and educator, was born August 7, 1836, in Darlington, South Carolina, the son of E. Augustus and Elizabeth Law. In 1856 he was graduated from the Citadel in Charleston, where he had been assistant professor of belles-lettres during his senior year. The following five years were spent teaching, first at the King's Mountain Military Academy at Yorkville, South Carolina, and later at the Military High School, Tuskegee, Alabama, of which he was co-founder with Robert Parks. In 1861 he recruited a company, largely from his school, and as captain took it into action at Pensacola. He served in all of the most important campaigns of the war in the East including the severe fighting against Thomas at Chickamauga and Hooker at Chattanooga. He fought at Gettysburg, where he claimed that the result might have been otherwise had Lee followed his advice and that of two other colleagues regarding the seizure of Round Top. After having been wounded at Cold Harbor, he transferred from the Army of Virginia to a cavalry brigade in Johnston's command. Just prior to the surrender he became major general.

Immediately after the close of the Civil War, Law administered the estate of William A. Latta, wealthy planter and railroad man, whose daughter, Jane Elizabeth, Law had married on March 9, 1863. He then lived for a time as a planter in Tuskegee and Yorkville and then resumed connections with the King's Mountain Military Academy until it closed in 1884. He dabbled in engineering and newspaper work. He moved to Barton, Florida, to fulfill a long-cherished plan of opening a school modeled after the Citadel and the Virginia Military Institute. After a year's existence as a private institution, this school was established as the South Florida Military and Educational Institute and received state aid through a system of county scholarships. It was a pioneer venture, with the attendance always small and resources meager. The students aided in the upkeep, and during the first year no fixed salaries were guaranteed the teachers. Nevertheless, high standards were maintained; and Law exercised a lasting influence on the student body. In 1903 he resigned from the Institute to devote the rest of his life to newspaper work—as editor of the *Barton Courier Informant* (1905–15)—and to his duties as trustee of Sumerlin Institute (1905–12) and as a member of the Polk County Board of Education (1912–20). He was especially interested in all state activities commemorating the Civil War. He served as commander of the Florida division of the Confederate Veterans (1899–1903) and aided in organizing the Barton chapter of the Daughters of the Confederacy.

When he died in 1920, he was the last of the major generals of the Confederacy. His reputation does not rest on his military record, however. His most lasting achievement was his part in establishing the foundation of the educational system in his adopted state, Florida.

E. M. Law

Fitzhugh Lee

Fitzhugh Lee was born at "Clermont," Fair County, Virginia, on November 19, 1835.

After an early education and special private schooling, Lee entered West Point in 1852. He showed greater skill in horsemanship than in his studies, graduating forty-fifth in a class of forty-nine in 1856. He was sent first to Carlisle Barracks, Pennsylvania, as a cavalry instructor, where he stayed for two years, and then to Texas as a second lieutenant in the Second Cavalry. Soon afterward he was wounded in a skirmish with Indians; however, he recovered once again to fight them.

West Point needed an instructor in the department of tactics. Lee was most happy to accept the offer and remained there from December, 1860, to May, 1861.

Like so many other Virginians, he submitted his resignation when the Civil War broke out and offered his services to his native state, Virginia. General Richard Ewell accepted him as a staff officer with the rank of first lieutenant in the regular army of the Confederacy. He also served in the same capacity under General Joseph F. Johnston during the Manassas campaign, after which he won his promotion to the rank of lieutenant colonel.

The Peninsular campaign proved his worth sufficiently to cause his superiors to elevate him to brigadier general. They saw how he had harassed the forces of McClellan.

It was Lee's delay in reaching the Rapidan that caused a complete postponement of the planned campaign to eliminate the forces led by Pope. In 1863 he had his own command in the battle of Kelly's Ford, and he showed great fighting power with only a small force against the superior army under General W. W. Averell.

It was at Chancellorsville that he performed a great military feat. He had a complete cavalry brigade under his command. It cooperated successfully with the main army sufficiently in guarding Jackson's march on May 2. Lee discovered that the right wing of the Union Eleventh Corps was in a somewhat "chaotic" state of organization on the field. He made a brilliant reconnaissance which enabled Jackson to place Rhodes' division to the left for decisive attack. The Army of Northern Virginia was grateful for his useful aid in the remaining months of 1863. Again he won a promotion, this time to the rank of major general.

In 1864 Lee's operations enabled the First Corps to take over that strategic crossroads, the Spotsylvania Court House. The main army used Lee's forces constantly to harass, cut down, and spread terror among the Union forces.

On September 19, 1864, at Winchester, Lee's luck ran out. He was severely wounded and taken out of action until early 1865. His superiors needed him so badly that they gave him a new command. He became head of the cavalry on the north side of James River. Soon afterward, with General Hampton losing command, he was made senior cavalry commander of the Army of Northern Virginia. He was absent from his division at the battle of Five Forks when it was mauled by the Union forces. He made a full retreat to Appomattox and realized that he was surrounded. With great chagrin, he surrendered on April 11, 1865. Not until 1886 did he enter politics. In that year he was elected governor of Virginia. In the Spanish-American War he became a major general of volunteers. After the war he became military governor of Havana. He died in 1905.

Robert E. Lee

Robert E. Lee was born on January 19, 1807, and when he had reached eighteen he became a cadet at West Point. In 1829 he graduated, second in his class, and obtained a commission in the Corps of Engineers.

Three years later, he married Mary Custis, the great-granddaughter of Martha Washington. They took up residence at Alexandria, Virginia, just opposite the national capital.

When the Mexican War broke out, Lee distinguished himself. As a captain with Scott's army he earned three brevets, was wounded at Chapultepec, and personally received an acclamation from the commander in chief for his brilliant reconnaissances on the advance to Mexico City.

In 1852 Lee was happy to become the commandant of West Point. For three years he endeavored to make durable improvements and succeeded sufficiently to win a promotion to lieutenant colonel of the Second Cavalry, stationed in West Texas. He became a full commander of a regiment in 1860.

While on leave at Alexandria, Virginia, Lee was called to put down John Brown's raid at Harpers Ferry. He led the Marines on an assault on the federal arsenal located there, captured the famous abolitionist and his men, and witnessed their historic execution.

General Scott recalled Lee from his command in Texas in February, 1861. Secession had created a national crisis, and Scott had great respect for Lee. He wanted the latter to remain in the federal army; but Lee felt, in all conscience, that this could not be since his loyalty to Virginia, in case of an invasion, was paramount. His feelings in the matter made dramatic history.

By April 17, Lee knew Virginia had seceded. He had his sad interview with General Scott, and on April 19 he resigned from the army.

On April 23, 1861, Lee addressed the Virginia convention and, in part, stated, "Trusting to Almighty God, on approving conscience, and the aid of my fellow-citizens, I will devote myself to the defense and service of my native State, in whose behalf alone would I have ever drawn my sword."

On May 25, Lee was allowed to take his Virginia troops and ally them with the Confederate States Army. He was given the highest rank then in Confederate service—brigadier general.

Jefferson Davis, President of the Confederacy, trusted Lee and kept him as his adviser, particularly utilizing his knowledge as an engineer for the location of batteries and troops on the different defensive lines.

President Davis kept Lee extremely active. Among his tasks was a plan to divert reinforcements from General G. B. Mc-Clellan. This plan was successfully carried out by his colleague, T. J. "Stonewall" Jackson; and the Shenandoah Valley was occupied by the Confederate Army by March, 1862.

For the next three years Lee took over command of the Army of Northern Virginia, replacing General J. E. Johnston, who suffered from severe wounds.

Lee proved himself equal to General McClellan when the latter advanced en masse on Richmond. Lee's master strategy checked the advance after seven days of fighting, and hurled back the Northern army. Lee achieved another decisive victory over Pope in the bloody Second Battle of Bull Run.

Lee next planned to invade Northern territory to lower the morale of the people, but this time McClellan's army held at the battle of Antietam in September, 1862.

At Gettysburg, though the terrible repulse of the Confederate assault on the third day of battle was due to his faulty orders, according to some military experts, no man blamed him. He put the blame on himself.

Yet another side of Lee's character became apparent in the days before the surrender at Appomattox Court House. Lee told General Pendleton, his colleague, "General, we have yet too many bold men to think of laying down our arms. The enemy do not fight with spirit, while our boys still do. Besides, if I were to say a word to the Federal Commander he would regard it as such a confession of weakness as to make it the condition of demanding unconditional surrender—a proposal to which I will never listen."

Here was the proud, true soldier. Yet when the war was over and he became head of Washington College, he told a mother of two sons who came before him, "Don't bring up your sons to detest the United States Government. Recollect that we form but one country now. Abandon all these local animosities, and make your sons Americans."

When Lee surrendered to Grant, not a man blamed him. They did not cheer him. Instead they gazed upon him with silent veneration. One of his colleagues, General Gordon, was later to write, "Lee was never really beaten. Lee could not be beaten! Overpowered, failed in his efforts, he might be, but never defeated until the props which supported him gave way."

Grant, on the other hand, regarded Lee's greatness as a misconception. "I never ranked Lee so high," he once stated, "as some others in the army; that is to say I never had so much anxiety when he was in my front as when Joe Johnston was in front. Lee was a good man, a fair commander, and had everything in his favor. He was a man who needed sunshine. . . . The illusion that heavy odds beat him will not stand the ultimate light of history. . . ."

Major General J. F. Fuller, in his *Grant and Lee* study, came to the conclusion, after gathering heavy evidence, that Lee in several respects ". . . was one of the most incapable Generals-in-Chief in history. . . ."

It must be remembered that Lee's patience and long suffering were not only valiant but almost fanatical. Obedience to orders was his central principle for all good soldiers, yet he was always content and shared the rations with his men. If he had a weakness it was, according to some of his staff officers, "his excessive amiability." He hated to hurt the feelings of his subordinates. In the final analysis, Lee as a general was a mixture of caution and audacity but no grand-strategist, for he refused to be influenced by policy or to influence it. To his army he said in his farewell address, "You will take with you the satisfaction that proceeds from the consciousness of duty faithfully performed." As President of Washington College he told his students, "we must look to the rising generation for the restoration of the country."

Lee died in 1870 and lies buried at Lexington, Virginia.

R E Lee

Stephen D. Lee

Stephen Dirk Lee was born in Charlestown, South Carolina, on September 12, 1833, of a well-known Southern family. He graduated from West Point in 1854 and served in the army until 1861, when he resigned after his native state had joined the Confederacy. He was aide-de-camp to General P. G. T. Beauregard in the attack on Fort Sumter. Later in 1861 he saw service in the Army of Northern Virginia, then commanded by Joseph E. Johnston. By the fall of 1862 he had risen to the rank of brigadier general because of gallantry in action and was sent to aid in the defense of Vicksburg, then besieged by Grant. He was taken prisoner, exchanged, and later promoted to major general and assigned to the command of a cavalry division.

Lee harassed Sherman's forces in the Meridian area and took over Polk's command of the Department of the Mississippi. When Hood was given the command of the Army of the Tennessee, Lee was made a lieutenant general and assumed command of Hood's old corps. He played a prominent part in the battle of Atlanta although Logan and Howard checked his bitter attack. He was with Hood in the battles of Franklin and Nashville where, along with Cheatham and Stewart, he engaged Steadman and Schofield. Even though his center had been driven in and the Hood forces were repulsed, Lee kept his forces closed up and fought a three-day rear-guard action in which he was eventually wounded. Upon his return to active duty he served under Johnston, with whom he surrendered in April, 1865.

After the war he settled in Mississippi and devoted his remaining years to farming. He died at Vicksburg on May 28, 1908.

S. D. Lee

John Alexander Logan

One of the most colorful and resourceful Union generals during the Civil War was the politician-turned-general, John Alexander "Black Jack" Logan.

Logan was born in what is now Murphysborough, Illinois, on February 9, 1826. Though he had no formal schooling until he was fourteen years old, he managed to study for three years at Shiloh College and served as lieutenant of volunteers in the Mexican War.

Logan graduated from the Law Department of Louisville University in 1851 and practiced law with ample success. During this period he entered politics as a backer of Stephen A. Douglas. He became a staunch Democrat and was rewarded by the people with election to Congress.

When the Civil War broke out, he fought at Bull Run before returning to Washington to give up his seat in Congress; and he then entered the Union Army as a colonel with a volunteer regiment which he had organized.

In Grant's campaign ending in the capture of Vicksburg, Logan fought so valiantly that he won promotion to major general of volunteers.

He became a corps commander in the Army of the Tennessee under McPherson and took part in Sherman's march from Chattanooga to Atlanta. He fought against such Confederate generals as Polk, Hardee, and Cheatham at Camp Creek and on the Resaca-Atlanta line. When McPherson was surprised and killed near Decatur by Hardee's men, Logan took over his command.

Logan moved troops to the aid of Blair, then fighting Hardee and Cheatham. The courageous Logan mounted a parapet and yelled "come on," breaking Cheatham's attack with a loss of 8,000 and throwing the Confederates back into Atlanta.

When Thomas, besieged in Nashville in December, 1864, was exasperatingly slow and apparently impervious to the orders from Halleck and officials at Washington, Grant became annoyed with him and sent Logan west to take over command.

This was unnecessary because Thomas came out of Nashville and destroyed Hood's army. In the final days of Sherman's campaign through Georgia and up through the Carolinas, Logan commanded the Fifteenth Corps. He was with Sherman when the defeated and surrounded Johnston surrendered the remnants of a Confederate army to him at Columbia Court House a few weeks after Lee had laid down his arms at Appomattox.

General Logan has been criticized in some quarters over the burning of the city of Columbia, South Carolina. Hampton had to flee so rapidly that he was unable to burn it as intended; Logan's men were at his heels and put out the fires. Some of the inhabitants, however, wishing to curry favor with the Federals, plied the Union soldiers with liquor; and in the ensuing confusion the city was burned. Many slaves were freed, and the jails were emptied.

When the war ended, Logan continued his political career. He became a congressman elected from a Republican district and a United States Senator from 1879 to his death.

Bruce Catton, in one of his many excellent descriptions of Civil War leaders, said of Logan, "seated on his big black horse, he was highly visible in all this fighting. If Logan was a politician, before and after the war, he was a solid combat soldier while the war was going on and he was never more so than in the Battle of Atlanta."

He died in Washington, D.C., on December 26, 1886.

John A. Logan

James Longstreet

James Longstreet, one of the greatest Confederate soldiers, was born in Edgefield District, South Carolina, but moved in early childhood to the vicinity of Augusta, Georgia, where his father farmed until his death in 1833. James Longstreet was admitted to West Point in 1838, attended the Academy with such great soldiers as McDowell, Sherman, Halleck, Thomas, and Grant, and graduated fifty-fourth in a class of sixty-two in July, 1842. He was made second lieutenant of the Fourth Infantry and served at Jefferson Barracks, Missouri, and with the Eighth Infantry at St. Augustine, Florida. In the Mexican War he fought in the battle of Monterey and served General Scott during the expedition to Mexico City. At Chapultepec he suffered severe wounds.

Longstreet remained in the army until 1861. At the outbreak of the Civil War he submitted his resignation and joined the Confederate cause. He won his army commission as a Confederate brigadier general on June 17, 1861.

His employment of his troops at the First Battle of Bull Run and his skill in organization brought him a promotion to the grade of major general and he was given command of a division under Joseph E. Johnston. He fought under Johnston at Yorktown in 1862 and conducted the rear guard action at Williamsburg the same year.

On May 31 his slowness in taking position and his misunderstanding of an order contributed to the Confederate defeat. During the Seven Days' Battle around Richmond (June 25–July 1, 1862) Longstreet fought hard and well and won the full confidence of General Lee. After this battle Lee placed more than half his infantry under Longstreet and on August 13 sent him to reinforce Stonewall Jackson, who had to face the strong army under Pope. In the first stage of the campaign of the Second Manassas, Longstreet was slow in crossing the Rapidan; but on the morning of August 29 he brought his troops into position on the right of Jackson, who had completed his famous march to Manassas Junction. Lee wanted Longstreet to take the initiative and attack, but the latter deliberated on the attack and made repeated excuses for his delays. He didn't strike until August 30, but the Union Army was forced to flee. Longstreet

fought well at Sharpsburg (Antietam), and as a result he was made lieutenant general with Lee's approval.

Longstreet bore the brunt of the defensive fight at Fredericksburg. On February 17, 1863, he helped Pickett's and Hood's divisions guard the roads to Richmond. Lee wanted him to fight or rejoin the Army of Northern Virginia, but Longstreet was not given preemptory orders.

Longstreet's failure to send two of his divisions to aid Lee meant that the latter could not follow up the victory won at Chancellorsville on May 2–3, 1863.

After the death of Stonewall Jackson on May 10, 1863, Longstreet became Lee's trusted lieutenant. Longstreet, at the head of his corps, joined Lee in front of Gettysburg on July 1, 1863, and learned that Lee intended to attack Meade.

Longstreet was filled with misgivings of failure and revealed these by hesitant directions in using his own First Corps. His delayed action on July 2 caused the attack of July 3 to be almost a military necessity. The disadvantages which convinced Longstreet that it was dangerous for Lee to assume the offensive were due to Longstreet's tardiness.

Gettysburg virtually concluded Longstreet's service with the Army of Northern Virginia during the period of its major offensive operation. He was dispatched to Georgia in September, 1863, and did admirably at Chickamauga but was not successful in front of Knoxville. In November he was so close to despair that he contemplated resignation.

Aroused by the danger of a Federal invasion of Georgia, Longstreet planned to make an offensive in Tennessee and Kentucky. These plans, however, were unacceptable. Instead he was sent to Virginia in April, 1864, and stationed near Gordonsville by Lee. On May 6 he aided Hill's troops with a great rally on the second day of the battle of the Wilderness. In this great counterstroke he himself was wounded. He was then ordered to defend Richmond but finally surrendered his forces along with Lee's at Appomattox on April 9, 1865.

After the war he became head of an insurance company and went into politics. He died on January 2, 1904.

James Longstreet

Mansfield Lovell

Mansfield Lovell was born in Washington, D.C., on October 20, 1820. He entered West Point in 1842 and after graduation was commissioned a lieutenant of artillery. Like many of his student colleagues, he saw action in the Mexican War and, in fact, suffered severe wounds on the battlefield of Monterrey. He stayed in the army until 1854, when political life attracted him. He succeeded in becoming superintendent of street improvements and deputy street commissioner in New York City.

When the Civil War began, he chose to fight for the Confederate cause. He was appointed by his superiors to command the Department of the South with New Orleans as his headquarters and was quickly commissioned as a major general in the army.

When Admiral David Farragut attacked the city of New Orleans, Lovell was forced to surrender. He did this in the knowledge that the Admiral had already reduced Forts Jackson and St. Philip.

Because of the bitterness of New Orlean's Creole population and insults, vilification, and attacks on the Union forces, the Union general, Butler, clamped down martial law. General Butler created a great sensation by declaring that any woman who showed contempt or issued insults to any Union officer or his uniform would be looked upon as a prostitute. This bitterness between Butler's forces and the populace attracted such unfavorable world opinion that Lincoln removed Butler from command at New Orleans.

In the later phases of the war Lovell served in Mississippi, Georgia, and South Carolina.

For some years after the war he retired to a plantation near Savannah but subsequently served as assistant to John Newton in deepening the ship channel at Hell Gate in the East River, New York City. He died in that city on June 1, 1884.

George Brinton McClellan

George Brinton McClellan was born in Philadelphia on December 3, 1826. He received an elementary education and increased his schooling by attending the University of Pennsylvania Preparatory School.

He attended West Point and made a good showing, graduating in July, 1846, with distinction. He was immediately placed in a corps of engineers.

In September of the same year he was sent to Mexico, where he served under General Winfield Scott. He was given recognition for gallantry on the field of battle; and when the war was over, he was assigned to teach practical engineering at West Point.

In 1851 he was given the important task of supervising the construction of Fort Delaware. The following year he participated in the famous Red River expedition, and in 1853/54 he served as an officer of the Corps of Engineers in the newly settled Washington and Oregon Territory.

In 1855 McClellan received an assignment much to his liking—to study the art of war and the European military systems and practices. Specifically, he was asked to visit the Crimea, where he observed closely the siege of fortified Sevastopol. With two other commissioners he visited a number of countries and returning from Europe furnished an able report entitled *Armies of Europe*. He also designed a saddle which was adopted by the army and became known as "The McClellan."

In 1857 he resigned his commission in the army and became chief engineer and later vice-president of the Illinois Central Railroad.

When the Civil War broke over the nation, McClellan had to come to a quick decision. He had established residence at Cincinnati, Ohio; and when he offered his services to the Union cause he was given a command over Ohio volunteers. He held the rank of major general.

Following the Union disaster at the First Battle of Bull Run, McClellan was chosen to succeed General McDowell as commander. His promptness in the defense of Washington after he had been summoned by President Lincoln brought order out of chaos and raised the spirits of the demoralized Federal troops. He had a ring of fortifications and redoubts thrown about the city and whipped the raw recruits into excellent shape before the early spring of 1862.

McClellan soon was named commander of the army, replacing the aged General Scott, with whose policy of caution and careful preparation he so sharply differed.

McClellan's rise was phenomenal. Though a master strategist, he lacked sufficient experience to attempt an early attack on Richmond in the First Peninsular campaign. He gathered an army of 200,000 men with which to oppose the Confederate Joseph E. Johnston's 150,000 men.

McClellan led the troops in the battle of Gaines Hill, where Johnston was wounded. Longstreet took over command and held off the Union forces. McClellan blamed Lincoln for his slow progress and demanded that McDowell's 40,000 men, who were held by Lincoln to defend Washington, be sent to him. His sole motive was to use them in order to turn the Confederate flank and drive on to Richmond.

Robert E. Lee succeeded General Longstreet, and soon sent the latter and the two Hills—David B. and Ambrose—against McClellan. Meanwhile the wily Stonewall Jackson flanked General Banks and came within the suburbs of Washington.

When Porter was flanked, McClellan was forced to withdraw to Harrison Landing on the James River. Lee, however, failed to crush the Army of the Potomac.

Lee's frontal attack on the Union Army at Malvern Hill ended in defeat. Stonewall Jackson was too slow to close the gap, and McClellan was able to repulse the enemy and save the army.

McClellan, who had a hidden hostility to Lincoln and an open, haughty, insulting manner toward the President, blamed his failure on Lincoln. The President was reluctant to replace him abruptly, but he did so indirectly by putting Pope in command of a separate army group to be formed from McClellan's divisions.

Pope, however, was crushed in the Second Battle of Bull Run, and McClellan was again placed in command of the Army of the Potomac. When Lee attempted his first invasion of the North, he once more engaged McClellan at Antietam. The latter hoped to hold Jackson in check while he crushed Lee. However, the wily Lee was able to bring his army back through Virginia though he lost about 13,000 men.

Once again McClellan failed to follow the enemy but instead demanded more troops. Lincoln felt that the enemy forces must be divided, fought, and destroyed. He replaced McClellan with General Burnside. Once more the able enemy forces, led by Longstreet, Jackson, Stuart and others, kept the Union Army at bay. In succession, Burnside was defeated at Fredericksburg and Hooker at Chancellorsville, while the cautious Union General Meade allowed Lee to save his army after the latter's defeat at Gettysburg.

McClellan, in retirement, once again blamed his position on Lincoln's jealousy. He did not see his own shortcomings. He was nominated for President by the Democratic party in 1864. He refused to denounce the war effort and urge a negotiated peace. Above all, he insisted that the Union be preserved. The election campaign thus became a matter of personal selection—Lincoln or McClellan. When the results were counted Lincoln had won his reelection. McClellan carried only three states.

After the war, McClellan returned to his work as an engineer, becoming chief engineer of the Department of Docks in New York City. He sought to justify his military career by publishing *McClellan's Own Story*. He died in 1885 at the age of 59.

McClellan was probably the best strategist in the Union Army, a master of detail and organization. However, he was too cautious and irresolute to crush an aggressive adversary like Lee. The raw Army of the Potomac that he drilled into a steady fighting force was the machine with which Grant finally crushed Lee.

Geo B McClellan

John Alexander McClernand

One of the most ambitious generals in the Civil War was John Alexander McClernand. Born in Breckenridge County, Kentucky, on May 30, 1812, he was admitted to the bar in Shawneetown, Illinois, in 1832 and in the same year served as a volunteer in the Black Hawk War.

In 1835 he founded and edited the *Shawneetown Democrat* and became active in politics as a Democrat. He served five terms in Congress.

In his first term as a congressman he vigorously opposed the famous Wilmot Proviso. In his second term, however, he became a strong Unionist.

When the Civil War broke out, McClernand resigned from Congress and raised the "McClernand Brigade" in Illinois. He was commissioned a brigadier general of volunteers in the spring of 1861 and was second in command at the battle of Belmont, Mississippi, in November, 1861.

During the rest of the Vicksburg campaign, a good deal of friction developed between the slow-moving McClernand and his colleagues. He lied to Grant and issued an order of the day blaming Sherman and McPherson for not taking Vicksburg.

It was Grant's opinion that on several occasions McClernand had been dilatory, and Grant acted promptly. On June 18 McClernand was temporarily relieved of his command and sent home to Illinois.

General Halleck had succeeded the stormy Frémont in the campaign against the Confederate fortifications on both the Tennessee and the Mississippi rivers. Forts Henry and Donelson on the Cumberland River were the immediate objects of his attack.

Fort Donelson was commanded by the Confederate general Floyd, the former Secretary of War under Buchanan. Grant had three divisions in his army under the commands of C. F. Smith, Wallace, and McClernand. Floyd used some 8,000 men and after hard fighting checked McClernand. Grant, on the other hand, had Smith attack the fort on his left flank. Floyd had to face the new danger, thus allowing Wallace and McClernand to press on. Buckner was forced by Grant to "surrender unconditionally" after Floyd had fled. All Tennessee was in Union hands.

In the bloody battle of Shiloh, McClernand's forces were surprised and driven back by A. S. Johnston; but Grant came to his aid and stabilized the fighting lines. Grant's masterful efforts at Corinth made him a national hero.

McClernand, after the battle of Shiloh, went on a recruiting expedition, blasting Grant and praising himself. He even induced Lincoln to make him equal in command with the hero of Corinth. Over 30,000 men were recruited to the colors through McClernand's efforts.

McClernand never regarded Sherman and Grant with any great respect. It is interesting to note that he did not hesitate to accuse Sherman of stealing his troops around the Memphis area. Halleck had only contempt for McClernand and denounced him to Lincoln as a cheap politician. As a result, the President wired Grant that the latter was in "full and absolute authority." By 1864 McClernand's usefulness came to an end, and he resigned from the army.

He died on September 20, 1900, in Springfield, Illinois, after having spent his last years in bitterness and obscurity.

J. A. McClernand

Alexander McDowell McCook

Alexander McDowell McCook came from the famous family of "fighting McCooks." He was born in Dayton, Ohio, on June 12, 1831. As a youngster he received a good education and qualified for the military academy at West Point. He graduated in 1852, thirtieth in a class of forty-seven.

McCook saw service as a lieutenant of infantry on the frontier, fighting Indians and maintaining peace among them. For a time he became a tactical instructor at West Point.

When the Civil War broke out, McCook was commissioned colonel of the First Ohio Infantry and led it in the First Battle of Bull Run. Early in September, 1861, he was appointed a brigadier general of volunteers and placed in command of a division of the Army of the Ohio. He commanded the Second Division of Buell's army corps in the battle of Shiloh, where he had been sent to the aid of General Grant. In July, 1862, he was promoted to major general of volunteers and saw service at Corinth and Nashville.

Following the Nashville campaign he was put in command of the First Corps of the Army of the Ohio and anchored the Union left flank in the battle of Perryville, where he was bitterly attacked by Cheatham and Hardee.

At the battle of Stone River, McCook was in charge of the Third Division of Rosecrans' army. His superiors ordered him to attack the left flank of Bragg's army, but the wily Confederate turned the tables on McCook and knocked out his division in the fighting.

Thomas and Sheridan, however, held fast; and Bragg's overall plan to crush Rosecrans failed to materialize.

McCook became the commander of the Twentieth Corps in the Shelbyville-Chickamauga campaign, commanding the right flank. Once again he faced the veteran Confederate Hardee. He was blamed for the Union fiasco in failing to crush Bragg in these engagements, but the true blame lay in the fact that his corps had been too far South from the main army. Though a court inquiry cleared him of blame, he was transferred to a different theater of war.

In the closing months of the war, March–April, 1865, McCook was placed in command of the Eastern Division of Arkansas and here won a much-deserved promotion to brigadier general of the regular army.

After the close of hostilities he continued in the army as an aide to General Sherman. In 1894 he received the rank of major general, and the following year he retired from the army. On June 12, 1903, he died in his home town of Dayton.

A. McD. McCook

Irvin McDowell

Irvin McDowell was born near Columbus, Ohio, in 1818. He studied at the College de Troyes, in France, and graduated from West Point in 1838. During the United States–Canadian border troubles he was stationed on the Niagara and Maine frontiers. In 1841 he served at West Point as assistant instructor in tactics, becoming adjutant in 1845. Early in the Mexican War he went to Mexico as aide-de-camp to General Wood and for gallant conduct at Buena Vista in 1847 was promoted to brevet captain. Shortly afterward he was given the rank of assistant adjutant general.

Following the Mexican War McDowell was stationed at the War Department in Washington and in 1856 was raised to the rank of brevet major. He was on General Wood's staff at the outbreak of the Civil War and assisted in inspecting and organizing the volunteer Union troops in the defense of Washington. In May, 1861, he was made brigadier general of volunteers and given command of the Army of the Potomac. Forced by the impatience of the Northern leaders, McDowell moved in July to meet the Confederates; but despite his carefully laid plans he met a disastrous defeat at Bull Run on July 21, 1861, due partly to the imperfect organization of his raw recruits. When McClellan was given command of the army, McDowell was retained as head of one of its five corps. In 1862 he was promoted to major general of volunteers and placed in command of the First Corps, which became the Army of the Rappahannock, stationed to guard Washington. In August, 1862, he received command of the Third Corps of the Army of Virginia and fought under Pope at the battles of Cedar Mountain and Rappahannock Station, and the Second Battle of Bull Run, where his actions caused some criticism. He was removed from his field command in September, 1862. Considering this action by the War Department as a direct reflection made upon his military services, he asked for an investigation, the result of which was favorable to him.

From May to July, 1863, McDowell was president of a board appointed to investigate alleged cotton frauds and during the following ten months presided over the board for retiring or disabled officers. In July, 1864, he was placed in command of the Department of the Pacific Coast and in March, 1865, was made brevet major general in recognition of his gallant services at Cedar Mountain. In 1872 he succeeded General Meade as major general in the regular army and was in command of various military departments until 1882, when he retired. The last years of his life were spent in California. He died in San Francisco on May 5, 1885.

Irvin McDowell

James Birdseye McPherson

James Birdseye McPherson was born at Sandusky, Ohio, on November 14, 1828. His great ambition was to enter West Point, and in 1852 he graduated from the Academy at the head of his class. Among his classmates were Sheridan, Schofield, and Hood. His superiors immediately appointed him as an instructor of practical military engineering.

A year later he went to New York City on an engineering assignment; and in 1857 he was sent as superintendent engineer to San Francisco, becoming first lieutenant within the year.

When the Civil War began, he was promoted to the rank of captain; and by the end of 1861 he had become a lieutenant colonel and aide-de-camp to General Halleck.

In the spring of 1862 he served Grant as chief engineer. He remained with Grant during the Shiloh campaign; but when Halleck needed an engineer-adviser, McPherson was ordered to his aid during the siege operations against Corinth. He fought bravely as head of an infantry brigade at the battle of Corinth and soon became major general of volunteers and commander of a division.

In the second advance on Vicksburg, McPherson commanded the famous Seventeenth Corps. After the fall of Vicksburg he was strongly recommended by Grant for the rank of brigadier general in the regular army and received this promotion on August 1, 1863.

McPherson's brilliant performance and courage caused his superiors to give him command of the famous Army of the Tennessee—Grant's and Sherman's old army—this appointment being made by Sherman with Grant's complete approval. McPherson commanded one of Sherman's divisions at the actions of Resaca, Dallas, and Kennesaw Mountain.

On July 21, 1864, when the Confederates under Hardee made a sudden and violent attack on the lines held by the Army of the Tennessee, McPherson dashed to the woods to meet the enemy's firing line and was immediately killed in action. Grant was deeply moved by the death of his best friend. It is said that Sherman wept openly at the great tragedy, for he had hopes that McPherson would supersede both Grant and himself as supreme Union commander.

L. J. McPherson

John Bankhead Magruder

Confederate general John Bankhead Magruder was born in Winchester, Virginia, and graduated from West Point in 1830. He was stationed at various army posts until the Mexican War, in which he gained a name for reckless daring.

In 1861, at the outbreak of the Civil War, he resigned his commission and joined the Confederate Army. He soon won an engagement at Big Bethel, frequently called the first battle of the war; and he was promoted to major general. He won great fame in the Peninsular campaign, though this was dimmed somewhat by his actions in the Seven Days' Battle and Malvern Hill. He served as head of the Department of Texas from 1862–64 and later commanded the Department of New Mexico and Arizona. His capture of Galveston from the Federals on January 1, 1863, was his principal achievement.

Following the war he served in the Mexican imperialist army until the death of Maximilian.

He died in 1871.

G.J. Rogers dr

William Mahone

William "Little Billy" Mahone was born in Southampton, Virginia, on December 1, 1826. His father was a tavern keeper, and young Bill worked at various jobs including post riding and, following his attendance at the Virginia Military Institute, school teaching.

In the years preceding the Civil War he worked as an engineer and manager of a small railroad. When the war began, Mahone joined the Southern cause and became a colonel with the Sixth Virginia Regiment. He was a brigadier general within the year and aided in the capture of the Norfolk Navy Yard and in the defense of the James River. He saw action at Malvern Hill, Fredericksburg, Chancellorsville, Gettysburg, the Wilderness campaign, and Spotsylvania. He was wounded in the Second Battle of Bull Run but was promoted by Lee to major general because of his work at Petersburg.

By the time he was thirty-eight years old he had become the leader of the "most remarkable shock troops" of the South.

He was quick, alert, and precise and had built up a great *esprit de corps* in what was called "Mahone's Brigade"—the Irish brigade.

Following the war he returned to the railroad business and also became active in national politics as a Republican in the midst of a Democratic "solid South."

In 1869 he helped soften the Reconstruction policy in the South through his control of the *Richmond Whig*, and with the aid of the powerful Senator Cameron he was elected a United States Senator in 1880. The Southern Democrats called him a traitor because of his activity in the National Republican party; and he was criticized for his activity as a lobbyist in the interest of railroads, particularly those in receivership. He was unpopular also because he sought to protect Negro voting rights in the new South.

Mahone died in Washington on October 8, 1895, and is buried in Petersburg, Virginia.

John Sappington Marmaduke

John Sappington Marmaduke was born on a farm near Arron Creek, Missouri, in 1833. His family was rather prominent in the West during the decades preceding the Civil War. His father, Meredith M. Marmaduke, came from Westmoreland County, Virginia, and was prominent in Missouri politics, serving as lieutenant governor and later as governor.

John Marmaduke received his education in the country schools of Saline County and at Masonic College, Lexington, Missouri. He attended Harvard before eagerly accepting an appointment to West Point. He graduated from the Academy in 1857 and was soon commissioned as a second lieutenant in the Seventh Regiment, United States Infantry. When the so-called "Mormon War" broke out, he saw action for two years (1858–60), serving under the capable Albert Sidney Johnston.

When the Civil War began, Marmaduke was on duty in New Mexico; and after a long discussion with his father, who favored the Union cause, he resigned his commission in the army and joined the Confederate cause. He was made a colonel of the militia by Governor Jackson of Missouri.

Disgusted with the poor showing of his troops at the battle of Booneville in June, 1861, Marmaduke resigned his colonelcy and went to Richmond, where he was commissioned a first lieutenant in the Confederate Army. He saw service for a short period as lieutenant colonel in Arkansas and later was made a colonel and given command of the Third Regiment under his old commander, Albert Sidney Johnston.

For gallant service under this leader at the battle of Shiloh, he was commissioned a brigadier general. After Shiloh he was placed in charge of Confederate forces in Arkansas. His force was not large enough to undertake big-scale operations, but he did make several raids into Missouri.

Early in 1863 he attempted an attack on Springfield which failed, but he soon followed this with a successful raid into southern Missouri. Following minor victories in several skirmishes he was forced to make a hasty retreat back into Arkansas. For his capable exploits around Helena, Fayetteville, and Little Rock he was made a major general in March, 1864.

As the leader of cavalry under General Price, Marmaduke displayed great courage and gallantry in the fighting around Kansas City, in which two horses were shot out from under him. In the retreat from this battle a few days later, he was captured while directing a rear-guard action and was kept a prisoner at Fort Warren, Massachusetts, until the summer of 1865.

After the war Marmaduke entered the insurance business in St. Louis. He was editor of the *St. Louis Journal of Agriculture* from 1871 to 1875 and from 1880 to 1885 was a member of the Missouri Railway Commission. He was defeated for the Democratic party nomination for governor in 1880 but four years later was nominated and elected governor of his home state. He died while in office, at Jefferson City, in 1887, just one year before the completion of his term.

John S. Marmaduke

George Gordon Meade

General George Gordon Meade, the victor of Gettysburg, was born December 31, 1815, in Cadiz, Spain, where his father, Richard Worsam Meade, was naval agent for the American government. When the latter, after having lived comfortably in Spain, died in poverty, young Meade turned his attention toward West Point, where he became a cadet on September 1, 1831. He was not a brilliant student while at the Academy, and in fact he planned to resign from military service as soon as he could find the opportunity. He was graduated nineteenth in a class of fifty-six.

As brevet second lieutenant of the Third Artillery, Meade was ordered to Florida. He arrived at the outbreak of the Seminole War and after serving a year in southern Florida was stricken with a fever which rendered him unfit for duty. After recovering from his illness, he was sent north to do ordnance detail work; but the work was dull to him, and he resigned from the army on October 26, 1836.

Meade went to work as an assistant engineer of the Alabama, Florida, and Georgia Railroad. In 1839 he acted as principal assistant engineer on a survey of the mouth of the Mississippi and the following year served on the joint commission to establish the boundary line between the United States and Texas. During the same year he returned to Washington, where he married Margaretta Sargent, daughter of painter John Sargent.

With the new responsibility of marriage, he applied for reinstatement in the army. Accordingly, on May 19, 1842, he was appointed a second lieutenant of the Topographical Engineers. As a military engineer he worked on the northeastern boundary survey until the end of 1843, when he was transferred to Philadelphia to work on the construction of lighthouses in the Delaware Bay.

In August, 1845, he was ordered to Texas with General Taylor's army of occupation. He arrived at Corpus Christi in September, 1845. During the Mexican War he engaged in the battle of Palo Alto and was brevetted a first lieutenant on September 23, 1846, at Monterrey. He was then transferred to General Scott's column, fighting in the siege of Vera Cruz.

From 1847 to 1849 he returned to the construction of lighthouses in Delaware Bay and to making surveys and maps of the Florida reefs. In 1850 he again saw active service against the Seminoles. On August 4, 1851, he was promoted to first lieutenant of Topographical Engineers. Five years later he became a captain of the same service and was ordered to Detroit, Michigan, on a geodetic survey of the Great Lakes.

When the Civil War broke out Meade, through the efforts of General Andrew Curtin of Pennsylvania, was made a brigadier general of volunteers on August 31, 1861. It was at this point that the close friendship between General Reynolds and Meade began, only to end when the former was killed at Gettysburg. Meade saw active service in the defense of Washington, D.C.; and in March, 1862, he was transferred, with his command, to McDowell's army. Three months later he was ordered to the Peninsula under General McClellan and was promoted to major in the Topographical Engineers of the regular army.

At the battle of Glendale Meade received the wound which was to trouble him for the remainder of his career. But in spite of this wound, he remained on his horse and gave orders to his subordinates, leaving the field of battle only because of great loss of blood.

The following year, having recovered, he rejoined his command, participating in the Second Battle of Bull Run late in August, 1862. When Reynold's division lost its leader at South Mountain on September 14, 1862, Meade was placed in temporary command. At Antietam he again pressed forward with courage and skill; and when Hooker fell, Meade was placed in temporary command of the First Corps. He fought under McClellan in the pursuit of Lee to Falmouth, Virginia, and by November, 1862, was a major general of volunteers. On January 26, 1863, he was placed in command of the Third and Sixth Corps.

Because of Meade's insight and initiative, he was placed in command of the Army of the Potomac. He was not happy with this appointment, feeling unready for this command; but he felt it was his duty to accept. At Gettysburg Meade generally handled his troops well though he did not escape heavy criticism for his failure to counterattack. It must be remembered, however, that he had held his command for only five days prior to the battle.

On January 28, 1864, he received the thanks of Congress "for the skill and heroic valor which, at Gettysburg, repelled, defeated and drove back, broken and dispirited, beyond the Rappahannock, the veteran army of the Rebellion."

Following Gettysburg, he was promoted to brigadier general in the regular army. When Grant became lieutenant general of all the Union forces in March, 1864, Meade's powers were decreased considerably, forcing him to assume the role of tactician and affording him much embarrassment. However, he remained loyal to Grant; and the latter was considerate of the delicate situation. In August, 1864, he won the promotion to major general in the regular army; and at the close of the war, he was placed in command of the Military Division of the Atlantic and, later, that of the South.

In the last days of his life, he was commissioner of Fairmount Park, Philadelphia, and died in that city on November 6, 1872.

210

Geo. G. Meade

Wesley Merritt

Wesley Merritt was born on June 16, 1834, in Salem, Massachusetts. In 1855 he chose a military career and entered West Point, graduating in 1860 as a second lieutenant. A year later he earned his promotion to first lieutenant, and General George Crook appointed him as his aide-de-camp. The General was in command of a cavalry division in the famous Army of the Potomac.

As a young cavalry officer recently promoted to brigadier general, he along with Custer saw action in the crucial battle of Gettysburg. A year later he became a major general of volunteers; and when Sheridan was given command of the newly formed Army of the Shenandoah, Merritt, along with other young and dashing officers like Custer, Torbert, and Devin, formed the fast-moving cavalry wings of Sheridan's forces.

Along with Custer he helped defeat and destroy General Jubal E. Early's forces in the battles around Cedar Creek and Fisher's Hill. He led one of the wings of the cavalry, Custer the other. Together these men and their forces pinned down General Early's men.

Following the end of the war, Merritt served in the West, helping to put down several Indian disturbances. He was superintendent at West Point from 1882 to 1887 and in the years 1895–97 took over command of the Departments of Missouri, Dakota, and of the East, respectively.

When war broke out with Spain, he commanded the U.S. forces in the Philippine Islands, cooperating with Admiral Dewey.

Merritt died on December 3, 1910, at the age of seventy-five.

W. Merritt

John Hunt Morgan

John Hunt Morgan was a professional soldier to the day he died.

Born in Huntsville, Alabama, on June 1, 1825, he was raised in Lexington, Kentucky. During the Mexican War he rose to first lieutenant in a cavalry regiment.

When the Civil War began, he joined the Confederate forces and was appointed leader of a cavalry squadron because of his talents and record as a scout.

Following the battle of Shiloh, he won a well-deserved promotion to colonel. It was then, in July, 1862, that he and his forces began their famous raids, threatening Louisville and even Cincinnati.

Bragg used Morgan's talents in the invasion of Kentucky. Before the year was over he successfully destroyed the strong garrison at Hartsville, Tennessee; and once again he earned a promotion, this time to brigadier general. Time after time he protected Bragg's forces with his dreaded raids into Indiana, Ohio, and Kentucky.

In the latter state he captured a garrison at Lebanon, and continued his advance as far as the suburbs of Cincinnati. He was repulsed by the Union forces at Portland near Buffington Island with the loss of over 600 men. On July 26, 1863, he was forced to surrender to the Union commander at New Lisbon.

For several months he suffered humiliation as a prisoner in the penitentiary situated at Columbus, Ohio. On the night of November 27, 1863, he escaped and within a few weeks was back in Confederate territory.

In the spring of 1864 he was placed in command of southwestern Virginia. Six months later he received command of the forces stationed at Jonesboro, Georgia. When he and his men reached Greenville, Tennessee, he was betrayed to the Federals and was shot down while walking alone in a garden.

Jno H Morgan

John S. Mosby

John S. Mosby was a bold, audacious, and crafty leader who spread terror among countless numbers of Union soldiers.

He was born in Powhatan County, Virginia, in 1833 and after the usual progress in education entered the University of Virginia in 1852.

When the Civil War broke out, he was engaged in the practice of law in Bristol, Virginia. Jeb Stuart was happy to use the brilliant services of this "pint-sized, small-town lawyer." Mosby began his partisan operations in northern Virginia, using not more than two hundred men on raids against Union forces, moving swiftly and secretly.

Each man in Mosby's Rangers furnished his own food, horse, arms, and uniform. These men seized and divided public and private property alike and were regarded by the Union commanders as thieves. However, Mosby personally never received any stolen goods.

Stuart had only high praise for Mosby's Rangers, considering them the only really efficient partisan group, though he deplored the depredations of those outlaw bands operating under the guise of war.

The raiders succeeded in destroying supplies, smashing communications, and burning crops in the Shenandoah Valley. The region between Brandy Station and Alexandria became known as "Mosby's Confederacy."

One of the most famous exploits of Mosby was his brilliant capture of General Edwin H. Stoughton at Fairfax Courthouse in March, 1863. A price was put on Mosby's head, but the partisans in the area helped Mosby's Rangers to elude the strong Union forces.

When Lee surrendered, Mosby was taken prisoner; but he received a parole from Grant.

Following the war, he returned to a lucrative law practice. In 1876 he joined the Republican party and helped Rutherford B. Hayes win the presidency. He coined the term "solid South" in his correspondence.

He died in 1916 at the age of eighty-three.

His published works include *War Reminiscences* and *Stuart's Cavalry Campaigns*.

Jno. S. Marsh

Peter Joseph Osterhaus

Peter Joseph Osterhaus was born in Coblenz, Germany, and served in the Twenty-ninth Infantry Regiment at Berlin. He became involved in the Revolution of 1848; and when the government triumphed, he emigrated to the United States, settling in Belleville, Illinois, where he was employed as a drygoods clerk. He later moved to Lebanon, Illinois, and operated a general merchandise business before moving to St. Louis in 1851.

At the outbreak of the Civil War, Osterhaus volunteered as a private in the Twelfth Missouri Volunteers. He was soon commissioned captain and was promoted to major on April 27, 1861. In a sharp engagement at Big Black River, Missouri, on May 17, 1863, he was injured by a shell fragment. Under temporary command of General Hooker, Osterhaus led his troops over Lookout Creek, climbed to the summit of Missionary Ridge, took literally thousands of prisoners, and drove the Confederate southern wing from the crest of the ridge. On July 23, 1864, he was made a major general of volunteers.

Osterhaus served as United States Consul to France from June 18, 1866, until August 16, 1877, residing at Lyons. His term included the period of the Franco-Prussian War, and his reports show keen insight into the economic problems involved in French compliance with the conditions of peace imposed by Germany. When relieved by his successor, he returned to the United States and engaged in the manufacture and export of hardware. It was not until July 27, 1902, that Congress authorized an additional pension for his services as a major general of volunteers. This pension was stopped March 20, 1905; for on March 3, 1905, Congress by special act had appointed him brigadier general of the United States Army, and on March 17 he was placed on the retired list. He died on January 2, 1917 at the age of ninety-four.

Osterhaus

John C. Pemberton

John C. Pemberton was born in Philadelphia on August 12, 1814. He received an elementary education in the same city and was later tutored in a number of languages including Hebrew, Greek, and Latin. He attended West Point for four years and graduated with a commission as second lieutenant, determined to pursue a military career in the field of artillery.

For two years, 1837 to 1839, he saw active service, fighting the Seminole Indians in Florida. From 1840 to 1842 he was stationed on the Canadian border.

When the Mexican War broke out, he became first lieutenant and fought in the battles of Palo Alto, Resaca, and Vera Cruz. In the years that followed, he fought the Mormons in Utah and Indians in the Northwest; during this period he was promoted first to captain and then to major.

Like so many other officers he faced a decision when the Civil War broke out. He was determined to give up his army commission and went straight to Richmond, Virginia. The authorities there elevated him to the rank of lieutenant colonel, and he was put in charge of artillery and cavalry with a new title —colonel.

He served as commander of the Departments of South Carolina, Georgia, and Florida.

In 1863 he took over the defenses of Vicksburg, feeling that it was imperative to hold the town. When his superiors insisted that he surrender Vicksburg to the enemy, he only reinforced the defenses; but in July, 1863, he was forced to capitulate to Grant when his men began dying from starvation.

He resigned his commission, stating that he had failed in his objectives; but his superiors appointed him inspector of ordnance with the rank of colonel until the close of the war. He died on July 13, 1881, and was buried in his native city, Philadelphia.

J.C. Pemberton

George Edward Pickett

George Edward Pickett, a legendary infantry leader, was born in Richmond, Virginia, on January 25, 1825. He graduated last in his class at West Point in 1846 and was assigned to the Eighth United States Infantry. He served with distinguished valor in all the battles of General Winfield Scott in Mexico, including the siege of Vera Cruz and the storming of Chapultepec, where it is said he was the first to scale the parapets and raise the flag of the United States over the castle.

After peace was restored Pickett was transferred to the Washington Territory, where he was destined to play an important role in the Northwest boundary controversy. He prevented the landing of British troops in 1859 when he occupied San Juan Island.

Like many other Virginians in the United States Army, he resigned his command after the outbreak of the Civil War. In June, 1861, he offered his services to the Confederacy and was immediately given a captaincy, earning the rank of colonel after a brief period in the service.

The following year he was put in command of a Virginia brigade of infantry with the rank of brigadier general. It was an active year; for he participated in the bloody battles of Williamsburg, Seven Pines, Gaines Mill, in which he was wounded, and Fredericksburg.

Pickett was a picturesque figure of a fighting man in the early phases of the Civil War. He was tall and thin, wore a goatee, and had auburn hair. He was greatly admired for his courage, and his brigade was known as the "Game Cock Brigade."

In the fierce battle at Gettysburg Pickett's division made history on July 3 when it led a courageous attack on Cemetery Hill. The charge belongs to the great stories of military history, but the losses in men and material were astounding.

Pickett, it is told, had been engaged to be married to a lovely young lady in Richmond. When it became certain that his reserve brigade of the Longstreet Corps was to storm the Union center at Gettysburg, Pickett gave the general a letter for his fiancée.

On the back of the envelope Pickett had written, "if old Pete's (Longstreet) nod means death, goodby and God bless you, you little one!" Seeing this, an officer offered him a drink, saying "Take a drink with me, in an hour you'll be in Hell or Glory." Pickett refused.

His charge with the brigade at Gettysburg was immortalized, and Pickett emerged as a legend on both sides of the war. However, as the war drew to a close, Pickett became dissatisfied and quarrelsome. He had to be reprimanded by Lee in person for his petty bickering with his fellow officers.

He also distinguished himself in his assault on Grant's line at Cold Harbor, covering his failure at Newburn to defeat the Union forces.

In the battle of Five Forks in 1865, Pickett with a depleted corps was told to anchor the Petersburg line at all costs and to protect a valuable railroad at Five Forks. He failed in his efforts and was cut off from Lee's army by Sheridan, Warren, and Griffin. Pickett, in fact, was almost captured. Lee was desperate and so angry at the results that in the mad retreat which followed, noticing Pickett passing by, he exclaimed, "Is that man still around?"

After the war Pickett entered the insurance business. He died in 1875.

G E Pickett

Albert S. Pike

One of the most suspicious and controversial officers to emerge from the period of the Civil War was Albert S. Pike. Born in Boston, Massachusetts, on December 29, 1809, he attended Framingham Academy and later became a teacher. For a short period he attended Harvard, where he studied the classics. He taught school at Gloucester and Framingham and in 1831 moved to St. Louis and later to Santa Fe.

In 1833 he taught in Pope County, Arkansas, and engaged in some literary work. He wrote letters to the daily press on politics and attracted the attention of the editor of the Little Rock *Arkansas Advocate,* later becoming an associate editor.

In 1837 Pike began the practice of law and rose to considerable prominence. He is credited with compiling the first law reports of the Arkansas Supreme Court and won great fame as a lawyer for the Creek Indians.

When the Civil War began, Pike was rather reluctant to join the Southern cause; but he did so, becoming a brigadier general in August, 1861. He led a force of Indians into the battle of Pea Ridge, gaining a bad reputation for the bloody losses among his troops. Shortly thereafter, he became engaged in a conflict with his superiors; and he resigned from the army. Though he spent the rest of the war in Texas and Arkansas, both sides were suspicious of him.

In 1865 he moved to New York City, but his connection with the Indian atrocities at Pea Ridge made him unwelcome. On August 30, 1865, he was pardoned by President Andrew Johnson. In 1867 he moved to Memphis to resume the practice of law and later went to Washington, D.C. He was greatly interested in Masonic work, especially in the Scottish Rite promotion. He died in the House of Scottish Rite in Washington, D.C., on April 2, 1891.

Albert Pike

Alfred Pleasonton

Alfred Pleasonton was best known for his keen display of ability in the great Peninsular campaign of 1862.

Born in 1824 in Washington, D.C., he studied at West Point, graduating in 1844. He soon saw active service in the Mexican War, and when this ended, volunteered to fight on the frontier in the bloody Indian wars.

When the Civil War broke out, Pleasonton served without particular distinction until the Peninsular campaign, when his brilliance won him the rank of brigadier general of volunteers.

This general had no fear of the great Stonewall Jackson and his leadership. He fought well against him at the bloody battle of Chancellorsville. His superiors admired his ability to defend himself against the fierce attacks made by Jackson.

When the turning point of the war occurred at Gettysburg, Pleasonton with his valiant cavalry aided the Union armies in the field and forced Lee to beat a retreat back to Richmond. His service was invaluable. He made a fine record in many other engagements with the Confederates.

Pleasonton's superiors felt that he could defeat the forces under General Sterling Price, stationed in Missouri. In two bloody engagements Pleasonton broke the back of these Confederate forces, and the threat to the Union forces in the West was over. The general survived the war and lived until 1897.

A. Pleasonton

Leonidas Polk

Leonidas Polk was born in Raleigh, North Carolina, on April 10, 1806. He received his military education at West Point but gave up his commission only six months after graduation. In 1831 he took orders in the Protestant Episcopal Church and seven years later was given the title of Mission Archbishop of the Southwest. This included such states as Arkansas, Louisiana, Alabama, and Mississippi and even Indian territory. In 1841 he was made Bishop of Louisiana. His efforts were mainly in the field of education, and he was one of the founders of the famous University of the South.

When the Civil War broke out, Polk sought a commission in the Confederate Army and dropped his Episcopalian duties as a church dignita y. He was so well known by the people that the army gave ' im rapid promotion up to the rank of major general. He was assigned to an important post at Columbus, Kentucky, which he fortified heavily enough to withstand the offensives of the Union forces at Belmont.

The following spring, Polk was put in command of a fighting corps under Generals Albert Sidney Johnson and Pierre T. Beauregard. They respected his ability as demonstrated at Shiloh. In October, 1862, he earned a promotion to lieutenant general and received command of one of the three corps in the Army of the Tennessee under General Bragg. Friction developed between the two in the fighting at Chickamauga. Bragg gave Polk the task of leading his corps to Ringgold in the overall plan to crush Crittenden. Polk moved too slow for the general; and when the latter found him reading a newspaper instead of fighting, curses of a sulphurous nature rent the air. Jefferson Davis was quickly informed of Polk's insubordination.

Polk was transferred to one of Joseph E. Johnston's corps, where he took command alongside Hood and Hardee in the fighting around Resaca and Pine Mountain. Osterhaus, the Union commander, gave him a hard fight at Resaca. However Polk, along with Hood, was able to attack Schofield near Cassville.

When Polk's corps arrived near Marietta on June 14, 1864, Sherman was making observations. He spied a group of officers and ordered a battery nearby to "give them a shot." A shell landed among the Confederates, killing Polk. His command was given to General Loring.

Leonidas Polk

John Pope

John Pope was born in Louisville, Kentucky, on March 16, 1822. After graduating from West Point in 1842, he received a commission in the engineering branch of the army. He saw action in the Mexican War and subsequently he spent his time working in the fields of exploration and engineering. In 1856 he earned the rank of captain.

When the Civil War called men to the colors, Pope was put in charge of the District of Missouri, as brigadier general. He vigorously put down heavy guerilla activity in that area.

With the aid of a gunboat flotilla under the command of Commodore A. H. Foote, Pope succeeded in capturing the defenses of New Madrid and Island No. 10. General Halleck used his services in the great siege of Corinth, and following this Pope became a major general.

Pope was looked upon as an energetic, able leader. A new Army of Virginia was created, and Pope set forth on a new campaign. At the very outset a most ill-advised order allowed him to combine the Western troops with his own Army of Virginia. The campaign began to fail, and soon Pope lost the confidence of his officers and men. When the Army of the Potomac was sent to his support, his operations led to the disastrous defeat at the Second Battle of Bull Run. There was a great clamor for his removal. He related his failure to the ill-advised order, but to no avail. He resigned from his command.

After a time he was placed in command of the Department of the Northwest. There he once again showed his skill and keen ability to lead men. However, he did not regain his former rank until the year 1882, when he was made a major general.

Jno Pope

David Dixon Porter

David Dixon Porter was born in Chester, Pennsylvania, on June 8, 1813. His formal education was meager. At the age of ten, he made a cruise with his father to the West Indies and three years later to Mexico City, where he became a midshipman in the Mexican navy. He saw his first active service on the ship *Esmeralda,* commanded by a relative, David H. Porter.

On February 2, 1829, he was appointed a midshipman in the American navy. He sailed for the Mediterranean area on board the ship *Constellation.* In 1836 he was appointed to the Coast Survey. He spent his time making hydrographic surveys and compiling field notes. In 1841 he was appointed to the rank of lieutenant.

When the Mexican War broke out, he sought active service but was disappointed when he was sent to New Orleans to act as recruiting officer. However, he took a large number of recruits to Vera Cruz in February, 1847, and was put in charge of the steamer *Spitfire.* He was elevated to the position of first lieutenant, and with a landing party of seventy sailors he fought cleverly and bravely enough to capture the fort at Tabasco. Commander Matthew C. Perry, his superior, praised him for this gallantry in action and rewarded him with his first permanent command of a naval vessel. When the war ended he once again returned to the Coast Survey. He desired more action, however, and in 1849 he took command of the merchant steamer *Panama,* which sailed the Pacific.

In 1857 Porter obtained an opportunity to become first lieutenant of the Portsmouth Navy Yard, but again he saw no active service. He then obtained an assignment once again to serve the Coast Survey on the Pacific coast.

Secretary of State William H. Seward needed an able man to head a joint expedition to relieve Fort Pickens, Florida. Porter was chosen on April 1, 1861, to perform this secret task. However, the plans were sidetracked by Secretary of the Navy Gideon Welles and by President Lincoln. Instead, Porter headed for Pensacola with the intention of taking the city. He was again sidetracked by Washington strategy. Porter remained near Pensacola for six weeks, maintaining blockade duty. Finally, in disgust, he determined to blockade Mobile and succeeded. His performances won his recognition, and he was promoted to the rank of commander.

Porter had an idea that the main fleet should be accompanied by a mortar flotilla when a fort was to be bombarded. He tested his idea on April 18, 1862, on the Forts St. Philip and Jackson just below New Orleans. The commanders of the forts capitulated only after Porter granted favorable terms.

Once again, at Vicksburg, the mortar flotilla was used effectively, convincing Commodore Farragut of its usefulness. On October 9, 1862, Porter became commander of the Mississippi Squadron with the rank of rear admiral. In January, 1863, he helped to capture Arkansas Post and was formally thanked by Congress.

When Porter helped Grant in his famous assault on Vicksburg and the siege that followed, the latter showed his appreciation for valuable services rendered.

Although Porter's Red River expedition failed in 1864, his superiors had great faith in him. He was put in command of the North Atlantic Blockading Squadron, set to destroy Fort Fisher, at Wilmington, North Carolina. It took more than two months of hard fighting to subdue the fort. Porter had used more than sixty ships in this attack! Again, Congress thanked him for a great victory.

In August, 1865, Porter was made superintendent of the Naval Academy. He instituted many practical changes and increased the professional knowledge required by the navy.

When his superior, Farragut, became admiral, Porter was chosen vice admiral in July, 1866.

Three years later President Grant installed Porter as a naval adviser to the Navy Department. In 1870 Porter became admiral of the navy upon Farragut's death. Porter died on February 13, 1891.

David D Porter

Fitz-John Porter

Fitz-John Porter was born in Portsmouth, New Hampshire, on August 31, 1822. He was the son of a naval officer and nephew of the later famous David Porter of the frigate *Essex*. He graduated from the United States Military Academy in 1845 and in the Mexican War won brevets for gallantry. At the close of that war he served at West Point as instructor and adjutant.

With the outbreak of the Civil War he was transferred to staff duties in the eastern part of the nation. He became colonel of a new regiment of regulars and soon afterwards was made a brigadier general of volunteers. Under McClellan he commanded a division of infantry in the Peninsular campaign, directed the Union siege against Yorktown, and was soon afterward placed in command of the Fifth Army Corps. When the Seven Days' Battle of the Wilderness began, Porter's corps had to sustain the full weight of the Confederate attack; and though defeated in the desperately fought battle of Gaines Hill, the steadiness of his defense was so conspicuous that he was immediately promoted to major general of volunteers and brevetted brigadier general in the regular army. His corps, moreover, had the greatest share in the successful battles at Glendale and Malvern Hill. Soon afterwards, the Fifth Corps was sent to reinforce Pope in central Virginia. Its inaction on the first day of the disastrous Second Battle of Bull Run led to Porter's subsequent disgrace; but it made a splendid fight on the second day to save the army from complete rout.

On the same day on which McClellan was relieved of his command, Porter (his friend and supporter) was suspended and tried by court-martial on charges brought against him by Pope. On January 21, 1863, he was sentenced to be "cashiered" and forever disqualified from holding any office of trust under the government of the United States. In 1878 Porter's friends succeeded in procuring a review of the case by a board of distinguished general officers. General Grant took Porter's part and wrote an article in the *North American Review* (vol. 135) entitled "An Undeserved Stigma." Against much opposition, a relief bill finally passed in Congress; and on August 5, 1886, Porter was restored to the United States Army with the rank of colonel and then placed on the retired list without compensation.

Following the Civil War he engaged in business in New York City and held successively many important municipal offices.

He died in 1901.

F. J. Porter

Sterling Price

Sterling Price was one example of the politician-turned-soldier who aroused so much suspicion and distrust in both the Union and Confederate ranks.

Price was born in 1809 in Prince Edward County, Virginia. After the usual formal education he entered Hampden-Sydney College to study law. After graduating he moved to Missouri and set up his law practice, later entering politics. In 1844 he was elected to Congress.

In 1846 Price resigned from Congress to take command of a regiment in the Mexican War. Kearney elevated him to the position of military governor of New Mexico, and he succeeded in keeping the state free of Mexican and Indian raids during his term. He made an equally splendid record as governor of Missouri from 1853 to 1857.

In 1861 Price vehemently opposed secession, making a number of political enemies. When the war began, however, he joined the Confederate camp, taking command of the Missouri militia. In August, 1861, he fought the Union forces at Wilson Creek and defeated them but was forced to retreat under the constant pounding by General S. R. Curtis.

Fighting under Van Dorn, Price suffered a defeat at Pea Ridge in March, 1862. His campaigns for the next two years were generally unsuccessful. Finally, Price achieved some measure of success in his raids through Missouri in 1864, until he was turned back at Westport. This was the last Confederate threat in the West.

Price died in 1867.

Sterling Price

John A. Rawlins

John A. Rawlins achieved fame as the little Illinois lawyer who struck up a strange friendship with the silent "Sam" Grant, the Union bulldog who chewed up and destroyed the Confederate Army.

Rawlins was born at Galena, Illinois, in 1831. He was admitted to the bar in 1854 and within three years became a city attorney.

A fiery advocate of the Union cause, his speech in Galena favoring armed coercion of the Southern states was listened to and favorably received by many people, among them Ulysses Grant.

When Grant became commanding general in the Mississippi River campaign, he appointed Rawlins as his assistant adjutant general. These two men seemed attracted to each other, and their friendship lasted throughout the war and even after Grant was elected President.

Though drinking was a common practice among the officers of the army, Grant seemed to have acquired an unenviable reputation as a heavy and habitual drinker; and his seedy appearance lent credence to the rumors.

Many high officials at Washington, including Stanton and Dana, were perplexed about Grant. Though the great military talents of this general caused them to overlook his drinking weakness, they desired to give him a companion who could look after his affairs. Congress then made Grant a lieutenant general and made Rawlins his chief of staff.

The latter, in turn, became a brigadier general in the regular army and later a brevet major general. He proved a very able executive, relieving Grant of many cumbersome details. He accompanied him on almost two years of bitter campaigning before Lee's army was destroyed.

Rawlins did not hesitate to express his views on military questions; and Grant, with great patience and understanding, listened to him. Rawlins supported Sheridan's plan to cut off Lee's supply line and destroy the rebel defenses at Dinwiddie and at Five Forks. In the closing days of the fighting, Rawlins at Farmville told Grant that Lee was stalling and urged an attack. Grant replied, "Rawlins, Lee is only trying to get let down easy." The cocky Rawlins told Grant that it was his "duty to capture or destroy his army."

Rawlins was with Grant when Lee surrendered at Appomattox. When Grant was elected President, Rawlins was appointed Secretary of War in the new administration.

Yours truly
Jno. A. Rawlins

Beverly Holcombe Robertson

Beverly Holcombe Robertson became the subject of criticism and controversy in his native South during the height of the Civil War.

Though not as famous or well known as many of his fellow officers on both sides of the struggle, Robertson gained considerable and varied experience in the conflict under such generals as Longstreet, Stuart, and Beauregard.

Robertson was born in Virginia in 1826. Like so many other Southerners he decided upon a military career, entering West Point during the closing days of the war with Mexico. He graduated in 1849, twenty-fifth in a class of forty-three. Assigned to the dragoons, he was to serve nearly two decades in the cavalry.

Before the outbreak of the Civil War he spent some twelve years in scouting and fighting Indians along the frontier. He was dismissed from service on August 8, 1861, some four months after Beauregard had opened fire on the Federal arsenal at Fort Sumter.

However, the South was ever-ready to make use of the services of young officers trained at West Point. He was commissioned colonel of the Fourth Virginia Cavalry on November 19, 1861, and from May to September, 1862, saw considerable action in the Virginia theater of the war.

Appointed a brigadier general on June 9, 1862, he commanded his cavalry brigade at Cedar Mountain, the Second Battle of Bull Run, and Antietam. Here he had a taste of action in a theater dominated by Lee, Jackson, and Longstreet on the Confederate side and by McClellan and Pope on the Union side. In addition, he had a chance to see the veteran Army of Northern Virginia in action as it swung north on its "victory march" singing "Maryland, My Maryland," with the gray-bearded Uncle Robbie Lee at its head. True, the legendary Stonewall Jackson was dead; but Robertson could still see such great Southern brigade and corps commanders as A. P. Hill, Longstreet, Ewell, Hood, Pickett, and the ubiquitous Jeb Stuart—the greatest or at least the most celebrated of Southern cavalry leaders.

Though he had been sent to North Carolina in the fall of 1862, he returned to Virginia in April, 1863, in time for the great Confederate-Union rendezvous at Gettysburg.

In May, 1863, he and his cavalry brigade served under the redoubtable Jeb Stuart in guarding the passes in South Mountain, and the following July he saw some action at Gettysburg. In the fall of the same year, October, 1863, after Lee had safely shepherded his beaten army back into Virginia, Robertson was named to command the second military district under Beauregard. In November, 1863, he went with Longstreet to Knoxville to try to bolster the sagging Confederate forces in the Tennessee theater.

Charged with making "mutinous" remarks to his brigade, he was removed from his command but was later restored to active service and was sent to help the dying Confederate hopes in the South.

In 1864 he served in South Carolina, joining the forces of Joseph E. Johnston in March, 1865. He was with that unhappy commander when he surrendered to General Sherman in April, 1865.

After the war he settled down to a life of business in Washington, D.C. He died in 1910.

William Rosecrans

Among the Civil War generals who caused considerable friction and controversy was William Rosecrans. Born in Kingston, Ohio, on September 6, 1819, Rosecrans was graduated from West Point in 1842 as a second lieutenant of engineering. He served as an assistant professor of engineering at West Point from 1849 to 1854, later turning to private practice as a civil engineer.

At the outbreak of the Civil War he volunteered his service to the Union and helped organize the Ohio Volunteers. In June, 1861, he won promotion to brigadier general and commanded a brigade in the army of occupation of West Virginia at Rich Mountain. He later succeeded Pope in command of the Army of the Mississippi and saw action with the Army of the Cumberland. He advanced south from Corinth with 6,000 men to cut off General Price from the main Confederate force, but he failed to accomplish this mission though he did repulse an attack by General Van Dorn.

Rosecrans is best known for his unfortunate campaign against the wily Bragg in the bitter fighting around Chickamauga, Strong River, and Chattanooga. Rosecrans and Bragg faced each other in the winter of 1862, with the Union forces resting in Nashville. Later in the summer of 1863, Rosecrans took his three army corps, commanded by McCook, Crittenden, and Thomas, to Murfreesboro; and he and Bragg fought the bloodiest battle of the war up to that time. Bragg had a force of 67,000. Rosecrans, with 56,000 men, checked Bragg's attack at Stone River; but his own army was too badly mauled to follow up the advantage. He notified Washington that "we have fought the greatest battle of the war and we won." He was, however, beaten in the battle of Chickamauga on September 19–20, 1863, and was relieved of his command. General Thomas succeeded him.

Rosecrans was put in reserve and waited orders for another command. This came in June, 1864, when he was transferred to the Department of Mississippi. He received the thanks of Congress for his conduct at Stone River in the fighting against Bragg.

He retired from the army in 1867 and soon after was appointed United States Minister to Mexico. He retired to a life of ranching and politics in California. From 1881 to 1885 he represented that state in Congress and from 1885 to 1893 became Register of the United States Treasury.

Shortly before his death in 1898, he was given the rank of brigadier general and placed on the retired list.

W. S. Rosecrans

Thomas L. Rosser

One of the most colorful and famous field officers of the Civil War was "Big Tom" Rosser, the leader of the gallant and nationally known cavalry division—the "Laurel Brigade."

Thomas L. Rosser was born on a farm in Campbell County, Virginia, on October 15, 1836. When a boy, his parents moved to Texas; and there he experienced early life on the frontier.

Rosser entered West Point on July 1, 1856; but since his class did not graduate until May, 1861, he decided to resign from the Academy upon the outbreak of the Civil War.

Rosser joined the Confederate Army and was wounded in the Peninsular campaign. Jeb Stuart, then colonel of the Fifth Virginia Regiment, noted Rosser as "a fine artillerist, as well as a bold cavalier."

Rosser saw action in the Second Battle of Bull Run, Chancellorsville, and at Gettysburg as commander of the Laurel Brigade. He was best known for his exploits in the several raids on Union supply lines and supply depots, especially in West Virginia.

Rosser's cavalry brigade was attached to Lee's army in the closing year of the war. He commanded his brigade in the fighting around Five Forks, assigned particularly to protect Pickett's line of supply. Pickett was then in command of the Confederate "Petersburg" defense line at Five Forks. During this campaign occurred the famous "fish fry" at Hatcher Run. Rosser had gotten a few fine shad and decided to invite both Fitzhugh Lee and Pickett to be his guests at his headquarters.

While these three well-known Confederate generals were enjoying the food and drink, the Union forces broke through on the White Oak Road and nearly captured Pickett.

In the last week of the war, Lee ordered Rosser to hold High Bridge to assure a road of escape, even if a temporary one, for the helpless rebels. During the clash with the Union forces, Rosser was wounded and one of his favorite subordinates was killed.

While Lee prepared to surrender at Appomattox, Rosser joined Gordon in a desperate effort to break through the Union lines and escape the inevitable. In the ensuing final clash the Laurel Brigade displayed a reckless but futile courage.

After the war Rosser secured employment on the western frontier building railroads. Part of his job was to run the railroad through the hostile Sioux country under the protection of army troops commanded by General Custer. Custer had been Rosser's classmate at West Point, and they had faced each other during the war.

From 1881 to 1886 Rosser was chief engineer of the Northern Pacific Railroad. In 1898 he was commissioned by President McKinley to train volunteer troops at Chickamauga for service in the Spanish-American War. Following the war he became postmaster at Charlotte, North Carolina. He died on May 29, 1910.

Thos L Rosser

John McAllister Schofield

John McAllister Schofield, was born in Chautauqua, New York. He graduated from West Point in 1853, a second lieutenant in the artillery.

At the start of the Civil War he was appointed major of the Missouri Volunteers. From February 15 to September 26, 1862, he commanded the military district of Missouri and was then put in charge of the Army of the Frontier. This army drove the Confederates in Missouri below the Arkansas River.

Schofield led Sherman's left wing in Georgia and also took part in engagements at Lost Mountain and Kennesaw Mountain in northern Georgia. He helped in the siege and capture of the city of Atlanta on September 2, 1864. He fought in the battle of Nashville and defeated Hood in the bloody battle of Franklin, Tennessee, on November 30, 1864. He was brevetted major general in March, 1864, and acted as commissioner in the sad details of the surrender of Johnston's forces to Sherman on April 26, 1865, at Durham Station, North Carolina.

After the war Schofield became United States agent in France from 1865 to 1866. It was he who warned Napoleon III and his government to withdraw the French troops from Mexico.

On June 2, 1868, he was appointed Secretary of War under President Andrew Johnson. In 1872, as commander of the Division of the Pacific, he recommended that the U.S. acquire Pearl Harbor, Hawaii, as a naval base. He served as superintendent of West Point and from 1888 to 1895 was commanding general of the army under President Grover Cleveland. He died in St. Augustine, Florida, on March 4, 1906.

Winfield Scott

Winfield Scott made American military history with his brilliant career as a general.

Born near Petersburg, Virginia, on June 13, 1786, he studied law at the College of William and Mary. When it seemed that England and America would go to war in 1807, he offered his services to the military authorities in Washington and was commissioned a captain of artillery. In 1812 he became a lieutenant colonel in the same field and was sent to New Orleans.

Captured at Queenston, Scott was exchanged in January, 1813. A year later he was promoted to brigadier general. He participated in the fierce battles of Lundy's Lane and Chippewa and was seriously wounded. Both Congress and the State of Virginia gave him full recognition for his military services.

Scott's services to the outbreak of the Mexican War included expeditions against the Seminole Indians in Florida and various Indian tribes in Alabama, Georgia, Tennessee, and North Carolina. In addition, he put down Canadian insurgents who violated American neutrality.

Scott made a remarkable record in the Mexican War as senior officer of the American army. He led the famous expedition against Vera Cruz in 1847 and achieved a number of other brilliant victories as well.

When the Civil War broke out, Scott was the commanding general of the U.S. Army, but nearing seventy-five, he was in no condition to direct a major war.

When hostilities began, Scott ordered the digging of trenches around the capital and placed artillery on the Anacostia River. He felt that 300,000 men and three years of fighting would crush the South. He suggested that a line of forts be erected on the Mississippi River, that the Confederacy be cut in half, that every Southern port be closed, and that a large army be trained before taking the field on a large scale.

This "Anaconda" policy of careful consideration aroused a storm of opposition in the North, more so when the Union forces were beaten at Bull Run. The cry was "On to Richmond," and Lincoln was compelled to support McClellan against Scott. The old warrior retired in humiliation.

He died at West Point in 1866.

Winfield Scott.

John Sedgwick

"Uncle" John Sedgwick was born at Cornwall, Connecticut, on September 13, 1813. He graduated from West Point in 1837 and served against the Seminoles in Florida. Volunteering his services at the beginning of the Mexican War, he saw action in the battles of Cerro Gordo, Contreras, Churubusco, and Chapultepec.

At the beginning of the Civil War, Sedgwick was commissioned brigadier general of volunteers and was assigned to the Army of the Potomac. His efficient services in the battle of Fair Oaks won the day for the Union Army. He made a good record for himself at Antietam and continued to show gallant service by effectively shelling Lee's army on Marye's Heights at Fredericksburg and pushing through Early's cavalry. Through the terrible defeat of the Union forces at Chancellorsville, Sedgwick continued to hold the line against Lee and his men.

At Gettysburg Sedgwick made valiant efforts to check both Generals Hood and Longstreet, who were trying to seize the important Union positions on Little Round Top.

Sedgwick was a great admirer of McClellan and was quite skeptical of Grant's ability to succeed with the Army of the Potomac. He had bluntly declared that "the truth is that we are on the wrong road to Richmond."

When Meade reshuffled his army commands, he followed a suggestion from Stanton and decided to remove Sedgwick from the Sixth Corps and give him command in the Shenandoah instead. Lincoln, however, had already given that command to General Sigel. Sedgwick was fully aware of these staff maneuvers but felt that it was to his best interests to direct his attention to his own duties.

Sedgwick was proud of his corps; for they rendered conspicuous service in the fierce fighting in the battle of the Wilderness, fought valiantly at Germanna Ford, and stood up to Lee's army at Orange Turnpike. In the latter action they successfully resisted Lee's flank movements despite the grave fears of Grant and Meade. In this battle Sedgwick was observed plunging into the very front lines and shouting to his men, "Let them come up before you! Let them have it!"

With all his fine qualities of courage and good common sense, admired so much by his men, Sedgwick was essentially a shy man, tired of war and carnage.

He met with fatal tragedy in the fighting around Spotsylvania Court House when a sharpshooter shot him below the left eye on May 9, 1864. When Grant heard of his death, he declared that "to lose him was worse than to lose a whole division of troops."

John Sedgwick

Raphael Semmes

Raphael Semmes was born in Charles County, Maryland, on September 27, 1809. He became a midshipman in the navy in 1826, but did not see real action until the Mexican War, when he superintended the landing of troops under the command of General Scott at Vera Cruz in March, 1847. In the ensuing battles in the Valley of Mexico, he served as an aide to General Worth.

In 1855 Semmes became naval secretary of the Lighthouse Board situated in Washington, D.C. When the Civil War broke out, he resigned his commission as commander and returned to the home which he had built in Alabama. Southern leaders who had planned secession immediately offered him the rank of commander in the Confederate Army.

Semmes fitted out a packet, *Sumter,* and made a record capture of seventeen Northern merchant vessels. In August, 1862, he was made commander of the *Alabama,* which had been built in England. The 1,016 ton ship built up a greater record than any other Confederate ship by capturing sixty-seven Northern ships.

In 1864 the Union cruiser *Kearsarge* challenged the *Alabama* to a life and death duel. The battle was fought off the French coast and raged for seven hours. The *Alabama* was finally sunk, but Semmes was rescued by an English witness of the battle. Upon his return home he was given the rank of rear admiral and was made commander of the powerful Confederate fleet stationed in the James River. Soon after the capture of Richmond, he was forced to blow up his ships and joined the forces of General Joseph E. Johnston.

When the Confederate forces surrendered, Semmes returned to his home in Mobile, Alabama, and set up a law practice.

He died in 1877.

Raphael Semmes

Philip Henry Sheridan

Probably the greatest cavalry leader in American history was Philip Henry Sheridan, born in Albany, New York, on March 6, 1831.

Through his own endeavors he secured an appointment to West Point, graduating from the Academy in 1853. He gained some experience in fighting Indians on the frontier before the outbreak of the Civil War. A first lieutenant at the time, he was promoted to captain and in the spring of 1862 became colonel of the Second Michigan Cavalry, serving under Halleck in Tennessee. He was soon raised to the rank of brigadier general of volunteers as a result of his skillful conduct in the battle of Boonesville.

Sheridan commanded the Eleventh Division of the Army of the Ohio first under Buell in the battle of Perrysville and then under Rosecrans at Stone's River, winning promotion to the rank of major general of volunteers. In the summer of 1863 he effectively supported Rosecrans in maneuvering the Confederates under Bragg out of Tennessee. In September, 1863, Rosecrans met with a signal defeat at Chickamauga; and his army was driven back in confusion to Chattanooga. Sheridan's cavalry division, although driven back in the course of defeat, helped to cover the retreat. In the subsequent fighting around Chattanooga, Sheridan won considerable distinction, especially in his daring and brilliant charge up Missionary Ridge.

Sheridan's bold, energetic action attracted the attention of Grant who, when he became lieutenant general in March, 1864, and assumed command of the Army of the Potomac in Virginia, placed Sheridan in charge of his cavalry. Sheridan assumed command in April, 1864, and soon proved himself to be the ablest cavalry leader in the Union Army. He protected Grant's flanks, and his corps was active in the battle of the Wilderness and Spotsylvania Court House. While Grant hammered Lee's lines, Sheridan was sent on a raid toward Richmond, in the course of which he cut the Confederate communications by destroying railroads and cutting telegraph lines. He returned to the main army in time to participate in the battle of Cold Harbor. Soon afterward he set out upon a raid to Charlottesville (June 7–26) to aid Hunter in the Shenandoah Valley, at that time a Confederate granary and the "back door" to Washington.

The success of these expeditions led to his appointment to the command of a newly formed Army of the Shenandoah on August 7, 1864, with instructions to clear the valley of the Confederates. This was probably the greatest opportunity of his military career, and he proved himself fully equal to it. His campaign was ruthless, devastating, and brilliant. He defeated Early at Winchester and again at Fisher's Mill and Cedar Creek. He pursued a military policy that was so active that he has often been severely censured for it. In order to make the region useless to the Confederates, he destroyed all means of subsistence so that one of the most fruitful regions of the South was left in utter desolation, with noncombatants on the verge of starvation. As one critic said, "If a crow flew through the valley, it would have to carry its own rations."

Sheridan was now raised to the rank of brigadier general of the regular army. Sheridan was at Winchester when the main body of his army was thrown into confusion by a surprise attack from Early at Cedar Creek. Mounting his horse, he made his famous twenty-mile ride and rallied his troops while shouting, "Turn, boys, we're going back," turning defeat into victory.

Commissioned major general of the regular army, he soon made another raid in the early spring of 1865 from Winchester to Petersburg, again defeating Early at Waynesboro. In April, 1865, he turned Lee's flanks at Five Forks and forced him to retreat to Appomattox, where he surrendered to Grant on April 9.

A month later Sheridan was placed in command of an American force on the Mexican border to watch the struggle between Maximilian, who had been set up as Emperor of Mexico by Napoleon III in 1864, and Mexican liberals who were seeking his overthrow. Sheridan's presence greatly aided the effectiveness of American diplomatic protests to the French government, thus hastening the collapse of the ill-starred venture.

In the spring of 1867 Sheridan was placed in charge of the Fifth Military District, embracing Louisiana and Texas, and was stationed at New Orleans. An advocate of extreme measures in dealing with the conquered South, he soon came into conflict with President Johnson, who opposed such policies. He was removed in 1867 and placed in charge of the Department of Missouri.

During the winter of 1869 he conducted a successful campaign against the Indians and was made lieutenant general by President Grant. He traveled to Europe, where he was attached to the general staff of the German Army as guest of the King of Prussia. When Sherman retired in 1884, Sheridan was made commanding general of the U.S. Army. Five years later, shortly before his death, he was raised to the rank of general. He died at Monquitt, Massachusetts, on August 5, 1888.

He crowned a life of war with a little romance when he married Irene Rucker, the daughter of a general of the Union Army, in 1875.

In physical appearance Sheridan was short, rather stout, and harsh of features. To those who opposed his policies in both peace and war, he seemed gruff and needlessly severe, but to his friends he appeared to be kind. Exceptionally gifted with personal magnetism, he was popular with his troops. As a military leader, he combined reckless courage with careful, brilliant tactics. Grant admired him intensely for his courage, aggressiveness, military ability, and resourcefulness. In fact, Grant looked upon "little Phil Sheridan" as one of the world's great leaders and commanders.

Phil. H. Sheridan

William Tecumseh Sherman

William Tecumseh Sherman is considered by many military experts as a pioneer of modern warfare. His mastery of tactics and strategy was in the realm of near genius. Yet he had no real appetite for war. He told the world for all time that war was hell and not a chivalrous or gentlemanly game.

Sherman was born on February 8, 1820. His father became a judge of the Ohio Supreme Court when William was nine. At fourteen he began preparations for West Point. Friends of his father gave him an early orientation in many of the required subjects, and in 1836 he entered the Academy.

As a second lieutenant stationed in Florida during the Seminole War, Sherman demonstrated mature insight. Writing to his sweetheart he noted, "You doubtless little sympathize with me in hunting and harassing a poor set of people who have had the heroism to defend their homes against such odds for such a period of time."

In 1846 Sherman was sent to the Pacific coast to help drive out the Mexicans from their California territory. Landing at Monterey, he became a junior officer, a subordinate of General Kearney's. When the latter departed after a dispute with Colonel Frémont, Sherman found himself acting as adjutant general to the newly appointed Colonel Mason.

In 1848 he witnessed the historic gold rush in California and became interested in its business possibilities. He determined to resign from the army but was dissuaded from this rash act.

On May 1, 1850, Sherman married Ellen Ewing, daughter of the Secretary of the Interior, and four months later was promoted to captain with the Commissary Department. He was, however, restless and finally resigned his commission to enter banking business. His energetic measures in the field made him a profit, but in 1855 a financial crisis forced him out of business.

Major D. C. Buell, assistant adjutant general in the War Department suggested to Sherman that he apply for a position at the newly established Louisiana Military Academy. Sherman applied and was accepted, but talk of secession disturbed him. He wrote to his wife that "if the Southern states should organize for the purpose of leaving the Union I could not go with them."

Events came thick and fast; and on January 18, 1861, Sherman handed in his resignation as superintendent of the Academy to Governor Moore. He was offered an opportunity to become assistant Secretary of War but declined, instead taking a commission as a colonel in the regular army.

He experienced his first mortification at the First Battle of Bull Run. He was ashamed at the terrible rout and defeat. In August he was made a brigadier general of volunteers and was sent to Kentucky. There he succeeded Robert Anderson of Fort Sumter fame.

When the Battle of Shiloh took place in April, 1862, Sherman distinguished himself as divisional commander and earned a promotion to major general. By December, 1862, he had taken command of the District of Memphis.

It was in the Vicksburg campaign that Sherman led his famous Fifteenth Corps to victory. He was made a brigadier general in the regular army, and a dream had come true.

Grant realized Sherman's military acumen and abilities as a field commander. He appreciated his vast knowledge of communications. When Grant assumed supreme command in the West, Sherman became commander of the Army of the Tennessee. Within a year, Sherman destroyed Confederate communications and supplies all along the Mississippi. In March, 1864, Grant turned over his commandership in the West to Sherman. Then followed the great Atlanta campaign, planned deliberately to break the morale of the people of the South. Sherman allowed the "scorch the earth" policy to prevail. He left behind him ruined and devastated land. On November 15, 1864, Sherman burned most of Atlanta, and with 60,000 men began his famous march to the sea. On December 21, 1864, Savannah fell, and the South was on the road to ruin.

Sherman turned northward, determined to close in on the helpless Lee from the rear. When Sherman marched through South Carolina, he devastated and destroyed that state with an avenging sword.

When Lee surrendered, Johnston fought a losing battle at Bentonville and immediately afterward approached Sherman with terms of surrender. Sherman offered his generous terms similar to those given by Grant to Lee at Appomattox. Official surrender came on April 26, 1865.

Sherman succeeded Grant as commander of the United States Army after the latter had been elected President. He held that post until he retired from the army in 1884.

Sherman died on February 14, 1896.

W.T. Sherman

Daniel Edgar Sickles

Daniel Edgar Sickles, congressman, diplomat, and soldier, was born in New York City on October 20, 1823. He secured his education in that city and attended New York University. As a young man he turned to the study of law under Benjamin Franklin Butler and was admitted to the bar in 1846. Within a year he entered politics and was successfully elected to the state legislature.

In 1853 he met Theresa Bagiole, the seventeen-year-old daughter of an Italian music teacher, and married her. That same year he was appointed corporation counsel but resigned when he was offered the opportunity to become secretary of the United States delegation at London. He held that position for two years, and returning to the United States was again elected to the New York State Senate.

In 1859 Sickles shot and killed Philip Barton Key, grandson of Francis Scott Key, because of Key's attentions to his wife. In a celebrated trial that brought him considerable notoriety, he was acquitted.

Although he was a Democrat at the outbreak of the war, Sickles offered his services to President Lincoln early in March, 1861. The President requested him to raise troops; and Sickles immediately organized the Excelsior Brigade in New York, becoming their colonel and commander. He led this brigade in the First Peninsular campaign.

In 1863 he won promotion to the rank of major general with command of the Third Army Corps. He served well in the Chancellorsville campaign, where it was the Third Corps that discovered the march of Stonewall Jackson around the Federal army flank. Sickles reported this fact and after some delay was instructed to attack the enemy.

When a surprise attack by the Confederates on the Eleventh Corps caused it to break, Sickles fell back with his men well in hand, attacked the victorious Jackson, and after bloody fighting stopped the Confederate advance.

The last campaign in which Sickles fought was Gettysburg. On the second day of fighting, July 2, his Third Corps was ordered by Meade to cover the Round Tops, two hills anchoring the Union left flank. Sickles decided, without taking orders from his superiors, to advance to the famous Peach Orchard salient in front of Cemetery Ridge.

Meade examined the new positions and suggested to Sickles that it was best to retreat to stronger positions. However, Longstreet made a sudden violent attack on Sickles' forces; and half of the latter's forces were lost by nightfall. In time, Union forces checked the onslaughts of Longstreet and his men; and valuable ground was held. As the battle came to an end, Sickles was hit by a shell fragment, losing a leg.

Sickles would have been in a good position if Meade had planned an offensive battle, but the latter had in mind defensive action. He criticized Sickles' conduct in his reports, and this meant the end of Sickles' military career. He was sent on a confidential mission to become governor of the Carolinas, but President Johnson found him so strenuous in the performance of his duties that he was dropped in 1867.

Sickles retired from the army with the rank of major general. In May, 1869, he was appointed Minister to Spain, where the complications of the Cuban problem and the Virginius affair proved too much for him. His actions were so vigorous that he was called the "Yankee King." But his actions were lacking in tact and he resigned in December, 1871.

Sickles continued to live abroad for seven years; and when he returned to the United States, his wife refused to go with him. They were reconciled more than three decades later at his deathbed, through the efforts of their son.

Sickles became chairman of the New York State Monuments Commission in 1886 but was relieved of that position because of mishandling funds. Separated from his family, continually involved in financial troubles and altercations, the "old, irresponsible, and cantankerous" gentleman spent his last years in New York City, where he died on May 3, 1914. His one undisputed claim to honor was his successful effort to obtain Central Park for New York City.

D Sickles

Franz Sigel

Franz Sigel was born at Sinsheim in Baden on November 18, 1824. After completing his studies in the Gymnasium of Bruchsal, he entered the military school at Carlsruhe. He graduated from there in 1843 and became an officer in the grand ducal service.

When the Baden insurrection broke out, he became a leader on the Revolutionary side in the brief campaigns of 1848 and 1849. His liberal political views brought him into conflict with the existing regime. In 1847 he fought a duel with an opponent and severely wounded him. He resigned from the military service and in 1848 led an army of 4,000 men against the government. He was defeated and fled to Switzerland.

In 1852 he came to the United States, working in turn as a journalist and schoolmaster in New York City and St. Louis. He became a major in the Fifth Regiment of the New York Militia, and in 1857 accepted the position of teacher of history and mathematics in the German-American Institute of St. Louis and director of schools in that city.

When the Civil War broke out, Sigel was active in raising and training Federal volunteer corps. He organized the Third Missouri Infantry and became its commander with the rank of colonel. His efforts saved the city of St. Louis, and he was given command of the Second Missouri Brigade with an appointment as brigadier general of volunteers.

At the Battle of Pea Ridge, Arkansas, on March 7, 1862, Sigel commanded two divisions in Fremont's army. He showed bravery and skill on the battlefield and contributed greatly to the Union victory that settled the critical situation in Missouri. He was then promoted to major general of volunteers and ordered to go to Virginia. There he was put in command of a corps in the Army of Virginia, led by Pope.

In the Second Battle of Bull Run Sigel fought valiantly. A month later his corps was transferred to the Army of the Potomac as the Eleventh Corps.

Owing to bad health, Sigel gave up his command until the summer of 1863, when he returned to duty in a subordinate command in the Department of the Susquehanna. A year later he was given full command of a corps in the Shenandoah Valley but was badly defeated by Breckenridge at New Market on May 15, 1864.

One year later, he resigned his commission and became an editor of a German journal in Baltimore, Maryland. In 1867 he left that city to go to New York City, where he obtained the position of Collector of Internal Revenue. He died in New York City on August 21, 1902.

F. Sigel

Henry Warner Slocum

Henry Warner Slocum was born in 1826 at Delphi, Onondaga County, New York. He taught school and also courses at the state normal school until 1848, when he obtained an opportunity to enter West Point. Four years later he graduated with honors, seventh in a class of forty-three. He was commissioned a second lieutenant in the artillery.

When Lincoln called for volunteers, Slocum gladly volunteered his services. On May 21, 1861, he was made colonel of the Twenty-seventh New York Infantry; and the First Battle of Bull Run saw him in action. His brilliance in the field won him a promotion to brigadier general of volunteers.

By 1862 he gained a second promotion to major general of volunteers. He and his division were sent to Alexandria, Virginia, after the withdrawal of McClellan's army from the Peninsula, with orders to assist in covering the withdrawal of Pope's troops.

Slocum was placed in command of the entire campaign in Maryland, where he engaged in fierce fighting at South Mountain and Antietam. In October he took over the Twelfth Army Corps, which participated in the campaign of Fredericksburg.

In the fall of 1863, after the bloody battle of Chickamauga, Slocum was ordered to reinforce Rosecrans' troops. A month later his corps and Howard's corps were transferred by rail to Tennessee. Slocum was at odds with General Hooker, who was assigned to command these two corps. When Slocum heard that Hooker was to take over this command, he immediately offered his resignation; but his superiors made an arrangement whereby personal contact between the two would be avoided.

This great transportation by rail of more than 24,000 troops over a distance of 1,200 miles within a period of nine days made military history.

In 1864 Slocum was given the Twentieth Corps and the left wing of Sherman's army, made up of the Fourteenth Corps. Near the end of the war, he took command of the Army of the Mississippi, located at Vicksburg.

After the war Slocum went back to the practice of law. He resigned from the army on September 28, 1865, and soon turned to politics. He was elected as a Democratic congressman in 1869–73, and 1883–85. He died on April 14, 1894.

Edmund Kirby Smith

Edmund Kirby Smith, soldier and educator, was born in St. Augustine, Florida, on May 16, 1824. Graduating from West Point in 1845, he was commissioned as a second lieutenant in the Fifth Infantry. When the Mexican War broke out, he fought at Palo Alto, Resaca de la Palma, and Monterrey. He was brevetted first lieutenant for bravery at Vera Cruz and Cerro Gordo and soon after became a captain for gallantry at Contreras.

In 1849–52 Smith served as captain in the Second Cavalry. After hard fighting in several Indian campaigns, he reached the rank of major.

When Florida seceded in 1861, he resigned from the U.S. Army and was commissioned colonel in the Confederate Army, later in the year attaining the rank of brigadier general.

In the First Battle of Bull Run, Smith was severely wounded. Following his recovery, he became major general and was given command of the Confederate forces in the Cumberland Gap region. He led the advances of Bragg's army in the Kentucky campaign and August 30, 1862, defeated the federal troops under Nelson near Richmond, Kentucky. His plan included an attack upon Cincinnati, but he was forced to withdraw toward Frankfort when Bragg failed to come to his support. He was promoted to lieutenant general and took part in the battles of Perryville and Stone River.

On February 19, 1864, Smith was appointed general in command of the Trans-Mississippi Department. He organized the governments of Louisiana, Arkansas, Texas, and Indian territory, and established a vigorous foreign trade by successfully running the blockade at Galveston.

In the same year he fought Banks in the Red River campaign. He was the last Confederate general to surrender, on May 26, 1865.

Following the war, Smith became, in turn, president of the Pacific and Atlantic Telegraph Company (1866–68), president of the Western Military Academy (1868–70), chancellor of the University of Nashville (1870–75), and professor of mathematics at the University of the South, Sewanee, Tennessee, from 1875 until his death on March 28, 1893.

E Kirby Smith

George Stoneman

George Stoneman was born in Lakewood, New York, on August 8, 1822. He graduated from West Point in 1846. As a brigadier general and major general in the Union Army during the Civil War, he fought in a number of important actions and distinguished himself in the battle of Williamsburg on May 5, 1862.

When Hooker faced Lee's army of 65,000 at Chancellorsville in May, 1863, the former had almost 113,000 men. He resolved upon a daring, wide flanking movement, including an effort to flank Lee and cut him off from any retreat to Richmond. Stoneman was ordered to cross the Rappahannock, circle Lee's flank, disrupt his supply line, and cut off any possibility of retreat.

Stoneman, in carrying out these orders, fell into conflict with Fitzhugh Lee; and the resultant loss of 7,000 horses and Stoneman's inactivity deprived Hooker of needed cavalry aid in the ensuing battle of Chancellorsville.

Stoneman served with Kilpatrick's cavalry in Sherman's Atlanta campaign. He made an attempt to cut Hood's supply but was ambushed and captured near Macon in August, 1864. He retired from the army in 1871 and served as governor of California from 1883 to 1887. He died in Buffalo, New York, on September 5, 1894.

George Stoneman

James Ewell Brown Stuart

"Jeb" Stuart was born on February 6, 1833. His ancestors distinguished themselves during the colonial and revolutionary periods and in the War of 1812.

After studying at Emory and Henry College, Virginia, he entered West Point, and upon his graduation in 1854 was commissioned a lieutenant.

After serving with the mounted riflemen against the Apaches in Texas, he was transferred to Fort Leavenworth, where he served in the First Cavalry. Shortly thereafter he married the daughter of Colonel Philip St. George Cooke and was promoted to first lieutenant. In the attack upon John Brown he was an aide to Colonel Robert E. Lee.

In April, 1861, Stuart was promoted to captain; but he had already decided to join the Confederate cause. His resignation was accepted on May 7, 1861. He offered his services to his native state and three days later was commissioned a lieutenant colonel of Virginia infantry.

Reporting to Stonewall Jackson at Harpers Ferry, he again won promotion to colonel with the command of 350 cavalrymen.

Stuart's services at the First Battle of Bull Run were brilliant. General Jubal A. Early wrote that "Stuart did as much toward saving the battle as any subordinate who participated in it." After the victory had been won, he pursued the Federals for twelve miles, gaining the heights in sight of Washington, with headquarters on Munson's Hill.

On September 24, 1861, he was promoted to brigadier general. In the spring of 1862 he covered the retreat from Yorktown and opened the battle at Williamsburg. For his daring raid around McClellan's army, just before the Seven Days' Battle, Stuart won the applause and hearty admiration of both friend and foe and on July 25, 1862, was promoted to major general. Stuart won additional fame through his raid around Pope's army, in which he captured that general's headquarters and a part of his staff at Catlett's Station; through his raid, in conjunction with General Tremble, upon the federal depot supplies at Manassas; through his services in screening the movement of Lee's army into Maryland; through the brilliant fighting of his troopers at the passes of South Mountain; and through the skill with which he managed his horse artillery on the Confederate left at Antietam, where he powerfully assisted in the repulse of Sumner's gallant charge.

In October, 1862, after the battle of Sharpsburg, Stuart led his bold horsemen to Chambersburg, Pennsylvania, and on his return, thwarting every effort of the Federal cavalry to intercept him, passed between McClellan's army and Washington, and with little loss recrossed the Potomac into Virginia. This expedition caused great demoralization in the Federal cavalry and by delaying McClellan's advance gave the Army of Northern Virginia several weeks for rest and preparation against a new invasion.

After the death of Stonewall Jackson and the disabling of A. P. Hill, Stuart took command of Jackson's corps, and by his audacious attack upon greatly superior numbers completed the work so brilliantly begun by Jackson when Lee commenced his movement into Pennsylvania. Stuart, after defeating the Federal cavalry at Fleetwood, or Brandy Station, passed again between the Federal army and Washington with orders to meet Early at York. Marching almost without rest for eight days and nights, the last three with almost constant fighting, he joined Lee's army at Gettysburg, bringing with him a large train of captured Federal supplies. On the third day of the battle he led a fierce attack upon the cavalry on the right flank of the Union line.

On May 5, 1864, Stuart guided the movement of A. P. Hill's corps against Grant's advance. On May 7 he warned Lee of Grant's flank march to Spotsylvania Court House and held it in check until the Confederate infantry could be thrown across Grant's path.

When Sheridan attempted to make a sudden dash into Richmond, Stuart barred his way at Yellow Tavern and saved the Confederate capital; but he received a mortal wound and died the next day, May 12, in Richmond.

John Cooke has written thus of Stuart's last moments. "As his life had been one of earnest devotion to a cause in which he believed, so his last hours were tranquil, his confidence in the mercy of heaven unfailing. When he was asked how he felt, he said, 'Easy but willing to die, if God and my country think I have done my duty.' His last words were: 'I am going fast now, I am resigned. God's will be done.' As he uttered these words he expired."

In every battle in which he took place, Stuart's black plume was clearly visible. In every arm of the service he won the highest honors. Gay and rollicking in camp, merry on the march, he was always fully awake to the demands of duty and equal to any emergency.

J.E.B Stuart

Edwin Vose Sumner

Edwin Vose Sumner was born on January 30, 1797. At the age of twenty-two he earned a commission as second lieutenant in the Second Infantry, and in 1833 he became a captain in a newly-organized body of men called the First Dragoons. Sumner fought in a number of Indian wars until 1846, when he was called to the colors in the war with Mexico as a replacement for Colonel William S. Harvey.

Sumner made a brilliant record leading his troops throughout the campaign. At Cerro Gordo, where he suffered severe wounds, he was brevetted for bravery on the battlefield. In July, 1848, he became a lieutenant colonel of the First Dragoons. When New Mexico lost its governor, J. S. Calhoun, Sumner acted temporarily in his place.

A keen rivalry developed between Generals Sumner and Harvey. This rivalry revealed itself in the fall of 1852 when Harvey ordered Sumner to prepare for a spring campaign against various Indian tribes. After marching with his regiment for four hundred miles, Sumner turned back against orders. Harvey pressed charges for disobedience, but the War Department vindicated Sumner's actions.

During the "bloody Kansas" days of 1856, Sumner preserved order and destroyed guerilla bands of partisans on both sides.

The Cheyenne met their match when Sumner fought them in Kansas in 1857. The following year, he took command of the region.

General Scott had great confidence in Sumner and chose him to accompany President-elect Lincoln to Washington, D.C. On January 5, 1861, Sumner wrote to Scott, "I have belonged to a general government for forty years and I consider it my government and so long as it lasts, the only government to which I owe fealty. As I view this obligation I feel bound in honor to devote myself to the preservation of the Union."

With the beginning of the war, Sumner was promoted to brigadier general, commanding the Second Corps in the Peninsular campaign at Antietam. The following year McClellan wrote to the War Department recommending Sumner to a higher rank, major general of the volunteers. McClellan was impressed with the latter's "extreme gallantry" in action on the battlefield and with the judgment and energy displayed at the Battle of Fair Oaks. Sumner received his appointment.

As a friend of General Burnside, Sumner was placed in command of the right wing of the Union Army at Fredericksburg. Burnside, as commander of the Army of the Potomac, ordered a frontal attack on Lee, who was entrenched in the hills beyond Fredericksburg. Sumner revealed great courage in battle, leading his troops made up of the Second and Fourteenth Corps. However, he was driven back with a loss of 5,000 men.

Shortly thereafter, Sumner fell ill and died early in 1863 as he prepared for a new command.

E V Sumner

George Thomas

One of the most famous and respected generals in American history was George Thomas, "the Rock of Chickamauga."

Thomas was born in Southampton County, Virginia, on July 31, 1816. He graduated from West Point in 1840 and served as an artillery subaltern in the war against the Seminole Indians in Florida in 1841. In the Mexican War he took part in the battles of Fort Brown, Resaca de la Palma, Monterrey, and Buena Vista, receiving three brevets for distinguished gallantry in action. From 1851 to 1854 he was an instructor at West Point and in 1855 was appointed by Jefferson Davis, then Secretary of War, to be a major of the Second Cavalry. His regimental superiors were A. S. Johnston, R. E. Lee, and W. J. Hardee. All three resigned at the outbreak of the Civil War to join the Confederacy, but Thomas finally decided to remain loyal to the United States. He soon won promotion in rapid succession to lieutenant colonel, colonel in the regular army, and brigadier general of volunteers.

As a division commander in the Army of the Cumberland, Thomas attacked the Confederate general Zollicoffer at Mill Springs on January 19, 1862, and gained the first important Union victory in the West. He commanded three divisions at Nashville to check Bragg, if attacked. Under Rosecrans he was entrusted with getting behind Bragg and cutting his communications. Bragg, with superior forces and reinforced by Longstreet, planned to destroy Thomas and then cut Union forces into segments and destroy them. In the early fighting around Chickamauga, Thomas' Westerners flung back all Confederate attacks. Bragg saw he could not crush Thomas; but Longstreet broke through the Union center, scattered the divisions of Brannan and Van Cleve, and forced Sheridan and Wood back. Rosecrans' defeated troops were compelled to retreat to Chattanooga.

It was in this battle that Thomas gained the name of "the Rock of Chickamauga," when, with the aid of Granger, he checked the enemy and saved the day.

Thomas succeeded Rosecrans as commander of the Army of the Cumberland shortly after the great victory of Chattanooga. He was made a major general in the regular army and received the thanks of Congress.

After the Civil War Thomas commanded the military departments in Kentucky and Tennessee until 1869, when he was transferred to the Division of the Pacific with headquarters at San Francisco. Here he died on March 28, 1870, a legend in his own time.

Geo H Thomas

Alfred T. A. Torbert

Alfred T. A. Torbert was born at Grozton, Delaware, on July 1, 1833. His father was a farmer and a local preacher. Young Torbert attended the local schools and entered West Point in 1851, graduating twenty-first in a class of thirty-four.

Assigned as a second lieutenant of infantry, Torbert saw service on the frontier and fought the Seminoles in Florida and the Indians in New Mexico, besides participating in the Utah expedition of 1857.

In the fall of 1861, Torbert was chosen colonel of the First New Jersey Volunteers. He led his regiment in the fighting around Yorktown, Gaines Mill, and the Second Battle of Bull Run. He commanded a brigade of the Sixth Army Corps at Antietam, where he was wounded in action, as well as at Chancellorsville and Gettysburg.

During 1862 Torbert was made a brigadier general of volunteers. In April, 1864, he took command of the First Cavalry Division and saw action in the Peninsular campaign and in the Shenandoah Valley. He fought at Rappahannock Station, North Anna, and Cold Harbor. Sheridan was happy to have him in command of the cavalry division of his Army of the Shenandoah; and in the closing months of the war, he served as the left flank of Sheridan's rapidly moving forces. He defeated a Confederate force under Wade Hampton at Trevilian Station in June, 1864; but he was repulsed with heavy losses.

As head of the middle section of Sheridan's army, Torbert was deeply involved in the battles of Winchester, Waynesboro, and Cedar Creek. At Winchester his envelopment of Early's left flank secured victory for Sheridan's army. He defeated the famous rebel cavalry general, Rosser, at Tom's Brook on October 9, 1864; and his calm, resolute action at Cedar Creek on October 19, 1864, helped hold the confused Union forces in line until Sheridan took over the direction of the battle.

On March 13, 1865, Torbert was made a brigadier general in the regular army because of his brilliant record in combat.

Torbert resigned his commission on October 31, 1866, and in 1871 became consul general at Havana. He was stationed in Paris for five years before resigning from the diplomatic service in 1871, to engage in business in Mexico City. Returning to New York in 1880, he died when the ship on which he was traveling sank off the Florida coast.

As a soldier, he was staunch, sure, and victorious in carrying out assignments. He was a splendid cavalryman, equally admired by both officers and men.

A. T. Torbert

Emory Upton

Emory Upton was born in Batavia, New York, on August 27, 1839. The son of a farmer, he was a wiry, high strung, and introspective young man.

He entered West Point, graduating from the Academy in May, 1861. He was given the commission of second lieutenant and placed in the Fourth Artillery, where he was promoted to first lieutenant.

As an officer in General Tyler's command, he took part in the First Battle of Bull Run, where he was wounded, and in the Peninsular and Maryland campaigns of 1862.

Put in command as colonel of the One Hundred and Twenty-first New York Volunteers, he saw service at Fredericksburg and Gettysburg.

Grant felt that Upton was a valuable soldier, and he saw to it that he received a brigade of the Sixth Corps. The men under his leadership distinguished themselves at Rappahannock Station in November, 1863, and at Spotsylvania Court House. He led the bitter attack on Ewell's forces, capturing 1,000 men, but was finally driven back.

Upton's superiors rewarded him for his gallantry in battle by giving him the rank of brigadier general of volunteers and later, lieutenant colonel in the regular army.

In the Shenandoah Valley campaign against Early, Upton commanded the Union right wing; and in the fighting he plugged a gap in the lines and stabilized the fighting front. He was wounded during the action but ignored General Sheridan's order to go to a hospital. He told the General it was the clear duty of officers to remain at the front at all costs, and for this service he was brevetted major general of volunteers.

In the very bloody attack at Cold Harbor, Upton rode up and down the line shouting "Stand by me, we must hold the line. If the rebels come up here, catch them on your bayonets, and toss them over your head."

He subsequently served in Georgia and Alabama in command of the Fourth Cavalry Division under General James H. Wilson, and for his services at Selma was brevetted brigadier general in the regular army in July, 1866.

Remaining in the army after the war, he originated a system of military tactics which was adopted by the government. He served as superintendent at West Point from 1870 to 1875.

In 1880 he was assigned to command the Fourth Artillery at the Presidio at San Francisco. Here he committed suicide on March 15, 1881, because of an incurable brain disease.

His published writings are *A New System of Infantry Tactics* (1870); *Tactics for Nonmilitary Bodies* (1870); and *The Military Policy of the United States* (1878).

E. Upton

Earl Van Dorn

Earl Van Dorn was born near Port Gibson, Mississippi, on September 17, 1820. He graduated from West Point in 1842 and rose to the rank of captain by 1855.

Resigning his commission at the outbreak of the Civil War, Van Dorn joined the Confederate Army. His career in the war covered a period of only two years and included only three major engagements.

In the Battle of Pear Ridge in March, 1862, Van Dorn led a large Confederate command which included Price's retreating Missouri forces and McCulloch's army. The Confederate wings, driven into the Boston Mountains, became separated by the Union forces and were crushed on successive days.

Seven months later Van Dorn gathered a force of some 16,000 men in an attempt to protect Vicksburg, while Price concentrated an equal number of men at Tupelo. Price kept the Union Army in a state of expectancy, finally moving his army to Iuka, while Van Dorn moved toward Holly Springs with the obvious purpose of joining forces either to attack Corinth or turn north, cross the Tennessee River, and attack Buell's army from the rear.

Grant acted resolutely. He sent Rosecrans' corps, 9,000 strong, south from Corinth in an effort to cut off any retreat by Price. Rosecrans, however, failed to trap Price, who retreated southeast into Mississippi where he joined Van Dorn.

Van Dorn and Price then planned a raid on Grant's supply line, the Memphis-Corinth Railroad; but Grant had already given up hope of protecting this. Van Dorn then received a map of the forts at Corinth, sent to him by the rebel spy, Aurelia Burton, and immediately planned an attack.

Grant, meanwhile, learned of the map and the Confederate battle plans and set his defenses. When the attack on Rosecrans came, McPherson was to attack Van Dorn from the rear, while Ord was positioned to cut off any retreat at Holly Springs. The main Union force under MacArthur, Davies, and Hamilton, remained behind the line, with Stanley's division in reserve.

Van Dorn attacked the Union left under MacArthur, but the first rebel attack was checked. Maury, of Van Dorn's Corps, threw his brigade into the gap between MacArthur and Davies and routed the Union forces. Price attacked Hamilton, and the Union front began to dissolve. Rosecrans, however, brought in Stanley's reserves; and the attack was halted.

Van Dorn then ordered Herbert to attack MacArthur, while Price was to use his full force. Herbert did not attack, feigning illness; and Van Dorn, in a rage, flung his forces recklessly against MacArthur, whose men riddled the Confederate charge.

Van Dorn fell back and fought several minor skirmishes before gaining a measure of revenge by capturing the Union depot at Holly Springs early in December to slow Grant's advance on Vicksburg.

In May, 1863, at Spring Hill, Tennessee, Van Dorn was killed in a personal quarrel.

Louis Riel

Lew Wallace

"Lew" Wallace's reputation rests not only on his military record but on his world famous novel, *Ben Hur*.

Lewis Wallace, lawyer, soldier, diplomat and author, was born at Brookville, Indiana, on April 10, 1827, the son of David and Esther French Wallace. Early in his life he displayed a love for adventure, was irritated by school and ordinary tasks, and preferred to draw caricatures or play truant. When his father was elected governor of Indiana in 1837 and the family moved to Indianapolis, Lew's zest for reading was stimulated by the advantages of the state library. Before he was sixteen he began to support himself by copying records in the county clerk's office. About the same time, Prescott's *Conquest of Mexico* made such a deep impression on him that he determined to write upon the theme. During 1844 he reported the proceedings of the Indiana House of Representatives for the Indianapolis *Daily Journal* and soon afterwards began studying law in his father's office. When the Mexican War began, he raised a company of volunteers assigned to the First Indiana Infantry, of which he became second lieutenant.

In the presidential election of 1848 Wallace campaigned against Taylor and edited a Free-Soil paper, chiefly because of resentment against Taylor's treatment of the Indiana regiments. Following the campaign Wallace became a Democrat. Admitted to the bar in 1849, he began to practice law in Indianapolis but soon moved to Covington and in 1850 and 1852 was elected prosecuting attorney. In 1856 he was elected to the state senate, where he advocated a reform in divorce laws and in 1859 proposed the popular election of United States Senators.

After Fort Sumter was fired upon, Wallace raised a company of 130 men and was made a colonel of the Eleventh Regiment. He was soon at the front and helped to capture Romney on the south branch of the Potomac and to evict the enemy from Harper's Ferry. An excellent disciplinarian and popular with his men, he was promoted rapidly. On September 3, 1861, he was made a brigadier general and on March 21, 1862, after his service at the capture of Fort Donelson, was made a major general. Unfortunately, he incurred the ill-will of General Halleck, who twice removed him from command. The first time he was restored by President Lincoln, the second time by General Grant.

In November, 1862, Wallace served as president of the military commission that investigated the operations of the army under General Buell. The following year he saved Cincinnati from capture by General E. Kirby-Smith, after which the President gave him command of the Middle Division and the Eighth Army Corps with headquarters at Baltimore. With 5,800 men, a number of them inexperienced, he held a force of 28,000 under General Early at Monocacy Creek on July 9, 1864. Though defeated, he probably saved Washington from capture and was highly commended by Grant in his *Memoirs*. He served on the court which tried the assassins of Lincoln and was president of the court which tried and convicted Colonel Henry Wirz, the notorious commandant of Andersonville (Georgia) Prison.

At the close of the war Wallace undertook to procure munitions and raise a corps of veterans for the Mexican liberals and spent some time in Mexico. Returning to Crawfordsville, he practiced law and in 1870 was an unsuccessful candidate for Congress on the Republican ticket. In 1878 he was appointed governor of New Mexico Territory, serving until 1881, when the President appointed him Minister to Turkey, where he served with a high degree of success and prestige. In 1890 he declined an offer of the mission to Brazil tendered by President Harrison. He died at Crawfordsville, Indiana, on February 15, 1905.

Lew. Wallace.

Gouverneur Kemble Warren

Gouverneur Kemble Warren was one of the most interesting and tragic figures to emerge from the shadows of the Civil War. A youthful hero at Gettysburg and at the pinnacle of fame and admiration, he was, in a short time, plunged into a state of despair and disgrace.

Warren was born near West Point in Cold Springs, New York, on January 8, 1830. His father was a personal friend of Washington Irving.

Warren had a strong desire to attend West Point, and in 1850 he graduated second in his class and was assigned to the engineers corps. He served several years in army river-and-railway-surveys, especially in the Mississippi and Ohio River areas.

In 1859 he returned to West Point as assistant and professor of mathematics.

At the outbreak of the Civil War, Warren was made a lieutenant colonel and later colonel of volunteers. For gallant service at Gaines Mill he was made a brigadier general and later became chief of engineers in the Army of the Potomac under Meade.

He saw action at Malvern Hill, the Second Battle of Bull Run, Fredericksburg, Chancellorsville, and Gettysburg. At Chancellorsville he made effective use of artillery in his attack on Jackson's corps.

As chief of engineers under Meade at Gettysburg, he was sent by that officer to check on the Union left flank then anchored on Little Round Top. He was opposed by the redoubtable Longstreet and his division commander John B. Hood.

Warren climbed to the summit of Little Round Top just in time to detect Hood's men climbing up that hill. Without hesitation, Warren took part of Sykes' brigade and the Twentieth Maine Regiment to repulse Hood's attack and hold Little Round Top.

In the opinion of some experts, if Hancock saved the Union center in the desperate charge of Pickett's brigade, Warren saved the Union left flank from being rolled up, with a possible victory for Lee.

Wounded in action, Warren was magnificent in courage and leadership. Here he reached the heights of fame and prestige. He won promotion as a major general of volunteers and in 1864, when only thirty-four years of age, succeeded Sykes in command of the Fifth Corps.

Warren served with Grant in the bloody campaigns that finally destroyed Lee's army and smashed the Confederacy. He led Grant's right flank in the Spotsylvania Campaign and formed part of Grant's great infantry team of Hancock, Warren, and Sedgwick.

Because of the recurrence of an old wound, Warren did not take part in the bloody attack at Cold Harbor. But he was greatly affected by these happenings. Warren once told his colleagues, "It is terrible. All day long a perpetual funeral procession goes by my headquarters." At Petersburg, Warren stationed his men in the trenches threatening to cut off Lee's line of communication with Richmond. Lee gathered some 15,000 men and gave them to Pickett to anchor the Petersburg line at Five Forks. Sheridan drove hard on the Petersburg line, but the battle-weary troops of Warren were slow in supporting Sheridan's attack on the crumbling Rebel lines.

Warren, of late, had become somewhat of a problem in the matter of prompt execution of orders. Grant, aware of the situation, had ordered Sheridan to remove Warren when the latter felt it necessary. When Warren was late at Dinwiddie and also at Five Forks, the irate Sheridan shouted, "tell him he was not at the front." He sent orders to Warren ordering him to surrender his command to General Griffin and to report to Grant's headquarters. Warren asked Sheridan to reconsider an order that would wreck a soldier's career. Sheridan refused, saying, "Obey the order."

Warren was later put in command of the Department of the Mississippi and in 1865 was mustered out of volunteer service. He reverted to his regular status as major of engineers and in 1879 became a colonel. He died at Newport, Rhode Island, on August 8, 1882. A statue to his memory was unveiled on Little Round Top, Gettysburg, in August, 1888.

G.K.Warren

Alexander Stewart Webb

Alexander Stewart Webb was born in New York City on February 15, 1835. He graduated from West Point in the class of 1855 and was commissioned a second lieutenant in the Fourth Artillery, having finished thirteenth in a class of thirty-four.

Webb saw service against the Seminoles in Florida and on the frontier, later returning to West Point as professor of mathematics.

At the outbreak of the Civil War, Webb became major of the First Rhode Island Infantry. As an artillery officer he saw action in the First Battle of Bull Run and had a record of active service at Yorktown, Mechanicsville, Gaines Mill, Antietam, and at Chancellorsville, serving as inspector general.

At Gettysburg he displayed great courage in the bloody repulse of Pickett's desperate drive against Hancock. He served under Grant in the great Wildnerness campaign and at Spotsylvania, where he was wounded in action.

He won successive promotions until he achieved the title of major general of infantry and became chief of staff to Meade in the Petersburg siege. He left the army service at his own request on December 3, 1870.

Webb served as president of the College of the City of New York from 1869 to 1902. His forceful personality showed its beneficial effects in the progress of this college. He died in New York City on February 12, 1911. A statue to his memory was raised in the Bloody Angle (Spotsylvania), where he had been wounded in the bitter fighting with Lee.

Alex. S. Webb.

Joseph Wheeler

"Fighting Joe" Wheeler, a fine example of a soldier who made the most of his talents in war and peace, was born in Augusta, Georgia, in 1836. At the age of twenty-one and after a haphazard education, he was appointed to West Point. He was graduated from the Academy in 1859 with a splendid record and was brevetted a second lieutenant of dragoons.

When his home state joined the Confederacy, Wheeler sent in his resignation to the regular army on April 22, 1861. He became a first lieutenant in the Confederate Army and soon rose to the rank of colonel in charge of the Nineteenth Alabama Infantry. He led the Confederate cavalry in Bragg's operations in Kentucky and Tennessee, raiding General Thomas' supply train near Chattanooga. He commanded a brigade at the battle of Shiloh, where he gained a reputation for discipline and leadership.

On July 18, 1862, Wheeler was given command of the cavalry of the Army of Mississippi, in which he won a reputation almost equal to Jeb Stuart's.

After the action of Perryville, he won a further promotion to the rank of brigadier general and a year later, in 1863, became a major general.

In several campaigns of the West, particularly Chickamauga and Chattanooga, Wheeler was given full command of the cavalry of the Confederate Army. Soon afterward, he was shifted to the Georgia campaign, where he commanded the cavalry in the Confederate operation against Sherman. He attacked McPherson and later Kilpatrick in the defense of Atlanta.

On June 27, 1863, he was wounded for the third time. He is said to have participated in 200 engagements and 800 skirmishes; and his nickname of "Fighting Joe" was unquestionably well earned.

Lee linked Wheeler with Stuart as one of the two outstanding Confederate cavalry leaders. In breadth of military vision and in delicacy of touch, Stuart was undoubtedly the superior. Nathan Bedford Forest had a deadly simplicity of action more effective than Wheeler at his best; but the latter yielded to none in dogged aggressiveness, in hard hitting, and in reliability. Loyal to his superiors and to his associates, his enemies, even with superior forces of cavalry, never succeeded in mastering him. He was beloved and trusted by his men; and despite the fact that excesses were ascribed to his troops in the last days of the Confederacy, he enjoyed general popularity throughout the South.

After the war Wheeler established himself as a commission merchant in New Orleans. On February 8, 1866, he married Daniella Jones Sherrod, daughter of Colonel Richard Jones of Alabama. In 1868 Wheeler moved to Wheeler, Alabama, named in his honor, and engaged in cotton planting and the practice of law. He entered politics and in 1881 was elected to the Forty-seventh Congress and was reelected in 1883.

As a congressman Wheeler pushed various pensions bills and was instrumental in the Congressional rehabilitation of General Fitz-John Porter. His chief public contribution, however, was his untiring efforts toward reconciliation between the North and the South. During these years he built up such a state-wide reputation that he was chosen by Alabama as one of her two representatives in Statuary Hall in Washington.

At the outbreak of the Spanish-American War in 1898, Wheeler offered his services to President McKinley; and the President commissioned Wheeler as major general of United States volunteers. The presidential action was recognized and applauded as a significant effort to make the war an instrument for the North and South to close ranks. Wheeler commanded the cavalry division of Shafter's Santiago expedition in Cuba, participated in the engagement at Las Guasimas, and despite illness was present at the Battle of San Juan Hill. After the surrender at Santiago, he commanded the army convalescent and demobilization camp at Montauk Point, Long Island. Later he was sent to the Philippines in command of a brigade but soon returned to the United States. On June 16, 1900, he was commissioned a brigadier general in the regular army. On his sixty-fourth birthday, September 10, 1900, he retired.

In retirement, Wheeler lived quietly. He died in Brooklyn, New York, on January 25, 1906. He was buried in the Arlington National Cemetery.

Jos Wheeler

Alpheus Starkey Williams

Alpheus Starkey Williams was born at Saybrook, Connecticut, on September 20, 1810. He received his education at Yale University and traveled widely both in the United States and in Europe.

On his return, he became a lawyer in Detroit. Ultimately, he entered politics and obtained a position as postmaster at Detroit.

At the outbreak of the Civil War, Williams was appointed brigadier general of the Michigan volunteers and was given command of the First Brigade of Bank's division in the Army of the Potomac.

For his brilliant services he was transferred to the Army of Virginia under Pope, where he commanded the First Division of the Second Corps. He was in charge of the First Division Twelfth Corps at South Mountain, Antietam, Chancellorsville, and Gettysburg.

In the bitter fighting of Pope's army against Lee and Jackson at Cedar Mountain and Culpeper, Williams overextended his force and was pushed back by a flank attack by Jackson. However, the excellent work by the Union artillery prevented the Confederates from completing a rout of Williams' force.

During the fall of 1863, he led the First Division of the Twelfth Corps in the Army of Cumberland. Later he commanded the Twenty-first Corps in the Atlanta campaign and also in Sherman's march to the sea.

Williams served commendably to crush the last desperate stand of the Confederates before "Joe" Johnston surrendered on April 26, 1865.

Following the war he served as United States Minister to Salvador from 1866 to 1869 and was elected to Congress as a Democrat in 1876. Two years later, on December 21, he died while in office, at Washington, D. C.

James Harrison Wilson

James Harrison Wilson was born in Shawneetown, Illinois, on September 2, 1837. He was accepted at West Point and after graduating in 1860 joined the engineer corps.

With the outbreak of the Civil War, Wilson saw action in the battles of Port Royal Bay and Fort Pulaski, Georgia. For his gallantry in the latter action he was promoted to major and became, subsequently, aide-de-camp to McClellan. He fought side by side with the General in the battles of Antietam and South Mountain.

Wilson served as inspector general of the Army of the Tennessee in 1862, and the following year he was made brigadier general of volunteers for gallantry in action in the Chattanooga campaign. During the year he again won promotions for his conduct at the battle of the Wilderness, the siege of Petersburg, and the Shenandoah campaign.

In 1864 Wilson took over the cavalry of the Mississippi Division and fought in the battles of Franklin and Nashville.

In the last year of the war he made very heavy raids into Alabama and Georgia and even captured Jefferson Davis. As a result he won promotion to major general.

When the Spanish-American War broke out in 1898, Wilson once again took command and was leader of the First Division of the First Army Corps at Puerto Rico. Two years later was sent to China to help the American forces put down the Boxer Rebellion. The following year he retired from the army as brigadier general.

He died on February 23, 1925, in Wilmington, Delaware.

J. H. Wilson

Horatio Gouverneur Wright

Horatio Gouverneur Wright was born in Clinton, Connecticut, on March 6, 1820. He received the usual elementary education and attended West Point, graduating from the Academy in 1841.

In 1846 Wright supervised the building of Fort Jackson, Florida. From 1856 to 1861 he was assistant to the chief of engineers at Washington.

At the First Battle of Bull Run, Wright served as chief engineer of Heintzelman's division. He also participated in the famous Port Royal, South Carolina, expedition. In the same year he was made brigadier general of volunteers and led the expedition which captured Jacksonville and other Florida coastal towns.

In May, 1863, Wright joined the Army of the Potomac as divisional commander in the Sixth Corps. He led a division in the Wildnerness campaign and succeeded to the command of that corps when Sedgwick was killed in May, 1864, at the Spotsylvania Court House. He was promoted to major general of the volunteers after the fighting at the Bloody Angle.

Wright served as major general at the battle of Opequon Creek in September, 1864, and made a valuable contribution to Sheridan's decisive victory over Early at Cedar Creek in October, 1864. When Petersburg was captured, he was brevetted major general in the regular army for his services.

Wright was mustered out of service on September 1, 1866, and returned to the regular army as a lieutenant colonel of engineers. He became a brigadier general and chief of engineers on June 30, 1879, retiring from military service five years later.

He died in Washington, D. C. on July 2, 1899.

H. G. Wright.

BIBLIOGRAPHY

GENERAL REFERENCE WORKS

Campaigns of the Civil War. Civil War Press. New York, 1959.

Confederate Military History. 12 vols., 1899.

Confederate Veteran. 40 vols., 1893–1932.

Southern Historical Society Papers. 49 vols., 1876–1944.

Clark, Walter. *In the Great War.* 5 vols., 1901.

Cullen, George W. *Biographical Register of the Officers and Graduates of the United States Military Academy.* New York, 1868.

Evans, Clement. *Confederate Military History: a Library of Confederate States History.* 12 vols. Atlanta, 1899.

Freeman, D. S. *Lee's Confidential Dispatches to Davis.* 1915.

Fox, William F. *Regimental Losses in the American Civil War 1861–1865.* Albany, 1889.

Hamersley, Thomas H. S. *Complete Regular Army Register of the United States.* Washington, 1880.

Heitman, Francis B. *Historical Register and Dictionary of the United States.* Washington, 1903.

Hill, D. H. *The Land We Love.* 1866–69.

Johnson, Robert U., and Buel, Clarence C. *Battles and Leaders of the Civil War.* 4 vols., 1887–88.

Livermore, Thomas L. *Numbers and Losses in the Civil War in America, 1861–1865.* Boston, 1900.

Military Order of the Loyal Legion of the U.S.—Military Essays and Recollections. Illinois Commandery, 1907.

Moore, Frank. *The Rebellion Record: A Diary of American Events.* 12 vols., 1862–71.

Pratt, Fletcher. *The Civil War on Western Waters.* New York, 1956.

War Department. *Union and Confederate Armies.* 70 vols., 1880–1901.

War of the Rebellion—A compilation of the official records of the Union and Confederate Armies. 128 vols. Washington, D.C., 1902.

Wiley, Bell I. *The Life of Johnny Reb.* 1943.

EYE-WITNESS ACCOUNTS

Alexander, E. P. *Military Memoirs of a Confederate.* New York, 1907.

Anderson, Charles. *Texas Before and On the Eve of the Rebellion.* Cincinnati, 1884.

Bartlett, Napier. *A Soldier's Story of the War.* New Orleans, 1874.

Blackford, W. W. *War Years with Jeb Stuart.* New York, 1945.

Blake, N. M. *William Mahone.* Duke University, 1932.

Boykin, E. M. *The Falling Flag.* New York, 1874.

Buell, Augustus. *The Cannoneer.* Washington, 1890.

Casler, John O. *Four Years in the Stonewall Brigade.* Guthrie, Oklahoma, 1893.

Chamberlain, W. W. *Memoirs of the Civil War.* Washington, 1912.

Chamberlayne, C. G. *Ham Chamberlayne, Virginian.* Richmond, 1933.

Chestnut, Mary Boykin. *A Diary from Dixie.* New York, 1906.

Collins, R. M. *Chapters from the Unwritten History of the War between the States.* St. Louis, 1893.

Cooke, Giles B. *Just Before and After Lee Surrendered to Grant.* 1922.

Cooke, John Esten. *A Life of General Robert E. Lee.* New York, 1866.

———. *Wearing of the Gray.* New York, 1867.

Cox, Jacob D. *Military Reminiscences of the Civil War.* New York, 1900.

Dabney, R. L. *Life and Campaigns of Lieutenant General Thomas J. Jackson.* New York, 1866.

Dame, William M. *From the Rapidan to Richmond and the Spotsylvania Campaign.* Baltimore, 1920.

Davis, Jefferson. *The Rise and Fall of the Confederate Government.* New York, 1881.

Davis, Varina H. *Jefferson Davis.* New York, 1890.

De Fontaine, F. G. *Marginalia.* Columbia, S.C., 1864.

De Leon, T. C. *Four Years in Rebel Capitals.* Mobile, 1890.

Douglas, Henry K. *I Rode with Stonewall.* Chapel Hill, N.C., 1940.

Early Jubal A. *A Memoir of the Last Year of the War.* Lynchburg, Va., 1869.

Eggleston, George C. *A Rebel's Recollections.* New York, 1875.

Eisenschiml, Otto. *The Celebrated Case of Fitz-John Porter.* Indianapolis, 1950.

Fremantle, A. J. L. *Three Months in the Southern States.* New York, 1864.

Fletcher, W. A. *Rebel Private, Front and Rear.* Beaumont, Texas, 1908.

Gerrish, Theodore. *Army Life.* Portland, Maine, 1882.

Gibbon, John. *Personal Recollections of the Civil War.* New York, 1913.

Gill, John. *Reminiscences.* Baltimore, 1904.

Goode, John. *Recollections of a Lifetime.* Washington, 1906.

Gordon, John B. *Reminiscences.* New York, 1903.

———. *Reminiscences of the Civil War.* New York, 1904.

Gorman, J. C. *Lee's Last Campaign.* Raleigh, 1865.

Goss, Warren L. *Recollections.* New York, 1890.

Graham, James A. *Papers* (H. M. Wagstaff, ed.). Chapel Hill, N.C., 1883.

Grant, U. S. *Personal Memoirs.* 2 vols. New York, 1886.

Grimes, Byran. *Extracts of Letters of . . . to His Wife.* Raleigh, N.C., 1883.

Hamlin, P. G. *Old Bald Head: The Portrait of a Soldier.* Strasburg, Va., 1940.

Hancock, Winfield Scott. *Reminiscences of Winfield S. Hancock.* New York, 1887.

Haskell, Frank. *The Battle of Gettysburg.* Wisconsin History Commission, 1908.

Hassler, Warren W., Jr. *General George B. McClellan, Shield of the Union.* Baton Rouge, 1957.

Haupt, Herman. *Reminiscences of General Herman Haupt.* Milwaukee, 1901.

Hunter, Alexander. *Johnny Reb and Billy Yank.* Washington, 1904.

Jackson, Mary Anna. *Memoirs of Stonewall Jackson.* Louisville, 1895.

Johnston, Joseph E. *Narrative of Military Operations.* New York, 1874.

Jones, J. B. *A Rebel War Clerk's Diary.* Philadelphia, 1866.

Keyes, E. D. *Fifty Years' Observation of Men and Events.* New York, 1884.

Lee, Fitzhugh. *Chancellorsville.* Richmond, 1879.

———. *General Lee.* New York, 1894.

Lee, R. E. *The Letters of R. E. Lee to Martha Custis Williams.* Cambridge, Mass., 1935.

Lee, R. E., Jr. *Recollections and Letters of General Robert E. Lee.* New York, 1904.

Livermore, Thomas L. *Days and Events.* Boston, 1920.

Logan, Kate V. Cox. *My Confederate Girlhood.* Richmond, 1932.

Long, A. L. *Memoirs of Robert E. Lee.* New York, 1886.

Longstreet, James. *From Manassas to Appomattox.* New York, 1898.

Lyman, Theodore. *Meade's Headquarters.* Boston, 1922.

MacCartney, Clarence Edward. *Little Mac: The Life of General George B. McClellan.* Philadelphia, 1940.

McCarthy, Carlton. *Detailed Minutiae of Soldier Life.* Richmond, 1882.

McClellan, George B. *McClellan's Own Story: The War for the Union.* New York, 1887.

McClellan, H. B. *The Life and Campaigns of Major-General J. E. B. Stuart.* Richmond, 1885.

McGuire, Judith W. *Diary of a Southern Refugee.* Richmond, 1889.

McKim, R. H. *A Soldier's Recollections.* New York, 1911.

Maurice, Sir Frederick. *Charles Marshall.* Boston, 1927.

Meade, George Gordon. *The Life and Letters of General Meade.* New York, 1913.

Misson, Frank M. *Reminiscences of a Private.* Columbia, S.C., 1910.

Moore, Edward A. *The Story of a Cannoneer under Stonewall Jackson.* New York, 1907.

Morse, Charles F. *Letters Written during the Civil War.* Boston, 1898.

Mosby, John S. *War Reminiscences.* Boston, 1887.

Myers, Frank M. *The Comanches: A History of White's Battalion of Virginia Cavalry.* Baltimore, 1871.

Nicolay, John G., and John Hay. *Abraham Lincoln: A History.* New York, 1890.

Norton, Oliver. *Army Letters.* Chicago, 1903.

Oates, William C. *The War between the Union and the Confederacy.* Washington, 1905.

Owen, William M. *In Camp and Battle with the Washington Artillery of New Orleans.* Boston, 1885.

Peyton, John L. *The American Crisis.* London, 1867.

Pickett, George E. *The Heart of a Soldier, as Revealed in the Intimate Letters of General George E. Pickett.* New York, 1913.

Pinkerton, Allan. *The Spy of the Rebellion.* New York, 1883.

Polley, J. B. *Hood's Texas Brigade.* New York, 1910.

———. *A Soldier's Letters to Charming Nellie.* New York, 1913.

Porter, Horace. *Campaigning with Grant.* New York, 1897.

Pryor, Mrs. Roger A. *Reminiscences of Peace and War.* New York, 1904.

Quintard, Charles T. *Dr. Quintard, Chaplain C.S.A. and Second Bishop of Tennessee.* Sewanee, Tenn., 1905.

Reagan, John H. *Memoirs.* New York, 1906.

Russell, William Howard. *My Diary North and South.* London, 1863.

Scales, Alfred M. *The Battle of Fredericksburg.* Washington, 1884.

Sorrel, G. Moxley. *Recollections of a Confederate Staff Officer.* Washington, 1917.

Stiles, Robert. *Four Years under Marse Robert.* Washington, 1903.

Taylor, Richard. *Destruction and Reconstruction.* New York, 1879.

Taylor, Walter H. *Four Years with General Lee.* New York, 1877.

Townsend, E. D. *Anecdotes of the Civil War.* New York, 1884.

Townsend, G. A. *Rustics in Rebellion.* Chapel Hill, N.C., 1950.

de Trobriand, Regis. *Four Years with the Army of the Potomac.* Boston, 1889.

von Borcke, Heros. *Memoirs of the Confederate War for Independence.* London, 1866.

Walker, Francis A. *General Hancock.* New York, 1897.

Wallace, Lew. *An Autobiography.* 2 vols. New York, 1906.

Welch, S. G. *A Confederate Surgeon's Letters to His Wife.* Washington, 1911.

Wilson, James Harrison. *Under the Old Flag.* New York, 1912.

Wise, John S. *The End of an Era.* Boston, 1899.

Worsham, John H. *One of Jackson's Foot Cavalry.* New York, 1912.

BIOGRAPHIES AND OTHER STUDIES

Bradford, Gamaliel. *Confederate Portraits.* Boston, 1914.

———. *Lee the American.* Boston, 1912.

———. *Union Portraits.* Boston, 1916.

Brooks, W. E. *Lee of Virginia.* Indianapolis, 1932.

Butler, Benjamin. *Autobiography.* Boston, 1892.

Dahlgren, M. V., ed. *Memoirs of John A. Dahlgren.* Philadelphia, 1872.

Horn, Stanley F., ed. *The Robert E. Lee Reader.* Indianapolis, 1949.

Jones, J. William. *Personal Reminiscences, Anecdotes, and Letters of Robert E. Lee.* New York, 1874.

———. *Life and Letters of Robert E. Lee.* New York, 1906.

Lewis, Lloyd. *Sherman, Fighting Prophet.* New York, 1932.

Maurice, Sir Frederick. *Robert E. Lee, The Soldier.* Boston, 1925.

McCabe, James D., Jr. *Life and Campaigns of General Robert Edward Lee.* New York, 1866.

Michie, Peter S. *General McClellan.* New York, 1934.

Page, Thomas Nelson. *Robert E. Lee, Man and Soldier.* New York, 1911.

Thomason, John W. *Jeb Stuart.* New York.

Winston, Robert W. *Robert E. Lee.* New York, 1934.

Swanberg, W. A. *First Blood: The Story of Fort Sumter.* New York, 1958.

———. *Sickles the Incredible.* New York, 1959.

GENERAL WORKS AND MONOGRAPHS

Adams, George W. *Doctors in Blue.* New York, 1952.

Basler, Roger, ed. *Collected Works of Abraham Lincoln.* 8 vols. New Brunswick, 1953.

Boynton, Charles B. *The History of the Navy during the Rebellion.* New York, 1867.

Catton, Bruce. *Mr. Lincoln's Army.* Garden City, 1951.

———. *This Hallowed Ground.* New York, 1936.

Harwell, Richard B. *The Union Reader.* New York, 1958.

Hosmer, James Kendall. *The American Civil War.* New York, 1884

McClellan, G. B. *Report on the Organization and Campaign of the Army of the Potomac.*

Palfrey, Francis W. *The Antietam and Fredericksburg.* New York, 1882.

Ropes, John C. *The Army under Pope.* New York, 1881.

———. *The Story of the Civil War.* 6 vols. New York, 1899.

Steele, Matthew Forney. *American Campaigns.* Washington, 1922.

Stine, J. H. *History of the Army of the Potomac.* Washington, 1893.

Webb, Alexander S. *The Peninsula: McClellan's Campaign of 1862.* New York, 1881.

Wiley, Bell Irvin. *The Life of Billy Yank.* Indianapolis, 1952.

———. *Life of Johnny Reb.* New York, 1943.

Williams, Kenneth. *Lincoln Finds a General.* 4 vols. New York, 1949–56.

Williams, T. Harry. *Lincoln and His Generals.* New York, 1952.

Nevins, Allan. *Ordeal of the Union.* 2 vols. New York, 1947.

———. *The War for the Union, 1861-62.* New York, 1959.

Sandburg, Carl. *Abraham Lincoln.* 6 vols. New York, 1926–29.

Swington, William. *Campaigns of the Army of the Potomac.* New York, ———.

Wise, Jennings C. *The Long Arm of Lee.* Lynchburg, Va., 1915.

MAPS

Atlas to Accompany the Official Records of the Union and Confederate Armies.

Civil War Atlas to Accompany Steel's "American Campaigns"

West Point Atlas, Vol. I (Civil War). New York, 1960.

OTHER BIOGRAPHY

Cook, Roy Bird. *Family and Early Life of Stonewall Jackson.* Charleston, W.Va., 1948.

Davis, Burke. *They Called Him Stonewall.* New York, 1954.

Henderson, G. F. R. *Stonewall Jackson and the American Civil War.* London, 1900.

Hughes, Robert M. *General Johnston.* New York, 1893.

Hunter, Martha T. M. *A Memoir of F. M. T. Hunter.* Washington, 1903.

McElroy, Robert. *Jefferson Davis: The Unreal and the Real.* New York, 1937.

Pemberton, John C. *Pemberton, Defender of Vicksburg.* University of North Carolina Press, 1942.

Roman, Alfred. *Military Operations of General Beauregard.* 2 vols. New York, 1884.

Tucker, Glenn. *Hancock the Superb.* New York, 1960.

ADDITIONAL SOURCES

Angle, Paul M., ed. *The Lincoln Reader.* New Brunswick, 1947.

Boatner, Mark. *A Civil War Dictionary.* Philadelphia, 1959.

Catton, Bruce. *A Stillness at Appomattox.* New York, 1953.

———. *Grant Moves South.* New York, 1959.

Commager, Henry Steele, ed. *The Blue and the Gray.* 2 vols. Indianapolis, 1941.

Conger, A. L. *The Rise of U. S. Grant.* New York, 1931.

Freeman, Douglas S. *Lee and His Lieutenants.* 3 vols. New York, 1944.

———. *Robert E. Lee: A Biography.* 4 vols. New York, 1935.

PICTORIAL WORKS

A Pictorial History of the Confederacy. Lamont, Buchanan (New York: Crown, 1951).

Army Lineage Book, Infantry, Vol II. Dept. of the Army, U. S. Government Printing Office (Washington, D.C., 1953).

Campers and Battlefields. Rossiter Johnson (New York: The Blue and Grey Press, 1958).

Confederate Arms. William A Albaugh III and Edward N. Simmons (Harrisburg, Pa.: The Stackpole Co., 1957).

Divided We Fought. Milhollen, Kaplan, and Stuart (New York: Macmillan, 1956).

Face of Robert E. Lee. Roy Meredith (New York: Scribner's, 1947).

Frank Leslie's Illustrated Newspaper, 1861–65.

Gardner's Photographic Sketch Book of the Civil War. Alexander Gardner (New York: Dover, 1959).

Generals in Gray. Ezra J. Warner (Louisiana State University Press, 1959).

Harper's Weekly. 1861–65.

Mathew Brady—Historian with a Camera. James Horan (New York: Crown, 1955).

Mr. Lincoln's Camera Man. Roy Meredith (New York: Scribner's 1946).

Mr. Lincoln's Contemporaries. Roy Meredith (New York: Scribner's 1951).

Official Atlas of the Civil War. M. J. Wright (New York: Yoseloff, 1959).

Photographic History of the Civil War. Francis Trevelyan Miller (New York: Yoseloff, 1957).

Picture History of the U. S. Navy. Theodore Roscoe and Fred Freeman (New York: Scribner's, 1956).

The U. S. Marines—A Pictorial History. Lynn Montross (New York, Toronto: Rinehart, 1953).

They Who Fought Here. Bell Irwin Wiley (New York: Macmillan, 1959).